THE GOSPEL IN A PLURALIST SOCIETY

THE
GOSPEL
IN A
PLURALIST SOCIETY

Lesslie Newbigin

First published in Great Britain 1989 by
SPCK
Holy Trinity Church
Marylebone Road
London NW1 4DU

First published in the United States 1989 by
Wm. B. Eerdmans Publishing Co.
255 Jefferson Ave. S.E., Grand Rapids, Mich. 49503

British Library Cataloguing in Publication Data

Newbigin, Lesslie
  The gospel in a pluralist society.
  1. Christian life. Faith
  I. Title
  248.4
  ISBN 0-281-04435-X

Printed in the United States of America

Contents

Foreword

The witness of the church has always taken place within a pluralistic milieu. During recent years, however, new perceptions of this milieu have emerged, and pluralism is fast assuming the character of an ideology. Hence the need to understand afresh the nature and role of the church's mission in today's pluralistic world.

Lesslie Newbigin's book is an important contribution to the ongoing search within the ecumenical movement for an authentic expression of the meaning of the gospel and the mission of the church in the midst of a plurality of cultures and religions. Newbigin identifies the danger of relativism evident in a good deal of current discussion. He rejects the dichotomy between the "world of facts" and the "world of values." He regrets the consequent attitude of timidity or of anxiety on the part of Christians, especially in the West. *The Gospel in a Pluralist Society* is a call to renewed confidence in the gospel of Jesus Christ. It is an attempt to see "how as Christians we can more confidently affirm our faith in the kind of intellectual climate" in which we find ourselves.

Newbigin has the courage to take up a position and the conviction to defend it against what sometimes appear to be impossible odds. What he has to say—and says with refreshing clarity—comes out of his background of long pastoral experience, missionary commitment, ecumenical vision, and unwavering confidence in the gospel.

There is no dearth of books dealing with the status of the Christian faith and the task of the church in a pluralistic context. Many of them are written for academic audiences. Newbigin addresses a much wider readership. At several points he suggests how Christian people may respond in practical ways to the issues raised by our pluralistic situation. Such suggestions are consistently grounded in a particular understanding of the biblical testimony and the Christian heritage, but they raise the discussion to a level that has rarely been reached by books on this crucial theme. Thanks to Newbigin, we can look forward to discussions of pluralism and interfaith dialogue at congregational levels where they do not normally happen.

In the early chapters Newbigin analyzes the roots of the present crisis of Christian confidence. Much of what he says in these chapters, set within a theoretical and epistemological framework heavily influenced by Michael Polanyi, has a clear Western orientation and may well prove to be controversial. Nevertheless, it opens up issues in a new way, and provides a fresh frame of reference within which key missiological motifs can be fruitfully raised and pursued.

It is possible that not all readers will be satisfied with the measure of integration between the epistemological insights and the theological formulations that follow. One may also sense a certain tension between the perspectival and the story character of the gospel and the absolute claims that are made for the gospel. But here too it is a creative tension. It leads Newbigin to suggest that "the Christian story provides us with a *set of lenses,* not something for us to look *at* but to look *through.*" If such an approach is consistently followed through, "we may overcome the destructive conflict between liberals and fundamentalists within the church." He also points to the need for and the possibility of a "dialogue" between the Christian story and other stories. And he rightly observes that this calls for a healthy and vigorous participation by Christians in their tradition, with confidence and commitment, in thought and practice.

What Newbigin has to say on the mission of the church confirms and strengthens many of the ecumenical affirmations on mission and evangelism. The central role of congregations in mission and the urgent need to equip ministers whose primary task will be the enabling of grass-roots participation in mission are powerfully articulated in the book. Describing the congregation as "the hermeneutic of the gospel," Newbigin underlines the nature and purpose of the renewed communities of God's people. At a time when many churches are looking for ways of developing missionary congregations, the positive suggestions given here will be of immense help.

The discussion on the gospel in a pluralistic society must and will continue. Newbigin's valuable contribution to it will provoke those who take the pluralistic context seriously to face equally seriously the pertinent, foundational theological issues. It will challenge those who are tempted to opt for forms of relativism. Nothing less than the transformation of mind that Newbigin calls for can give us the kind of confidence in the gospel so indispensable for the life of our churches and the work of the ecumenical movement.

Christopher Duraisingh
Director, WCC Commission
on World Missions and Evangelism

Preface

What follows is in substance a series of lectures which I gave in Glasgow University as Alexander Robertson Lecturer for the year 1988. I am very grateful to Professor George Newlands and his colleagues in the Divinity Faculty both for the honor they did me by extending the invitation, and for the great kindness they showed my wife and me during our stay in Glasgow. I am also grateful to the students who attended the lectures and stimulated my thinking by their vigorous participation in discussion in smaller groups.

I can make no claim either to originality or to scholarship. I am a pastor and preacher, trying to make available to my fellow pastors and others such thinking as I have gleaned in my very unsystematic reading bearing on the topic I am trying to address. A scholarly work would contain references to all the relevant literature and evidence that the writer had taken account of all the various arguments. To have dignified my text with a proper apparatus of footnotes would have been to pretend to a kind of scholarship which I do not possess. It is better, in this foreword, simply to acknowledge some very massive debts to writers from whom I have borrowed without always acknowledging the fact. Throughout the work, and especially in the first five chapters, I have relied heavily on the work of Michael Polanyi, especially his *Personal Knowledge* (1958). At many points I have been indebted to Alasdair MacIntyre, especially his book *Whose Justice? Which Rationality?* (1988). In Chapter 9 I have drawn heavily on Hendrikus Berkhof's *Christ, the Meaning of History* (1966). And in Chapter 16 I have drawn ideas from Walter Wink's *Naming the Powers* (1984) and *Unmasking the Powers* (1986).

Like all people who have used the English language I have until recently been accustomed to using the masculine pronoun inclusively to refer to both halves of the human family. That this is, for valid reasons, no longer acceptable to many readers poses a problem for the writer. To use both pronouns ("he or she") at every point can make sentences intolerably convoluted. I have therefore used both "he" and "she" inclusively and—I hope—impartially. I hope that this will not expose me to any serious charge of moral delinquency.

I am very grateful to Dr. Dan Beeby and Dr. Harold Turner of the Selly Oak Colleges, who were kind enough to read my first draft and to help me with comment. They bear no responsibility for the defects of the final product.

Selly Oak   LESSLIE NEWBIGIN
Birmingham

1. Dogma and Doubt in a Pluralist Culture

It has become a commonplace to say that we live in a pluralist society—not merely a society which is in fact plural in the variety of cultures, religions, and life-styles which it embraces, but pluralist in the sense that this plurality is celebrated as things to be approved and cherished. In much of the Western world pluralism is contrasted with a situation perceived to have existed in earlier times in which there was an accepted public doctrine, shaped by Christianity, providing the norm by which all belief and conduct was to be judged. Pluralism is conceived to be a proper characteristic of the secular society, a society in which there is no officially approved pattern of belief or conduct. It is therefore also conceived to be a free society, a society not controlled by accepted dogma but characterized rather by the critical spirit which is ready to subject all dogmas to critical (and even sceptical) examination. It will be part of my business in these studies to consider how far these perceptions are true and what elements of myth are present in them. For it is quite certain that long-established dogma only gives way to critical attack when that attack is based on some other beliefs. Criticism does not come out of a vacant mind.

It is often said, or implied, that the dominance of the Christian worldview in western European society was overturned by the rise of modern science, but this seems to be an oversimplification. Graf Reventlow, in his massive work *The Authority of the Bible and the Rise of the Modern World*, shows how the attack has its origins, far earlier than the rise of modern science, in the strong humanist tradition which we inherit

1

from the classical Greek and Roman elements in our culture, and which surfaced powerfully in the Renaissance and played a part in the Reformation. This humanist tradition is itself composed of many elements which can be grouped into two main strands. There is the rationalist tradition, drawing especially on Greek and Stoic sources, which affirms human reason as the organ through which alone truth may be known; and there is the spiritualist tradition, drawing on still more ancient sources which Europe shares with India, the tradition which affirms the capacity of the human spirit to make direct contact through mystical experience with the ultimate source of being and truth. What these have in common is the conviction, one might say rather the unquestioned assumption, that historical events are not a source of ultimate truth. Truth can only be that which is accessible equally to all rational human beings apart from the accidents of history, through the exercise of reason and the experience of direct contact with the divine. The most famous expression of this is the much-quoted saying of Lessing that the accidental truths of history can never establish universal truths of reason. For the humanist tradition this had, and still has, the force of an axiom.

Graf Reventlow's study shows how, during the latter part of the seventeenth and through the eighteenth centuries, while ordinary churchgoers continued to live in the world of the Bible, intellectuals were more and more controlled by the humanist tradition, so that even those who sought to defend the Christian faith did so on the basis that it was "reasonable," that is to say, that it did not contradict the fundamental humanist assumption. Reviewing the story, one can see how the defense moved through successive tactical retreats. There was, to begin with, the view that God has provided two ways of making himself known to us: the book which we call the Bible, and the book of nature. Truths which we cannot by the exercise of reason read from the book of nature are provided for us, as a sort of supplementary source, from the Bible. We are not, in this view, part of a story, a drama of creation, fall, redemption, and consummation. We are in a timeless world where timeless truths, valid for all times and all peoples, are being communicated in two different ways. As the eighteenth century rolls on, we find that the really essential truths are available to us from the book of nature, from reason and conscience; the truths which we can only learn from the Bible are of minor importance, adiaphora about which we need not quarrel. But inexorably we move on to the point where the Bible is subjected to the scrutiny of reason and conscience and is found to be full of inconsistencies, absurdities, tall stories, and plain immorality.

What is striking about the books which were written, especially during the eighteenth century, to defend Christianity against these attacks, is the degree to which they accept the assumptions of their assailants. Christianity is defended as being reasonable. It can be accommodated within these assumptions, which all reasonable people hold. There is little suggestion that the assumptions themselves are to be challenged. The defense is, in fact, a tactical retreat. But, as later history has shown, these tactical retreats can—if repeated often enough—begin to look more like a rout.

Perhaps the experience of a foreign missionary may usefully illuminate the point I wish to make. When I was a young missionary I used to spend one evening each week in the monastery of the Ramakrishna Mission in the town where I lived, sitting on the floor with the monks and studying with them the Upanishads and the Gospels. In the great hall of the monastery, as in all the premises of the Ramakrishna Mission, there is a gallery of portraits of the great religious teachers of humankind. Among them, of course, is a portrait of Jesus. Each year on Christmas Day worship was offered before this picture. Jesus was honored, worshipped, as one of the many manifestations of deity in the course of human history. To me, as a foreign missionary, it was obvious that this was not a step toward the conversion of India. It was the co-option of Jesus into the Hindu worldview. Jesus had become just one figure in the endless cycle of *karma* and *samsara,* the wheel of being in which we are all caught up. He had been domesticated into the Hindu worldview. That view remained unchallenged. It was only slowly, through many experiences, that I began to see that something of this domestication had taken place in my own Christianity, that I too had been more ready to seek a "reasonable Christianity," a Christianity that could be defended on the terms of my whole intellectual formation as a twentieth-century Englishman, rather than something which placed my whole intellectual formation under a new and critical light. I, too, had been guilty of domesticating the gospel.

India was then, as it still is, a religiously plural society. Within the fairly rigid structure of the Indian social system, there was and is freedom to follow whatever religious path one chooses. Our society in Europe has moved, in the years since the war, a long way toward the same kind of religious pluralism. During the years when I was sitting in discussion with the Hindu friends, Britain was still nominally a Christian country. Apart from the small Jewish community there was no significant non-Christian presence. Preaching the gospel was calling people back to their spiritual roots. There was little distinction between evangelism and revival. Today the situation is different. Our large cities have substantial communities of Hindus, Sikhs, Buddhists, and Muslims. Their native neighbors soon discover that they are, in many cases, much more godly, more devout, and more pious than the average native Christian. What, then, is the meaning of evangelism in this kind of society? It cannot be the sort of "recall to religion" which has often been the way evangelism was understood. They do not need recalling to religion; they are generally very religious already. Is it not arrogance to thrust our religion on them when they have already a religion of their own which is clearly worthy of profound respect? From such very natural questionings as these, we soon reach the situation which was noted by one member of the recent General Assembly of the United Reformed Church: when thinking of our unbelieving English neighbors we speak of evangelism; when speaking of our Asian and West Indian neighbors we speak of dialogue. The gospel is, like the facilities in the parks in South Africa, for whites only. It is a conclusion which the Asian Christians in our cities find exceedingly odd.

I am of course touching here on profound questions about the Christian understanding of the great world religions, on which I shall have more to say later, but this reluctance to use the language of evangelism in a multifaith context is a symptom of something very fundamental in our contemporary culture. I spoke earlier of the conflict already present in the sixteenth and seventeenth centuries between the biblical and the humanist elements in our culture, between a worldview shaped by the Bible and a worldview shaped by the assumptions of rational and spiritual humanism. At that time both elements were part of the shared public view, even though in tension within it. The Bible and the catechism which purported to summarize its teaching were taught as public truth. The great thinkers whose work heralded the dawn of the modern world were Christian believers and took it for granted that theology belonged no less than physics or mathematics to the one seamless robe of truth. A large amount of Isaac Newton's intellectual energies were devoted to questions of theology, and there was no mental barrier for him between this and his work in mathematics, physics, and astronomy. Yet, as we have seen, there was a tension in which the humanist tradition proved the stronger of the two. The Bible had more and more to justify itself at the bar of reason and conscience. Insofar as it appeared that it could not do so, the tension grew into a separation. The Bible became the book through which the life of the soul, the interior life, the spiritual life was interpreted—at least for those who were content to remain under its influence. It could not hold its own in the public sphere. Scientists and philosophers were no longer theologians and biblical scholars. The catechism could no longer be part of the curriculum in the public schools. There could be what are called "religious studies" because religion is a fact of human life. But the things which religious people believe in are not facts in that sense. Only what can stand up under the critical examination of the modern scientific method can be taught as fact, as public truth: the rest is dogma. One is free to promote it as personal belief, but to affirm it as fact is simply arrogance. How, in this situation, does one preach the gospel as truth, truth which is not to be domesticated within the assumptions of modern thought but which challenges these assumptions and calls for their revision? That is what we shall be concerned with in these chapters.

It may be convenient to start from the word which I have just used, the word "dogma," for, as we know, the adjective derived from this word—"dogmatic"—stands in our language precisely for all that is ignorant and arrogant, for the very opposite of a sincere searching for the truth.

"Dogma" derives from *dokein*, "to seem." It is the word used to designate that which seemed good to a competent authority and was promulgated as such. It is so used in the apostolic decree of the Council in Jerusalem as recorded in Acts 16:4. More generally in the history of the Church it has been used to designate that which has been authoritatively given and is to be received in faith. It was so used for many centuries. In our contemporary world, by contrast, the readiness to question dogma is regarded as one of the marks of intellectual maturity and competence.

Now it is beyond question, however we may evaluate the fact, that Christianity began with the proclamation of something authoritatively given. Paul presents himself not as the teacher of a new theology but as the messenger commissioned by the authority of the Lord himself to announce a new fact—namely that in the ministry, death, and resurrection of Jesus God has acted decisively to reveal and effect his purpose of redemption for the whole world. Obviously the New Testament contains many differing interpretations of this fact, but it is always one fact which is being interpreted, what my old teacher Carnegie Simpson used to call "the fact of Christ." And, whatever their differences, New Testament writers are at one in regarding this fact as of decisive importance for all peoples everywhere.

This proclamation invites belief. It is not something whose truth can be demonstrated by reference to human experience in general. Rather, it is that by the acceptance of which all human experience can be rightly understood. It is the light by which things are seen as they really are, and without which they are not truly seen. It rests on no authority beyond itself. When challenged to show their authority, its spokesmen can only say, "In the Name of Jesus." But it is proclaimed with boldness as the truth, not as one possible opinion among others. And of course it can be rejected, and is rejected. The New Testament repeatedly affirms a radical contradiction between the apostolic message and the wisdom of the world. The affirmation of this contradiction reaches its terrifying climax in the Johannine accounts of the arguments between Jesus and the authorities of his own people. But it is implicit from the beginning in the words by which (according to Mark) Jesus began his ministry. The initial call was to repent, to be converted, to have a radically new "mind-set," to face the opposite way as the necessary precondition for being able to recognize the new reality—namely the presence here and now of the reign of God.

However grievously the Church may have distorted and misused the concept of dogma in the course of history, and it has indeed done so grievously, the reality which this word designated is present from the beginning and is intrinsic to the gospel. Something radically new has been given, something which cannot be derived from rational reflection on the experiences available to all people. It is a new fact, to be received in faith as a gift of grace. And what is thus given claims to be the truth, not just a possible opinion. It is the rock which must either become the foundation of all knowing and doing, or else the stone on which one stumbles and falls to disaster. Those who, through no wit or wisdom or godliness of their own, have been entrusted with this message can in no way demonstrate its truth on the basis of some other alleged certainties: they can only live by it and announce it. It is something given, dogma, calling for the assent of faith.

And of course it is at this point that the other strand in our culture, the humanist, rationalist element, is roused to protest. To subject every alleged truth to the critical scrutiny of reason is, in our culture as in the Greek world of Paul's day, the mark of a mature person. Perhaps our culture has prided itself more than any previous culture on its willingness and ability to subject every dogma to fearless criticism in the light of reason and experience. It is therefore natural that the missionary, the evangelist, with his confident assertion of a truth to be accepted in faith, should be the object of suspicion or at least of scepticism. Is he not simply a survivor from a previous epoch? Must we not all accept that truth is larger, richer, and more complex than can be contained in any one religious or cultural tradition? Is it not more fitting that we adopt the attitude of a humble seeker after truth, keeping an open mind, ready to listen to all that comes from the varied religious experience of the human race? Is it not more honest as well as more humble to stop preaching and engage rather in dialogue, listening to the experience of others and offering our own, not to displace theirs but to enrich and be enriched by the sharing of religious experience? Only an open mind can hope to reach the truth, and dogma is the enemy of the open mind.

One might make an immediate and rather superficial comment on this by saying that it is very obviously a view which we apply only to certain kinds of truth. In spite of the enthusiasm of many educational experts for encouraging their pupils to have an open mind and to make their own decisions about truth, a teacher who asks her class whether Paris is the capital of France or of Belgium will not appreciate the child who tells him that he has an open mind on the matter. The principle of pluralism is not universally accepted in our culture. It is one of the key features of our culture, and one that we shall have to examine in some depth, that we make a sharp distinction between a world of what we call "values" and a world of what we call "facts." In the former world we are pluralists; values are a matter of personal choice. In the latter we are not; facts are facts, whether you like them or not. It follows that, in this culture, the Church and its preaching belong to the world of "values." The Church is among the "good causes" which must be supported by good people, and without this support it will collapse. The Church is not generally perceived as concerned with facts, with the realities which finally govern the world and which we shall in the end have to acknowledge whether we like them or not. In this cultural milieu, the confident announcement of the Christian faith sounds like an arrogant attempt of some people to impose their values on others. As long as the Church is content to offer its beliefs modestly as simply one of the many brands available in the ideological supermarket, no offense is taken. But the affirmation that the truth revealed in the gospel ought to govern public life is offensive.

The purpose of these chapters is to examine the roots of this culture which we share and to suggest how as Christians we can more confidently affirm our faith in this kind of intellectual climate. Let me here make only a few preliminary points which will have to be developed later.

1. Dogma is not the unique peculiarity of the Church. Every kind of systematic thought has to begin from some starting point. It has to begin by taking some things for granted. In every domain of thought it is always possible to question the starting point, to ask "Why this rather than another?" or "What grounds are there for starting here?" It is obvious that this kind of questioning has no theoretical limit. One can go on questioning, but then one would never begin to form any clear conception of the truth. No coherent thought is possible without taking some things as given. It is not difficult to show, in respect of every branch of knowledge as it is taught in schools and colleges, that there are things taken for granted and not questioned, things which could be questioned. No coherent thought is possible without presuppositions. What is required for honest thinking is that one should be as explicit as possible about what these presuppositions are. The presupposition of all valid and coherent Christian thinking is that God has acted to reveal and effect his purpose for the world in the manner made known in the Bible. Of course it is open to anyone to ask, "Why choose this starting point rather than another—for example, the Qur'an, the Gita, or *Das Kapital*?" But then one has to ask the questioner about the assumptions from which he starts, and which perhaps have not been examined. It is obvious that for most of our time we take for granted the assumptions which the society of which we are a part takes for granted. It is difficult to question them, and normally it is only someone coming from outside who asks the questions about what "everyone knows to be true." Here we have something to learn from the sociologists.

2. We need to attend to what has been taught us in recent years by the sociologists of knowledge about the social conditioning of belief. Every society depends for its coherence upon a set of what Peter Berger calls "plausibility structures," patterns of belief and practice accepted within a given society, which determine which beliefs are plausible to its members and which are not. These plausibility structures are of course different at different times and places. Thus when, in any society, a belief is held to be "reasonable," this is a judgment made on the basis of the reigning plausibility structure. In discussions about the authority of the gospel the word "reason" is often used as though it were an independent source of information to be set alongside tradition or revelation. But clearly this is a confusion of categories. Reason does not operate

in a vacuum. The power of a human mind to think rationally is only developed in a tradition which itself depends on the experience of previous generations. This is obviously true of the vast edifice of modern science sustained by the scientific community. The definition of what is reasonable and what is not will be conditioned by the tradition within which the matter is being discussed. Within an intellectual tradition dominated by the methods of natural science it will appear unreasonable to explain things in terms of personal will and purpose. But if God exists and he is capable of revealing his purpose to human beings, then the human reason will be summoned to understand and respond to this revelation and to relate it to all other experience. It will necessarily do this within a tradition which determines whether or not any belief is plausible—in this case the tradition of a community which cherishes and lives by the story of God's saving acts.

It is no secret, indeed it has been affirmed from the beginning, that the gospel gives rise to a new plausibility structure, a radically different vision of things from those that shape all human cultures apart from the gospel. The Church, therefore, as the bearer of the gospel, inhabits a plausibility structure which is at variance with, and which calls in question, those that govern all human cultures without exception. The tension which this challenge creates has been present throughout the history of Western civilization.

3. A third point which may be made in this critique of doubt is as follows. There is an admirable air of humility about the statement that the truth is much greater than any one person or any one religious tradition can grasp. The statement is no doubt true, but it can be used against the truth when it is used to neutralize any affirmation of the truth. How does the speaker know that the truth is so much greater than this particular affirmation of it—for example, that "Jesus Christ is the truth"? What privileged access to reality does he have? In the famous story of the blind men and the elephant, so often quoted in the interests of religious agnosticism, the real point of the story is constantly overlooked. The story is told from the point of view of the king and his courtiers, who are not blind but can see that the blind men are unable to grasp the full reality of the elephant and are only able to get hold of part of the truth. The story is constantly told in order to neutralize the affirmation of the great religions, to suggest that they learn humility and recognize that none of them can have more than one aspect of the truth. But, of course, the real point of the story is exactly the opposite. If the king were also blind there would be no story. The story is told by the

king, and it is the immensely arrogant claim of one who sees the full truth which all the world's religions are only groping after. It embodies the claim to know the full reality which relativizes all the claims of the religions and philosophies. As Polanyi has trenchantly put it: "The emphatic admission of our fallibility only serves to re-affirm our claim to a fictitious standard of intellectual integrity . . . in contrast to the hidebound attitude of those who openly profess their beliefs as their final personal commitment" (Michael Polanyi, *Personal Knowledge,* p. 271).

In a pluralist society such as ours, any confident statement of ultimate belief, any claim to announce the truth about God and his purpose for the world, is liable to be dismissed as ignorant, arrogant, dogmatic. We have no reason to be frightened of this accusation. It itself rests on assumptions which are open to radical criticisms, but which are not criticized because they are part of the reigning plausibility structure. But if we are to meet the criticism, if we are to be faithful bearers of the message entrusted to us, I think that we have to pay attention to four points with which I conclude this first chapter.

a. Part of the reason for the rejection of dogma is that it has for so long been entangled with coercion, with political power, and so with the denial of freedom—freedom of thought and of conscience. When coercion of any kind is used in the interests of the Christian message, the message itself is corrupted. The truth is that it is the dogma rightly understood, namely the free gift of God's grace in Jesus Christ, which alone can establish and sustain freedom of thought and of conscience. We must affirm the gospel as truth, universal truth, truth for all peoples and for all times, the truth which creates the possibility of freedom; but we negate the gospel if we deny the freedom in which alone it can be truly believed.

b. Second, it is plain that we do not defend the Christian message by domesticating it within the reigning plausibility structure. That was surely the grand mistake of the eighteenth-century defenses of the reasonableness of Christianity. There is a profound confusion of thought when it is suggested that reason and revelation are two parallel paths to truth, or when, in a further development of this line of thinking, it is said that alleged revelation has to be tested at the bar of reason. All this kind of language involves a confusion about the terms we are using. The faculty which we call reason, the power of the human mind to think coherently and to organize the data of experience in such a way that it can be grasped in meaningful patterns, is necessarily involved in all knowing of any kind. The question at issue, for example, in the debates about the respective roles of reason and revelation is really about how the data of experience are to be understood. They are—to be more specific—debates about whether the events which are narrated in the Bible are to be understood entirely in terms of political, social, economic, and psychological categories such as are used in a secular writing of history, or whether, without denying the usefulness and relevance of these categories, we recognize this story as communicating the personal will of God acting in and through all the events recounted. Reason is not an independent source of information about what is the case. It is one aspect of the human activity by which we seek to understand the world and ourselves. The difference involved in the long-running debates about reason and revelation is not a difference between two sources of information: it is a difference between two ways of interpreting the data which are (potentially) available to all. The Christian believer is using the same faculty of reason as his unbelieving neighbor and he is using it in dealing with the same realities, which are those with which every human being has to deal. But he is seeing them in a new light, in a new perspective. They fall for him into a different pattern. He cannot justify the new pattern in terms of the old; he can only say to his unbelieving neighbor, stand here with me and see if you don't see the same pattern as I do.

Perhaps the most crucial example of the point I am trying to make is to be found in the way we interpret the story of the first Easter. In the effort to make Christianity acceptable to contemporary thought many theologians explain the scriptural accounts of the empty tomb and the appearance of the risen Jesus in purely psychological terms, as visions created in the minds of the disciples by their faith in Jesus. Thus the resurrection story is the result of a preexisting faith, in exact reversal of the biblical record, which affirms that unbelief was turned into faith by what happened on Easter morning. Here is a classic example of the domestication of the gospel, of the attempt to defend it by co-option into the reigning plausibility structure. It is obvious that the story of the empty tomb cannot be fitted into our contemporary worldview, or indeed into any worldview except one of which it is the starting point. That is, indeed, the whole point. What happened on that day is, according to the Christian tradition, only to be understood by analogy with what happened on the day the cosmos came into being. It is a boundary event, at the point where (as cosmologists tell us) the laws of physics cease to apply. It is the beginning of a new creation—as mysterious to human reason as the creation itself. But, and this is the whole point, accepted in faith it becomes the starting point for a wholly new way of understanding our human experience, a way which—in the long run—makes more sense of human experience as a whole than does the reigning plausibility structure. That the crucified Jesus was raised from death to be the firstfruit of a new creation is—in the proper sense—dogma. It is something given, offered for acceptance in faith, providing the starting point for a new way of understanding which, instead of being finally defined by the impassable boundary of death (our personal deaths and the final death of the cosmos), moves from death outward to an open world of infinite possibilities beckoning us into ever fresh regions of joy. One does not defend this new perspective by trying to demonstrate its compatibility with the old. One challenges the old with the demand and the offer of a death and a new birth.

c. But, and this is my third point, it is essential to the integrity of our witness to this new reality that we recognize that to be its witnesses does not mean to be the possessors of all truth. It means to be placed on the path by following which we are led toward the truth. There is indeed a proper place for agnosticism in the Christian life. There is a true sense in which we are—with others—seekers after the truth. The apophatic tradition in theology has always insisted on the fact that no human image or concept can grasp the full reality of God. Christians are—or should be—learners to the end of their days. But it is equally important to insist that this learning is, like all genuine learning, an exercise which is guided and disciplined by a tradition—the tradition which stems from God's decisive acts in Jesus Christ. No learning takes place except within a tradition whose authority is accepted as guidance for exploration. No seeking can be called serious which is without any clue. Wandering about in a twilight where all cats are grey is not seeking truth. When Christians affirm, as they do, that Jesus is the way, the true and living way by whom we come to the Father (John 16:4), they are not claiming to know everything. They are claiming to be on the way, and inviting others to join them as they press forward toward the fullness of the truth, toward the day when we shall know as we have been known.

d. And this leads to the final point. The dogma, the thing given for our acceptance in faith, is not a set of timeless propositions: it is a story. Moreover, it is a story which is not yet finished, a story in which we are still awaiting the end when all becomes clear. Here, I think, is the point at which we may well feel that the eighteenth-century defenders of the faith were most wide of the mark. The Christian religion which they sought to defend was a system of timeless metaphysical truths about God, nature, and man. The Bible was a source of information about such of these eternal truths as could not be discovered by direct observation of nature or by reflection on innate human ideas. Any valid defense of the Christian faith, I believe, must take a quite different route. The Christian faith, rooted in the Bible, is—I am convinced—primarily to be understood as an interpretation of the story—the human story set within the story of nature. Our dialogue as Christians, therefore, with the modern world, will be as much a dialogue with the historians as with the natural scientists. Every understanding of the human story, even more obviously than every understanding of the natural world, must rest heavily on a faith commitment—for we do not yet see the end of the story. But no human life is possible without some idea, explicit or implicit, about what the story means. The Christian faith is—as often said—a historical faith not just in the sense that it depends on a historical record, but also in the sense that it is essentially an interpretation of universal history. Its defense, therefore, will be as much concerned with how we act as with what we can say.

2. The Roots of Pluralism

That Britain is a plural society is a fact no one can deny. Peoples of many ethnic origins and of many different religious commitments live together in our cities and share our public life. This fact of plurality must, as I have said, be distinguished from an ideology of pluralism. It is pluralism to which we must now attend. Within this single term it is also necessary to distinguish between cultural pluralism and religious pluralism. Of course it is true that culture and religion are deeply interconnected. Religion is from one point of view an aspect of culture, but this is not the whole of religion. Religions may be multicultural, as Christianity obviously is. And people of different religions can share much of a common culture. Cultural pluralism I take to be the attitude which welcomes the variety of different cultures and life-styles within one society and believes that this is an enrichment of human life. I accept the truth of this, but qualify that acceptance with the obvious point that cultures are not morally neutral. There are good and bad elements in culture. I would not wish to see cannibalism or infanticide introduced into Birmingham, and I would not wish to see sexual promiscuity and abortion on demand introduced into Madras. Religious pluralism, on the other hand, is the belief that the differences between the religions are not a matter of truth and falsehood, but of different perceptions of the one truth; that to speak of religious beliefs as true or false is inadmissible. Religious belief is a private matter. Each of us is entitled to have—as we say—a faith of our own. This is religious pluralism, and it is a widely held opinion in contemporary British society.

But it is vital for clear thinking to recognize the severe limits of pluralism. There is a very large area in which the writ of pluralism does not run, the area of what are called "facts." About "beliefs" we agree to differ. Pluralism reigns. About what are called "facts" everyone is expected to agree. Of course there are differences of opinion about the facts, but we don't accept the differences as final. We expect eventually to sort them out, clear up misconceptions and mistakes, and get general agreement about the facts.

But what are "facts"? It is certainly not more than a hundred years since children in Scottish schools learned at an early stage the fact that "Man's chief end is to glorify God and enjoy him forever." This was as much a fact as the movement of the stars and the Battle of Bannockburn. Today it is not taught as a fact. It may be included in a syllabus of religious studies, along with the beliefs of Hindus, Buddhists, and Muslims, for it is a "fact" that some people do have these beliefs. But it is not itself a fact: it is a belief which some people hold. It is not part of the curriculum in the public schools. On the question of "the chief end of man"—the purpose for which human beings exist—we are pluralists. Each person is free to believe what he or she prefers. It is a matter of personal choice, of having "a faith of your own." We do not ask whether the belief is true, but whether the believer is sincere in holding the belief. On the other hand, it does not occur to us to ask whether a person is sincere in his or her beliefs about physics; we ask whether the belief is correct.

Of course there are other things about human life which are taught as facts. It is widely taught that human life is the accidental result of a struggle for existence in which the successful succeed, and we are the successful. This is taught as fact. It has obvious implications about what kind of human life is to be regarded as successful. But it is taught as what "we know," not as what we—or some people—believe.

The way we understand human life depends on what conception we have of the human story. What is the real story of which my life story is a part? That is the question which determines what we believe to be success and what failure. In our contemporary culture, as exemplified in the curriculum of teaching in the public schools, two quite different stories are told. One is the story of evolution, of the development of species through the survival of the strong, and the story of the rise of civilization, our type of civilization, and its success in giving humankind mastery of nature. The other story is the one embodied in the Bible, the story of creation and fall, of God's election of a people to be the bearers of his purpose for humankind, and of the coming of the one in whom that purpose is to be fulfilled. These are two different and

15

incompatible stories. One is taught as fact; the other—if it is taught at all—is taught as a symbolic way of expressing certain values in which some people, but not all, believe. The first is taught as what we know; the second as what some people believe.

This strange split between "We know" and "We believe" is to be the theme of my third chapter. Here I want to look at the origins of the split. Everyone knows that, in any investigation, the answers you get will depend on the questions you ask. And, in the whole vast enterprise of trying to understand what human life is and what the world is, the questions we ask will be determined by our interests. The spectacular success of the natural sciences in the past three hundred years has been due to their concentrating on tracing the cause-and-effect relation between happenings, and setting aside the question of purpose. There was a good practical reason for this. Purpose is a personal word. People entertain purposes and seek to realize them; things, inanimate objects, do not have purposes of their own. An inanimate object, such as a machine, may embody purpose, but it is the purpose of the designer, not its own. If I come across a piece of machinery or equipment and have no idea of its purpose, I can of course take it to pieces and discover exactly how it works. But that will not explain what it is for. Either the designer, or someone who knows how to use it successfully for the purpose for which it was designed, will have to tell me. There will have to be personal communication. Of course he might be a liar. He might be trying to play a trick on me. If I am to use the machine successfully I will have to trust him, at least provisionally, and try it out. And if the thing in question is something designed to save life from disaster—for example, a parachute—my decision to trust or not will be a life-and-death decision. This is very awkward!

Only if I know the purpose for which something was designed, can I say that it is good or bad. The mass of silk fabric in front of me may be good as a parachute, but bad as a bell tent or a bishop's rochet. If I do not know the purpose for which human life was designed, I have no basis for saying that any kind of human life-style is good or bad. It is simply an example of human life as it is. Judgments about what is good or bad can only be personal hunches. Each person will be entitled to her own. They will be, as we say, personal beliefs; and since there is no objective fact by which to test them, pluralism operates. If, on the other hand, it were a fact that the one who designed the whole cosmic and human story has told us what the purpose is, then the situation would be different. That would be a fact—a fact of supreme and decisive importance.

16

Our society does not accept it as a fact. It is not part of the "plausibility structure." In his runaway best-seller *The Closing of the American Mind* Allan Bloom, a Chicago academic philosopher, has described the resulting situation in the academic world as he sees it, a world where relativism and subjectivism reign. Bloom finds as the most significant sign of this the fact that the language of "values" has replaced the traditional language of "right" and "wrong." He traces this back through Max Weber to Nietzsche. Nietzsche, he says, was the first to realize that the operation of the modern critical principle would make it impossible any more to speak of right and wrong. The factual, ontological basis for using such language had been removed. There could only be personal choice. And what could guide that choice except the will? We choose what we want. So we are left with the will to power. This, it seems to me, perfectly explains the dichotomy of our usage between what we call "values" and what we call "facts." Facts are what we have to reckon with whether we like them or not. Values are what we choose because we want them—either for ourselves or for someone else. Middle-class parents want values to be taught to children in schools because life will be more pleasant if these values are adhered to. But they do not ask whether these values have any relation to the "facts" as taught in school. They do not ask whether it is possible to believe that concern for minorities, for the poor, for the disabled is important if the fact is that human life is the result of the success of the strong in eliminating the weak. If it is a "fact" that human life is the accidental result of the ruthless suppression of the weak by the strong, and it is not a fact that "Man's chief end is to glorify God and enjoy him forever," then "values" have no factual basis. They can only be the expression of what some people choose, and—inevitably—it will be the strong who prevail. The language of "values" is simply the will to power wrapped up in cotton wool. And we cannot use the language of right and wrong because it has no basis in the "facts" as we understand them.

How have we reached this point? Hannah Arendt, in her brilliant book *The Human Condition*, makes an interesting suggestion—no more than that. She suggests that it was the invention of the telescope that made people realize that things are not always what they appear to be. It sowed in their minds the suspicion that perhaps in what we all think are obvious facts we are being deceived. How can we be absolutely sure that we are not? The work of Descartes, she suggests, was a response to this anxiety. He sought for clear and distinct ideas based on truth which could not be doubted. As is well known, he found (or believed

17

that he had found) this indubitable starting point in his own thought: "I think, therefore I am." From this there developed that radical dualism which has so controlled European thinking ever since—a dualism similar to that which had been characteristic of Greek thought between the intelligible world of ideas known directly by the mind and the world of objects known through the sense of sight, sound, touch, and so on. This dualism, expressed in Descartes's distinction between *res cogitans* (thinking reality) and *res extensa* (reality extended in space) created a situation in which it was necessarily doubtful whether the gap between these two worlds could be bridged. A scepticism about whether our senses give us access to reality is the background of the major philosophical thinking ever since. In the thought of Kant, whose giant intellectual achievement has overshadowed the thought of Europe ever since, the real or noumenal world must remain forever impenetrable by our senses. We can only know what appears to our senses, the phenomenal world. And the orderly structure which enables us to grasp and deal with this phenomenal world is not inherent in it; it is provided by our minds which, for the necessities of our own reason, provide the rational structure by which we can make sense of the phenomena. The rational structure of the created world, which science seeks to understand, is not given to it by its Creator; it is furnished by the necessities of human thought.

It follows that guidance for living is not to be found through knowledge of things as they truly are, for this knowledge is unobtainable. If the statements in the Shorter Catechism about human nature and destiny are factually true, then questions about right and wrong conduct can be rationally discussed on the basis of the facts. But this is no longer possible. Ultimate reality is unknowable. Human nature, like everything else in our experience, is to be understood in terms of efficient causes and not in terms of final causes. The study of the facts, in this view, will enable us to understand how human nature in fact functions. Opinions about how it *ought* to function can only be personal opinions, and any assertion that the purpose for which human life exists has in fact been revealed by the One whose purpose it is, is treated as unacceptable dogmatism.

This is so much the accepted view of our time and place that it is hard to look at it critically. Yet we must do so; we must examine the dogma which undergirds this rejection of dogma. The generally held assumption that doubt is more intellectually respectable than assent to a creed is one that must itself be criticized. It is a product of the movement of thought which I have sketched. It assumes that ultimate reality is unknowable. It insists that truth claims about God and about the nature and destiny of humankind must be in the form "This is true for me," not in the form "This is true." Confident statements of belief about such things are regarded as arrogant. It is assumed that there are statements of what is called "fact" which have been—as we say—scientifically proved; to assert these is not arrogance. But statements about human nature and destiny cannot be proved. To assert them as fact is inadmissible. They can never be more than "How it seems to me," or "My personal experience," or—even more typically—"How I feel."

Just because these assumptions are so largely unquestioned and because it is these assumptions which underlie the contemporary religious and ethical pluralism, it is necessary to subject them to critical examination.

Let me suggest five points for consideration in this regard.

1. There is need for what Polanyi calls the critique of doubt. When we undertake to doubt any statement, we do so on the basis of beliefs which—in the act of doubting—we do not doubt. I can only doubt the truth of a statement on the ground of other things—usually a great many other things—which I believe to be true. It is impossible at the same time to doubt both the statement, and the beliefs on the basis of which the statement is doubted. Doubt may take two forms. It may be in the form: I doubt your statement because I believe that something else is true. I doubt it because it does not square with the rest of my beliefs. In that case the situation is clear. But there is also agnostic doubt, which again may take two forms. It may be: "Your statement is not proved," or "Your statement is of such a kind that it can never be proved, therefore I doubt it." But in both forms this assumes that the doubter believes that there are criteria of proof which would be applicable in this case, or he believes that there are no such criteria. In either case he is able to doubt only because of things which he believes without doubting.

2. This leads to my second point, which is about the relative roles of faith and doubt in the enterprise of knowing. If we consider what is involved in learning to know anything, we will see that knowing has to begin with an act of faith. We have to trust the evidence of our eyes and ears, or, if we are learning a language, or learning science or history or any other branch of knowledge, we have to begin by trusting those who undertake to teach us. There is no other possible way to begin. It is of course true that our eyes may deceive us and that textbooks may be

mistaken and that even university professors may be wrong. Doubt, the use of the sceptical, critical faculty, is therefore necessary as we proceed. We may have to question and revise what we first accepted. But (a) we have no other way of starting except by accepting a-critically the evidence of our senses and the guidance of the tradition represented by teachers and textbooks; and (b) when we do begin to doubt and to criticize, it is always and can only be on the basis of other things which we have accepted as true and which we have learned in the same way, by accepting a tradition. There is no other possible basis for rational doubt. It follows, therefore, that, while both believing and doubting have a necessary place in the whole enterprise of knowing, believing is primary and doubting is secondary. The contemporary opinion—very widely held—that doubt is somehow more honest than faith, is an entirely irrational prejudice. It is a form of dogmatism which is entirely destructive.

3. The work of philosophers and historians of science in the present century has shown very clearly that the whole work of modern science rests on faith-commitments which cannot themselves be demonstrated by the methods of science. This has been frequently pointed out and it is only necessary to refer briefly to it. The development of science as we know it would have been impossible without two beliefs: that the universe is rational and that it is contingent. The point has often been made and hardly needs to be repeated. If the universe did not have a rational structure, if different instrument readings at different times and places were simply random events which could not be brought into a coherent relation with each other, then science would be impossible. But the rationality of the universe is not something that science can prove; it has to be assumed as the starting point of scientific effort, and the assumption is a faith-commitment. So also, if the universe were not contingent, if it were (as Indian thinking has generally assumed) an emanation of the absolute spirit rather than the creation of a personal God who has, by the act of creation, given it a degree of autonomy, then science as we know it would be unnecessary. We would know ultimate reality by the exercise of pure contemplation and the whole business of testing hypotheses by laborious experiment would be unnecessary. It is therefore not an accident that modern science was born in a culture which had been shaped for many centuries by this belief.

If the historians of science have shown us that the roots of modern science are in a certain kind of believing, the philosophers of science have also shown convincingly that the popular dichotomy between "facts" (as what we know) and "beliefs" (of which we can only say, "This is true for me") rests on an illusion. Facts are only grasped by an activity of the knower which is impossible without long training. This training begins in infancy when the newborn child begins to make some sort of sense of the buzzing noises and the ever changing patterns of light and shade which surround her, and continues through the long business of being educated into the use of words, concepts, and patterns of thought which are part of the inheritance of a human culture. Facts do not imprint themselves on the brain like images on a photographic plate. They have to be grasped and understood. All so-called facts are interpreted facts. What we see depends on the way our minds have been trained. At one time people looking into the night sky saw chinks in the celestial sphere through which the light shone from beyond. Later they saw heavenly bodies moving around the earth; today they see the minute fraction of a universe vaster than the human mind can grasp, and know that they are only seeing a few of our nearest neighbors.

As Polanyi says, in discussing some of the great scientific controversies, "The two sides do not accept the same 'facts' as facts, and still less the same 'evidence' as evidence. . . . Within two different conceptual frameworks the same range of experience takes the shape of different facts and different evidence" (Michael Polanyi, *Personal Knowledge*, p. 167). What we see as facts depends on the theory we bring to the observation.

4. I have already given reasons for thinking that the fashionable preference for doubt as against faith, "honest doubt" as against "all your creeds," may conceal the very arrogance which it proposes to condemn. The fact that all our knowledge is limited ought not to be used to disallow such statements of what we can know as we are able to make. The believer, encountering such a move, is entitled to put the question: "How do you know that ultimate reality is greater than any possible statement about it?" To the Kantian one may put the question: "How do you know that the unknowable noumenon exists?" And to the one who says that the whole truth of God cannot be disclosed in Jesus Christ, the Christian may fairly ask, "What is the source of your knowledge that this is so?" How does the doubter know so much about the unknowable? And the point has to be pressed further. The most obvious feature of the unknowable reality is that each person is free to conceive it as he or she wants. The unknown god is a convenient object of belief, since its character is a matter for me to decide. It cannot challenge me or pose radical questions to me. It is likely to be, as Feuerbach saw, just the en-

larged image of my own ego thrown up against the sky like the Brock-enspetre.

Certainly if, in affirming what I believe to be the truth, I suggest that I *possess* the truth in such a way that I have nothing more to learn, I am rightly condemned. That is the element of validity in the position I am criticizing. There is surely always more truth to be discovered. That this is so is one of the things that lie at the heart of life—even of the life of animals and birds. The curiosity which is always seeking to discover more seems to be one of the necessary conditions of life. But seeking is only serious if the seeker is following some clue, has some intuition of what it is that he seeks, and is willing to commit himself or herself to following that clue, that intuition. Merely wandering around in a clueless twilight is not seeking. The relativism which is not willing to speak about truth but only about "what is true for me" is an evasion of the serious business of living. It is the mark of a tragic loss of nerve in our contemporary culture. It is a preliminary symptom of death.

5. The devaluing of belief-statements as merely subjective ("What is true for you but may not be true for other people") involves a logical absurdity. It presupposes the possibility of an "objective" knowledge which is not knowledge as believed to be true by someone. This bogus objectivity is expressed in Bertrand Russell's definition of truth as the correspondence between a person's beliefs and the actual facts. This definition is futile since there is no way of knowing what the actual facts are except by the activity of knowing subjects. The definition implies a standpoint outside the real human situation of knowing subjects—and no such standpoint is available. An outsider may say that my belief is false because he sees the facts differently. In that case there is room for discussion. But I cannot apply this definition of truth to test my own perceptions of truth, since there is no way in which I can stand outside my own perception of the facts. I cannot at the same time say: "This is what I believe" and "What is the case is something different from what I believe."

When I say "I believe," I am not merely describing an inward feeling or experience: I am affirming what I believe to be true, and therefore what is true for everyone. The test of my commitment to this belief will be that I am ready to publish it, to share it with others, and to invite their judgment and—if necessary—correction. If I refrain from this exercise, if I try to keep my belief as a private matter, it is not belief in the truth.

In the next chapter I shall discuss more fully the question of believing and knowing, but meanwhile let me look briefly at what is involved in this dichotomy between "I believe" and "I know," as it affects our role as Christians in our contemporary culture.

It is surely obvious that knowing has both a subjective and an objective pole. It is subjective in that it is I who know, or seek to know, and that the enterprise of knowing is one which requires my personal commitment and often the development of skills in which I have to invest long hours and days of effort. And it is subjective in that, in the end, I have to take personal responsibility for my beliefs. In this enterprise of knowing I am dependent on my culture; I cannot, of course, detach myself from my culture or the tradition by which I was formed. The ways in which I have learned to cope with experience and to grasp the nature of things are ways which I have learned from my culture through all the years of training since infancy. Nevertheless I am responsible both for learning the skills and faithfully using the tools for understanding that my culture furnishes, and also for criticizing, refining, and even perhaps changing these tools. This is all my personal responsibility, and the beliefs which I hold are beliefs for which I must accept responsibility. But, on the other hand, I am not holding them responsibly if they are merely a transcript of my feelings. I am responsible for seeking as far as possible to insure that my beliefs are true, that I am — however fumblingly — grasping reality and therefore grasping that which is real and true for all human beings, and which will reveal its truth through further discoveries as I continue to seek.

What seems to have happened in our culture is a falling apart, a disconnection between the subjective and the objective poles. We have on the one hand the ideal, or shall I call it the illusion, of a kind of objectivity which is not possible, of a kind of knowledge of what we call the "facts" which involves no personal commitment, no risk of being wrong, something which we have merely to accept without question; and on the other hand a range of beliefs which are purely subjective, which are, as we say, "true for me," are "what I feel," but which are a matter of personal and private choice. To suggest that these latter beliefs ought to be accepted as true for all is to be guilty of the unforgivable sin — dogmatism. And, as I have said, this dichotomy between knowing and believing is embodied in the curriculum of our public schools and universities. The dichotomy is seen at its sharpest in the United States where it is established and fortified by the Second Amendment. There is a legally enforced division between what is called science and what is called religion. The one may be taught as public truth, the other may not. To teach that human beings exist as the result of the successful elimination of weaker species by those which have accidentally inherited superior strength or skill is allowed. To teach that human beings exist to glorify God and enjoy him forever is not allowed. Yet both of these beliefs refer to what is believed to be true for all human beings. They are both—if true—extremely important. Both of them are affirmations about what is the case. One is held to be a matter of objectively true facts, even though the Darwinian theory is obviously incapable of proof; the other is held to be a matter of private opinion. It may be taught in churches which are voluntary associations of those who choose to belong to them; it may not be taught as part of public truth.

This falling apart of the two poles of the business of knowing—the objective and the subjective—is reflected in the life of the Christian churches. It would be surprising if it were not so, for our churches are from one point of view part of our culture. I am referring to the deep and tragic split which divides Christians between those who are usually labeled liberals and fundamentalists. Clearly we are dealing here with another form of the same malaise. There are on the one hand those who seek to identify God's revelation as a series of objectively true propositions, propositions which are simply to be accepted by those who wish to be Christians. And on the other hand there are those who see the essence of Christianity in an inward spiritual experience, personal to each believer, and who see the Christian doctrines as formulated during church history as symbolic representations of these essentially inward and private experiences. This falling apart, this dichotomy, is one manifestation of the more general situation which I have tried to describe, the falling apart of the objective and the subjective poles of knowing. They are the twin products of the movement of thought which came to full self-consciousness in the eighteenth-century Enlightenment and which still dominates what we call "modern" culture. Between them they are tearing the Church apart.

George Lindbeck of Yale, in his important book *The Nature of Doctrine,* tries to develop a third way of understanding Christian belief which would—he hopes—open a way for healing. In contrast to what he calls the "Propositional Model" of the fundamentalists and the "Experiential Model" of the liberals, he proposes what he calls a "Cultural Linguistic Model," in which Christian doctrines would be seen rather as rules of language, the rules which make it possible to speak truthfully about God's revelation of himself in Jesus Christ. I that this is a promising proposal, but I shall suggest (pp. 58f.) that this tragic split within Christendom can only be healed as part of the wider healing of the split in our culture as a whole, only through a resolute assault on the fundamental problem which is epistemology, the way we formulate an answer to the question: "How do you know?" In the next chapter I shall venture some thoughts on this, thoughts which I hope will be relevant to this dichotomy within the life of the churches.

There is one particular aspect of pluralism which has become very important for people in the Western world during the past thirty years. Although the world has been a religiously plural place for as long as we know anything of the history of religions, most people for most of history have lived in societies where one religion was dominant and others were marginal. What the sociologists call the "plausibility structure" was provided by the dominant religion. This was the situation during the period when European civilization developed, and it is still the situation in a country like Saudi Arabia, except perhaps in the urban centers. But in the past thirty years European peoples have become accustomed for the first time to the presence in their midst of large numbers of people of other faiths. It has not taken long for them to discover that many of these Hindus, Buddhists, Sikhs, and Muslims are devout and godly people, whose religion means much more to them than Christianity means to the majority of Europeans. If what matters about religious beliefs is not the factual truth of what they affirm but the sincerity with which they are held; if religious belief is a matter of personal inward experience rather than an account of what is objectively the case, then there are certainly no grounds for thinking that Christians have any right—much less any duty—to seek the conversion of these neighbors to the Christian faith. To try to do so is arrogance. Since the interreligious issue is usually compounded by the interracial issue, and since we are aware of the racism which infects us so deeply, there are the strongest emotional reasons for regarding religious pluralism as something to be accepted and welcomed. The Christian faith may be true for us; it is not necessarily true for everyone. To confess Jesus as Lord and Savior and to worship him in the language that we use in church is quite proper as an expression of our devotion. But this does not entitle us to make the same claim outside the context of the life and worship of the Church. Our creedal statements are not to be understood as statements of objective truth, that is to say, statements of what is the case and therefore what everyone in the end has to deal with. Jesus is my Lord and Savior, our Lord and Savior; others, with equal sincerity, look to other names as the recipients of their devotion. We have no right to

25

affirm, in such a society, that there is no other name given under heaven whereby we are to be saved. Here pluralism reigns. What matters is not the factual content of faith claims but the sincerity with which they are held. They are matters not of public knowledge but of personal faith. Knowing is one thing, and the schools are there to see that everyone knows what we all need to know about the real facts. Believing is something else, that is, it is a personal matter for each individual. Each of us should have a personal faith of our own.

In the next chapter we shall look more closely at this interesting dichotomy in our society between knowing and believing.

3. Knowing and Believing

I have suggested that there is an error in the frequently repeated state-ment that we live in a pluralist society. We are pluralist in respect of what we call beliefs but we are not pluralist in respect of what we call facts. The former are a matter of personal decision; the latter are a mat-ter of public knowledge. The difficulty of maintaining this absolute dis-tinction between knowing and believing has been illustrated in a num-ber of recent cases which have been going through the United States courts up to the Supreme Court. In one case the proposal to teach cre-ation along with evolution in the public schools has been declared ille-gal. One view of the origin, nature, and destiny of human beings may be taught in the public schools; another may not. In the long judgment handed down by the Court there is no suggestion that questions of truth or error were considered. The only question is whether the proposed view is science or religion. If it is science it may be taught—true or false; if it is religion it may not be taught—true or false. For science is what we all know, and religion is what some people believe. By contrast, in one of the state courts the school board has been successfully sued by a group of Christian parents on the ground that what is taught in the public schools is really a religion, namely secular humanism, which is a total view of human nature and destiny in which one may or may not believe. No doubt the judgment of the State Court will be appealed, and no doubt the Supreme Court will overturn it. But the point is: how and where do we draw the boundary between what we know and what we believe? A whole series of Supreme Court judgments in the United States depend on drawing this line. But can it be done?

There was a time when no such line was drawn. For most of human history it had been thought that all knowledge was one and that theology was as much part of human knowledge as astronomy or history. Even as late as the end of the seventeenth century, Isaac Newton was as much involved in theology as in astronomy and physics. How has the line come to be drawn?

As I mentioned earlier, Hannah Arendt has suggested that it was the invention of the telescope (and perhaps the microscope) that started the trouble. When people peered through these new instruments, they discovered that things were not exactly what they had been thought to be. How, then, are we to be sure that we are not deceived by appearance? How can we be certain? From the asking of this question—one can argue—there followed the whole program of the past three hundred years of European history, a program of systematic scepticism. Every supposed truth must be critically examined afresh. Old traditions and dogmas must be exposed to the acids of critical doubt, and only what survives is to be retained. The rest can be thrown away. That is the only safe path from the darkness of superstition, dogma, and tradition to the clear light of truth.

The name usually quoted as the great pioneer of this movement is that of Descartes. He sought passionately for a firm foundation for knowledge, something that no rational person could doubt, and for a way of building systematically on that foundation by means of clear and distinct ideas, words and concepts whose meaning was determinate. The ideal was to be found in mathematics, where everything is absolutely clear and distinct and everything is related to everything else in a coherent way which reason can grasp. And, as is well known, he found his starting point in the famous statement *cogito ergo sum,* "I think, therefore I am."

Let me suggest three questions about this program. In the first place there is already a great act of faith. How do we know that things are such that we can ever expect to enjoy this kind of total insurance against error? Why should we rule out the possibility that things are such that human life is intended to require the taking of risks? It seems, in fact, that both human and animal life requires taking risks. What grounds are there for thinking that this idea of total certainty is anything other than an illusion, a piece of wishful thinking which has no relation to reality? We know very well that insurance companies make large profits out of this desire to be safe against risk, but did God consult the insurance companies in designing the world? There is certainly no proof that this assumption is other than illusion.

Second, even if we should grant that the statement "I think, therefore I am" is proof against doubt, it is so only because it makes no contact with any reality outside the thinking self—outside Descartes's famous stove in which this great thought came to him. May it not be the case, as modern scientists have shown, that only statements which can be doubted make any contact with reality? We may take mathematics as our ideal of a kind of thinking which is not open to doubt, but mathematics is itself a construct of the human mind, and we should heed the words of Einstein: "As far as the propositions of mathematics refer to reality, they are not certain; and as far as they are certain, they do not refer to reality" (*Ideas and Opinions,* 1973, p. 233. I owe this reference to Professor T. F. Torrance).

Third, we have to examine the program for "clear and distinct ideas." This requires a more thorough examination. Ideas can only be handled by the use of words. We may have clear and distinct visual images and no verbal description will be a substitute for these, but ideas— if they are to have any interpersonal currency—have to be expressed in words. And words are useful only insofar as their meaning is indeterminate. If the meaning of words was to be absolutely clear and distinct, there would have to be as many words as there are things in the universe. Every word we use is useful only insofar as it is part of a whole language, and every language is a distinct way of grasping and ordering the experience of the people who use it. This is true even at the simplest levels. When I point to an animal and say: "That is a dog," the word "dog" is useful only because it can refer to a large range of animals of an enormous variety of shapes, sizes, colors, and habits. I can use it confidently only if I have enough experience of these animals to be sure that this specimen is one of that class. There might be some doubt in my mind (not being an expert) about whether it was a dog or a fox. In respect of many biological species one has to be an expert to know whether the specimen in question belongs to this or that species. The point is that the use of the species name is meaningful only because it has a reference which is not absolutely fixed. As Polanyi has put it, "Only words of indeterminate meaning can have a bearing on reality" (*Personal Knowledge,* p. 251). If the meaning of words were determinate, all verbal statements would be tautologies. Polanyi also quotes some words of A. N. Whitehead: "There is not a sentence which adequately states its own meaning. There is always a background of presupposition which defies analysis by reason of its infinitude" (Polanyi, *Personal Knowledge*, p. 88). Moreover, the full sense of the word depends on the culture in which the language has been shaped. In some cultures a dog is seen as a member of the household and an object of affection; in others it is primarily a scavenger and an object of contempt. The word "dog" has distinctly different meanings in the two cultures, and the full meaning of the word can never be exhaustively specified.

I hope that the importance of this point will become clearer in the course of the argument. As an introduction to the critique of the Cartesian program, let me take a famous statement of Bertrand Russell about the way in which scientific truth is established, the way in which we come to be able to say "We know," as distinct from "Some people believe." Russell writes:

> In arriving at a scientific law there are three main stages: the first consists of observing the significant facts; the second in arriving at a hypothesis which, if it is true, would account for the facts; the third in deducing from this hypothesis consequences which can be tested by observation. (*The Scientific Outlook*, p. 58)

In the ensuing discussion I am following the argument of Drusilla Scott, *Everyman Revived: The Commonsense of Michael Polanyi*.

This is beautifully clear, but does it explain what actually happens? Let us apply the critical method to each of the three stages.

1. "Observing the significant facts." We have to ask, "Significant for what?" There are billions of "facts" lying around all the time; which ones are significant? It depends, of course, on what you are interested in. For the scientist interested in solving a problem they are the facts which are significant for that purpose. If he simply examines facts at random he will get nowhere and waste his time. The scientist has to identify the problem and then judge which facts have significance in relation to that problem. That is a matter for personal judgment and there are no rules for deciding it. And it must be a good problem. Years have been wasted in the attempt to solve problems which led nowhere; witness, for example, the centuries spent in seeking the secret of perpetual motion, or of making gold out of base metals. There are many modern examples. A good scientist is one who can identify a good problem. But what is "a good problem"?

What, indeed, exactly is a problem? Here we touch a perplexity which has puzzled thinkers from Plato onward. What are you doing when you try to solve a problem? Are you looking for what you know or for what you do not know? If you know, there is no problem; if you do not know, how do you know what to look for? Indeed, how do you know that there is anything at the end of the trail? The answer seems to be that to recognize a problem is to sense, by a kind of intuition, that there is something to be discovered which has not yet fully revealed itself but of which there are hints. A good scientist is one who has a sound intuition about where that something lies, and on that basis is able to identify facts which may be significant for searching in that direction. But he has no proof in advance that his intuition is correct. It is a matter of faith, and he has to stake his professional life on it, in the sense that if the intuition is false he may waste years of his life in a futile quest. There are many tragic examples of such long and eventually futile efforts. And very clearly this is not a matter of clear and distinct ideas and of things which cannot be doubted. Here is how one of the greatest scientists has described the quest. I am quoting from Einstein's *The World as I See It* (p. 125). "The supreme task of the physicist is the search for those highly universal laws from which a picture of the world can be obtained by pure deduction. There is no logical path leading to these laws. They are only to be reached by intuition, based upon something like an intellectual love." This passionate search is the only context in which the scientist can begin to guess which facts are significant. It is a venture of faith, believing where one cannot yet see. Without this faith and this "intellectual love," science cannot begin.

2. We move to Russell's second stage, the framing of a hypothesis. Here again the history of science demonstrates that this is never a matter of step-by-step logical argument. There are no rules for framing hypotheses. It is much more a matter of intuition and imagination. Some of the most significant new theories have come from a vision or a dream. The immensely creative generalizations first formulated by Newton and by Einstein were in no sense the result of a process which could be described in terms of rules or fixed procedures. As one physicist has said of Newton's laws, "They are the achievements of the human imagination and insight hardly equalled by any poet" (Sir Arthur Vick, "The Making of a Scientist," *The Listener* 29.1.59). And Einstein is recorded as expressing his delight when the poet St. John Perse spoke to him of the importance of intuition in poetry. "But the same thing is true for the man of science," he said. "The mechanics of discovery are neither logical nor intellectual. It's a sudden illumination, almost a rapture. Later, to be sure, intelligence and analysis and experiment confirm (or invalidate) the intuition. But initially there is a great leap of the imagination." (The conversation is reported in Crossman, *The Dark Interval*, 1975,

p. 31.) If all knowledge were to come up to Descartes's specification, scientific discovery would never happen.

3. Finally we come to Russell's third step, the verification of a hypothesis by experiment. Here again there is a great oversimplification of the way scientists actually work. A true hypothesis will prove itself true in all kinds of unexpected ways, and scientists will be continually testing it in new situations. But every day, in laboratories all over the world, there are experiments which yield results different from what the theory would require. Probably the majority of these are put down to mistakes in procedure. Many of them are left aside as puzzles to be considered later. Only if they point the way to some new and interesting problem are they followed up; otherwise scientists would waste their time in useless experiments. And, finally, a theory is abandoned only when it has been shown that there is another theory which is more intellectually and aesthetically satisfying and which can account for more of the facts. It is well known that when a new theory is propounded, such as those of Copernicus or Einstein, there will usually be for some years a passionate debate between the defenders of the old and the advocates of the new. The outcome may be in doubt for some time. But one thing is certain: scientists do not abandon a theory simply because some experiments have yielded results which do not confirm it; they abandon it only when a better theory is available. This point is particularly striking in the field of biology. A succession of scientists have pointed out enormous inconsistencies and impossibilities in the Darwinian theory of evolution by natural selection among random mutations. Cosmologists have affirmed that the known time-span of the universe is insufficient even for the earliest steps of this process. There is an almost total blank in many of the places where the intermediate stages between species should be represented in the fossil record. These and many other facts which seem to make the theory untenable are widely recognized. But until a better theory is produced, this one remains in place. It can never be proved; it might reasonably be held to be disproved by many arguments. But it remains the accepted theory until something held to be more acceptable takes its place.

We have to conclude that Russell's account does not do justice to the way science actually works. If we attend only to the textbook writers and the popularizers of science we get the impression that all this is "fact," quite different from the worlds of imagination and intuition in which poets move and from the world of faith in which religious people move. But if we look at the way scientists actually work, we see that this is a false impression. There are not two separate avenues to understanding, one marked "knowledge" and the other marked "faith." There is no knowing without believing, and believing is the way to knowing. The quest for certainty through universal doubt is a blind alley. The program of universal doubt, the proposal that every belief should be doubted until it could be validated by evidence and arguments not open to doubt, can in the end only lead—as it has led—to universal scepticism and nihilism, to the world which Nietzsche foresaw and which Allan Bloom and other contemporary writers describe.

Let us then return to the problem which Descartes set himself to solve. It is of course true that our eyes can deceive us, that perception is fallible, that "seems to be" is not necessarily the same as "is." How do we in fact make any trustworthy contact with reality? How do we escape from the pure subjectivity into which Descartes has led us, from a situation in which we have lost confidence in our capacity to know things as they really are? Let us, following Michael Polanyi again, turn from using the visual sense—as most of the philosophers of the last three hundred years have done in their discussion of perception—to using the tactual image.

Polanyi invites us to consider our use of tools. We take a hammer and use it to drive in a nail. The impact of the hammer on the nail is felt through a pressure on the palm of the hand. But we are not (when we are intent on driving in the nail) conscious of what is happening in the palm of the hand. We are conscious of the impact of the hammer on the nail. That is where we focus. We are tacitly aware of the pressure on the palm, but focally aware of the impact on the nail. If we start thinking about what is happening in the palm, we shall miss the nail. Now transfer this to an activity which is concerned with exploring reality rather than with knocking in a nail. A surgeon uses a probe to investigate a cavity which cannot be observed directly. No doubt there is a slight pressure of the probe on his hand, but he pays no attention to this; he attends to what is happening at the end of the probe. One can almost say that the probe is an extension of his hand: he feels the lumps and hollows that the probe explores. He indwells the probe; it is an extension of himself. He may be tacitly aware of the feeling in his hand, but he is focally aware of what the probe is finding out about the patient's body. Note two more points: first, when he is a student learning the job and is introduced to this type of probe for the first time, he will have to attend to the probe, focus attention on it; but when he is an experienced surgeon he will only be tacitly aware of it, focally aware of what he is finding out through it. Second, while he is using the probe, he is relying on it. A time may come when he is no longer satisfied that it is the right instrument. He may need to discard it and find another. But while he is using it, he must trust it. He cannot at the same time rely on it and doubt it. He uses it a-critically.

Now, says Polanyi, consider that probe as an example of the means we are using all the time to understand reality. We use words. We have to learn to use them. When we learn a new word we have to attend to it, focus on it. If we come across a horrible new word like "eschatology" or "contextualization," we have to focus on it and find out exactly what it is supposed to be useful for. When we start using it, throwing it around in our theological essays, we do not attend to it focally: we attend to the meaning which we hope it conveys. While we use it we rely on it to do what we want. We make it our own. We *indwell* it, as the surgeon does the probe. We are tacitly aware of it, but focally we are attending to the meaning we are trying to convey. Like the surgeon, we may come to doubt whether it is the right word for the job. We may write a sceptical essay in which we talk about "contextualization" as a word which some people use but which we do not think helpful for understanding what is really involved in communicating the gospel. But if we use it without quotation marks, we are relying on it to do the job. And, obviously, since we cannot write an essay in which every word is in quotation marks, it means that we are relying on these words to do the job. We use them confidently, a-critically. If we did not, we would have to be totally dumb.

But words are obviously only the most elementary of tools. We can only use them as part of a language which is shaped by the experience of a whole people. Behind every word there is a history. I use the word "experience." Used in that way it is a fairly new word in English. It used to have the same meaning as "experiment"; it has come to have its present meaning in English theological writing during the past hundred years, partly as the result of developments in German philosophy. I have some reasons for doubting whether it is a useful tool. But while I use it (without quotation marks) I am using it a-critically, relying on it to make contact with reality. But it has no meaning apart from a set of concepts which it was used to express.

So we have words, languages, concepts—all tools on which we have to rely a-critically while we use them. And beyond these there is the vast language of mathematics, the apparatus of dictionaries, maps, computers, all the tools on which we tacitly rely while focally attending to the meanings we want to grasp or to communicate. And all these things are part of a larger entity which we usually call a culture—a whole way of understanding and ordering things which is embodied in language, story, and all the forms of social life which are made possible through a shared language and a shared story. Most of this we learn, or perhaps one might say absorb, during the first few years of our lives as we learn to talk, to read, and to share in the common story of our people. Normally we simply take it for granted. We are not conscious of it. Like the lenses of our spectacles, it is not something we look at, but something *through* which we look in order to see the world. The lenses of our spectacles are performing exactly the function that the lenses of our own eyes are made to perform. In that sense, they are part of us. We indwell them. So also with a vast amount of our culture—its language, its images, its concepts, its ways of understanding and acting. It is only when we are exposed to a totally different culture and a different language, shaped by a widely different history, that we can turn back and see that what we always took for granted is only one way of seeing things.

What is surely obvious about all this is that it is a risky business. Knowing things as they are is not something that happens automatically or that can be guaranteed against failure. Even the newborn infant has to learn how to focus the lenses of the eyes in order to make some sense out of the patterns of light and darkness all around. At every stage there has to be a personal commitment to probe and explore, and at every stage we have to rely on tools, instruments, which we have to trust while we use them. But we have also to be ready to examine and reshape the tools so that they may be more fitted to the reality to be explored. The commitment is a personal matter; it has to be *my* commitment. In that sense it is subjective. But it is a commitment which has an objective reference. It is, as Polanyi puts it, a commitment "with universal intent." It looks for confirmation by further experience. The test of its validity will be that it opens the way for new (and often unexpected) discovery. It has to be published, shared so that it may be questioned and checked by the experience of others.

If this is even an approximately true indication of what is involved in knowing, how has it come about that, in our culture, there is a dichotomy between what purports to be factual knowledge, public truth which everyone is expected to accept, and the world of beliefs and values about which we say that everyone is free to have his or her own? It is hard to answer this question, because we are questioning our own assumptions. We are asking whether what we take to be obvious is really true. We are being asked to take off the spectacles we have been using and take a look at the world through another pair. If a visitor from another culture, accustomed to seeing things through another pair of spectacles, were to try to understand the way we see things, how would he go about it?

I think he would find that, like many people, we have two pairs of spectacles and use them for different occasions. To understand this our visitor would need to know a little of our history. If he did, he would know that there was a time when we used just one pair of spectacles. For many centuries European people saw the world as a unified cosmos in which all things had their place and their significance in relation to God, who was their creator and sovereign. Within this unified view of things there were certain ways of behaving which were appropriate to a world so understood. Centuries of this belief and of this assumption about human behavior have worked so deeply into our collective consciousness that, especially when we are thinking about personal and domestic matters, these assumptions about what is proper human behavior still have a strong pull. Our ideas about what is good conduct are still rooted in that older view of the cosmos. In certain situations we revert to that older view, put on the old spectacles for short-range sight.

But our visitor would see that during the past three hundred years a quite different view of the cosmos has gained ground, first among a few intellectuals and then gradually throughout society as a whole. And this provides the spectacles which we use in public life. These give us a quite different view of things. Now the figure of God has disappeared into the shadows. He may exist or he may not; the question is not vital. We have learned to understand things in a different way. The way to "explain" things is to analyze them into their smallest parts and show how everything that happens is ultimately governed by the laws of physics. If a thing or a happening can be understood as the mathematically calculable interaction of its parts, then it is "explained." Things are not to be explained in terms of purpose, because purpose is a function of the beliefs and values of the person whose purpose it is. Things are to be explained in terms of their causes, of what makes them happen. All happenings have causes, and all causes are adequate to the effects they produce. The ultimate goal is to understand everything in terms of the physics and chemistry of its constituent parts. Human life is ultimately to be understood as the product of an endless series of random happenings in the physical world. Chance and causality are the sufficient "explanation" of all that is and all that happens. The main intellectual drive of our culture is in this direction—to understand everything in terms of the fundamental laws of physics.

The world so understood is the world of what are called "facts," the facts which we "know" and which everyone needs to learn. It is a closed world of cause and effect, a world from which purpose has been excluded as a category of explanation, and in which—therefore—there can be no judgment of "good" or "bad." It is a world, as we say, of value-free facts. I know, of course, that developments in science during the present century have called this picture radically into question. They have done so in at least two ways. First, the advance of particle physics has shown that—to put it paradoxically—the ultimate elements of what we call matter are not material. It is no longer possible to envisage the atom as a system of rotating particles like billiard balls. As far as modern physics has penetrated into the secrets of the atom, its ultimate constitution may be described as a pattern of relationships between non-material entities—relationships which can be represented mathematically but cannot be visualized. And, second, the development especially of quantum physics has shown that a picture of the cosmos which excludes the observing subject (as classical physics did) is not a true picture. The scientist, with his purposes, is part of the picture. The concept of a purely mechanical system operating without any place for purpose is mistaken. These developments in physics—and other developments resulting from the work of astronomers at the ultimate limits of human penetration—have certainly changed the picture of the cosmos which dominated the eighteenth and nineteenth centuries. But there has not yet been time for these far-reaching changes to be absorbed into popular thinking. Most ordinary people, and many practitioners of the human sciences such as sociology and economics, still operate with the myths of "value-free facts" and a mechanical universe. And in such a universe, the rules regarding human conduct which were based on a different and earlier view of what is the case have lost their ontological grounding. They have no firm basis in reality as science understands it. They can only be "values," matters for personal choice. They are what some people believe. They are not part of the world of "facts" which all human beings will have to take account of whether they like it or not.

The facts are "value-free" because the world of which they are a part is not the product of any purpose, but is the accidental result of the operation of the twin factors of chance and causality. Yet it does not take much reflection to see the absurdity of this. It has been seriously argued that a monkey with a typewriter could—given time—produce by chance all the plays of Shakespeare. I have not yet heard a scientist saying that the monkey could have manufactured the typewriter by chance. But the example is a nice one to end with, for the machine—a favorite model for this kind of thinking—is precisely that which can never be explained without invoking the concept of purpose. A complete mechanical, chemical, and physical analysis of the parts of a machine and of the interrelation between them is not an explanation of the machine. It is inexplicable without some concept of the purpose for which these pieces of metal were put together in this way. A machine which creates itself and exists for no purpose is something which in most periods of human history would have been thought to exceed the imagination of even the most credulous. Yet it is widely diffused and is still given credence by respected scientists. It is this concept of a cosmos without purpose which provides the validation for the division of our world into two—a world of facts without value and a world of values which have no basis in facts.

I called it a picture, but that is perhaps not accurate. It is rather a set of concepts *through* which people see the world. The world looks like that because these are the lenses through which it is seen. The lenses themselves are not seen. We do not look at them but see through them. I shall try to suggest later how another set of lenses is available. I shall suggest that the Christian story provides us with such a set of lenses, not something for us to look *at,* but for us to look *through.* Using Polanyi's terminology, I shall suggest that the Christian community is invited to *indwell* the story, *tacitly* aware of it as shaping the way we understand, but *focally* attending to the world we live in so that we are able confidently, though not infallibly, to increase our understanding of it and our ability to cope with it. I shall suggest that this approach provides us with a way along which we may overcome the destructive conflict between liberals and fundamentalists within the Church. And I shall suggest, in line with what I have said in this chapter, that this calls for a more radical kind of conversion than has often been thought, a conversion not only of the will but of the mind, a transformation by the renewing of the mind so as not to be conformed to this world, not to see things as our culture sees them, but—with new lenses—to see things in a radically different way.

4. *Authority, Autonomy, and Tradition*

The movement of the Enlightenment in the eighteenth century, the movement which brought our contemporary Western culture to its distinctive self-consciousness, was in an important respect a movement of rejection of tradition and its authority. Immanuel Kant summed up the central theme of the Enlightenment in the famous phrase "Dare to Know." It was a summons to have the courage to think for oneself, to test everything in the light of reason and conscience, to dare to question even the most hallowed traditions. That robust determination remains operative as perhaps the central thrust of our culture, of what is happening now in every part of the world under the name of "modernization." Any attempt to affirm and defend the Christian faith within our modern scientific worldview has necessarily to answer the questions the Enlightenment put to tradition and the authority of tradition.

The first thing to be said is that a movement of this kind is irreversible. One cannot go back. It is one thing to say "The Church has always taught" or "The Bible teaches," if one is part of a culture which accepts these as authoritative. But it is quite a different thing to say these things in a culture which does not. If, in a modern society today, I say "The Bible teaches," I will at once have to answer the question: "But why should I believe the Bible?" In this culture an appeal to the Bible is simply an expression of my personal choice of this particular authority among the many which I might choose from. This is the point Peter Berger makes in the title of his book *The Heretical Imperative*. In a pre-Enlightenment society there are only a few heretics in the original sense of the word, that is to say, only a few people who make their own decisions about what to believe. For the vast majority faith is not a matter of personal decision: it is simply the acceptance of what everybody accepts because it is obviously the case. There is no alternative and no personal choice. By contrast, Berger rightly says, in a post-Enlightenment society we are all required to be heretics, we are all *required* to make a personal choice. Everyone, as the saying goes, has to have a faith of his or her own. If, then, I appeal to the authority of the Bible or the Church, that is simply my personal choice. It does not settle any argument.

Of course one could point out, in response to Peter Berger, that his heretical imperative is not universal. There *are* elements in our culture where tradition is operative. No one, in our culture, suggests that each of us should have a physics of his own or a biology of her own. We know, of course, that there are arguments among physicists and biologists, just as there have always been arguments among biblical scholars and church theologians. But where there is a consensus among physicists, as there is across the vast range of matter which is included, for example, in a school textbook of physics, we accept that as authoritative. In this field, the statement "All physicists are agreed that . . . " is normally enough to settle an argument. There is no significant proportion of our society which simply dismisses the findings of the physicists as merely private, subjective preferences. In the case of statements about Christian belief, however, the situation is obviously different. A very large section of society simply dismisses the statements of theologians as expressions of personal opinion—opinion which they are entitled to hold but which does not rank as public truth, as factual knowledge in the sense that the statements of physicists do. If Christians then appeal to the authority of Scripture or of the Church, they know that others will regard this appeal as simply the expression of a personal choice. How, in this situation, can Christians affirm their statements as public, factual, objective truth?

My own first teacher in theology was John Oman, and there was no issue about which Oman felt so passionately as the issue of individual freedom and responsibility in pursuing and grasping the truth. His book *Vision and Authority*, with its subtitle "The Throne of St Peter," was a passionate assertion of the right and duty of individual search for truth over against the claims of ecclesiastical authority. He takes Jesus' command that we are to become as little children to be his authorization of a spirit of endless and relentless curiosity which refuses to be fobbed off with authoritarian answers. And in an unforgettable chapter entitled "The Authority of the Optic Nerve" he contemplates the fragility of the instrument through which we perceive the world, so small and so liable to failure, and asks the question: "Why is the channel of sight a nerve and not a sinew, a thread and not a cable? Why, if the Creator would grant a vehicle of knowledge of the outer world, is it so weak and delicate?" (*Vision and Authority,* p. 44). It would seem, in other words, that the Creator had intended fallibility to be part of our human nature, and that the appeal to an authority beyond our own fallible vision is an offense against our Creator. And so, in a chapter entitled "The Essential Attitude," Oman writes: "All man's faculties afford their own demonstration and require no external guidance, nay, err if they are subjected to any such interference" (*Vision and Authority,* p. 40).

There is surely a vital element of truth in this, and there are situations in which it is this element which needs to be emphasized. But it is a one-sided emphasis. A teacher of mathematics who has tried to teach her pupils the elements of geometry will not be content until the pupil can see for himself or herself that it is true that the three angles of every triangle add up to 180 degrees. The teacher will not be content if the child simply accepts it on her authority and—when questioned by someone who does not understand—can only say, "My teacher says so." And yet the child will certainly not reach the point of understanding without first accepting the authority of the teacher. We do not expect each fresh generation of schoolchildren to discover the whole of Euclid by the unaided exercise of native curiosity.

It is instructive to compare at this point the differing approaches to learning which are currently used in science and in religion. There is a great deal of contemporary literature about the teaching of religion which emphasizes almost exclusively the freedom and autonomy of the child, and which strongly condemns any attempt to impose on the mind of the child any particular view of religious truth. One may take as an authoritative example the report entitled "Understanding Christian Nurture," produced by the British Council of Churches in 1981 under the chairmanship of Bishop John Gibb. The report affirms as the purpose of Christian nurture the development in children of "critical openness" or "autonomy." Tillich's concept of theonomy as something distinct both from heteronomy and from autonomy is rejected, since either God must give me reasons for submitting to him or else theonomy is simply heteronomy. In the words of the report: "Either divine authority is presented to us with reasons, in which case we must discern them in critical openness in order to obey God, or, on the other hand, God is a dictator" (p. 19). Children are to be taught to use their critical faculties in respect of any claim to truth, and to be open to new truths which might call in question their previous ideas of truth. The Christian must learn to "act as if it were possibly the case that his beliefs were false" (p. 26). The problem, of course, is that one can only entertain rational doubt about a proposition on the basis of some belief which, at that moment, one does not doubt. To doubt all one's beliefs at the same time is impossible. The report recognizes this in a later section where it is said that "a certain element of dogmatism is necessary to balance the critical principle since without this the criticism itself would seldom be sufficiently sustained and penetrating" (p. 26). The problem here is that it is not possible to be both dogmatic and doubtful about the same beliefs at the same time. One can only be doubtful about some beliefs if one is at the same time firm in holding others. In spite of this concession to dogma, the report overwhelmingly emphasizes the critical principle as the one which is to be fostered in the nurture of children. The approach corresponds to the succinct statement made by the legal representative of the school board in a recent case in the U.S. courts, a case in which Christian parents were objecting to the things their children were learning in the state schools. "The schools seek to teach students to be autonomous individuals who can make their own judgments about moral questions. The schools believe that students should be able to evaluate and make judgments on their own, based on their experience and beliefs, not on those of their teachers."

The contrast between this approach and the approach to the teaching of science in schools is obvious. The science teacher has a clear and firm view of what is the case about—for example—the laws governing the expansion of gases, and he expects that as a result of the teaching the pupils will also believe the same thing. This "believing" must mean, of course, that the pupil has really understood it, believes it to be true because he or she sees that it is true; it will not be enough that the pupil learns to repeat what the teacher says; the pupil must also understand it as true. And that means that the pupil will have to be encouraged to ask critical questions. There is no other way by which the new truth can really be grasped. But the teacher will certainly not be satisfied if, at the end, the pupil has an open mind on the truth or otherwise of what is taught, nor will the teacher at any stage give the pupils the impression that the truth or otherwise of Boyle's Law is a matter of private opinion.

This "understanding" is more than a matter of logical argument. It is much more a kind of intuition. Most of us can, perhaps, remember early struggles with school mathematics. There is a time, sometimes a long time, when one simply cannot see what the point of it is. The teacher's words are clear and simple, but one cannot see the point. And then, suddenly, the penny drops. One sees that there is something true and beautiful and satisfying. Afterward it is impossible to see how we could not see it before. The logical steps the teacher took in explaining it are now quite clear, and we wonder why they were not clear before. It is a little like trying to learn how to ride a bicycle. You can be told all about the way balance is kept by turning the front wheel this way or that, but you still fall off. But then, suddenly, you know how to do it, and after that you soon reach the point where the actions needed to keep your balance are no longer a matter of deliberate decision. You have so internalized them that you no longer attend to them but think only about where you are going. While you are still learning and falling off, you have to accept in faith the belief that people *can* ride a two-wheeled machine without falling off. You have to submit yourself to the tradition of bicycle-riding until the point comes when you have internalized the tradition and it has become part of your own self. The same is true in respect of our learning in mathematics and science. As Michael Polanyi has said, "The authority of science is essentially traditional" (*Knowing and Being,* p. 66).

The statement of Polanyi stands in sharp contrast to the way science is popularly understood. One could quote as typical of the popular understanding of science some words of Bertrand Russell: "The triumphs of science are due to the substitution of observation and inference for authority. Every attempt to revive authority in intellectual matters is a retrograde step. . . . One of the great benefits that science confers upon those who understand its spirit is that it enables them to live without the delusive support of subjective authority" (B. Russell, *The Impact of Science on Society,* 1952; quoted by Polanyi, *Knowing and Being,* p. 94). How is one to explain these contradictory views of the place of authority in science? The answer is partly by reference to history. At the critical time when the new science was developing it was necessary to reject elements in the traditional teaching of the Church. It was necessary to set the actual visibility of the moons of Jupiter through the telescope against the traditional teaching that there could not be such moons. In this sense observable facts had to be set against the authority of a tradition. And such oppositions are obviously necessary at many points in the development of human thought. But it is an elementary mistake to assume, therefore, that the authority of tradition has no necessary part to play in the quest for truth. The actual practice of science shows that Polanyi is right. Polanyi has followed the advice of Einstein, who said that if you want to understand science you should not listen to what scientists say but watch what they do. In other words, we will get a better understanding of science if we look behind the finished product to the workshop, the laboratory where the creative work on the frontiers of science is done.

I began by looking at the experience we have all had in our first attempts to learn mathematics or physics. We have to rely on the authority of the teachers, but the purpose for which this authority is exercised is that we should come to see for ourselves that what is being taught is true. Clearly also the teacher herself has had to rely and continues to rely on the authority of the scientific tradition as embodied in the standard textbooks. But behind these textbooks lies a whole range of material—articles in learned journals, lectures and seminars in which the frontiers are being pushed back and new ideas are being explored. It is through this work that the tradition is being continually developed and reshaped—sometimes by gradual adjustments, sometimes by dramatic changes which Thomas Kuhn calls "paradigm shifts." But how do these changes, these new discoveries, take place? I have already touched on this in the previous chapter. There are no logical rules by which one can learn how to make new discoveries. There are certainly no logical steps by which one could argue from the premises of Newton's physics to the formulations of the special and general theories of relativity. It has much more to do with intuition and imagination—the intuition that there is a problem waiting to be tackled, a configuration of things waiting to be discerned, an orderliness not yet manifest but hidden and waiting to be discovered. And it is a matter of personal judgment between alternative possibilities for experiment and research, personal judgment also in distinguishing between a meaningful pattern and a set of random events.

None of this can be embodied in formal rules which could be applied without taking the risks involved in personal judgment. That is why the scientific tradition can only be passed on through personal contact between teachers and learners. This is true even at elementary levels. A child cannot grasp even elementary mathematics simply by reading a textbook; the help of a teacher is essential. A medical student is not qualified to become a doctor simply by reading all the textbooks on physiology, anatomy, and the like. When she has completed this she has to go through a long period of clinical training in which she learns through hour-by-hour contact with an expert as he does his work. She may have learned all she can from a textbook on diseases of the lungs, but she will still need this clinical practice with an experienced doctor before she can learn to interpret the lights and shades of an X-ray picture. She has to acquire this skill through a long period of practice, and there is no way of acquiring it except by submitting herself to the authority of a practitioner who is already acknowledged as possessing this skill, and certified by the scientific community as a competent teacher.

The same holds true from this elementary level right through to the highest levels of original research. Only after a long period in which the student has submitted herself to the authority of the tradition is she qualified to work alongside a scientist who is doing original research on problems which are not only unsolved, but perhaps not even recognized except by this scientist. It will only be by watching this scientist at work, seeing how he tackles difficulties, chooses lines of inquiry, evaluates ambiguous evidence, and projects fresh and original ideas that the student will learn the skill of research. There are no impersonal and mechanically applicable rules by which such original research can be guided. There are no objective criteria by which the work of the scientist can be judged: he, along with his peers, is the one who sets the standards and determines the criteria, and—in doing so—accepts the risks of failure as well as the possibility of success. The question of success or failure may not be settled for a long time. Einstein's theories were, after much debate, accepted on the basis of their intrinsic beauty and completeness, but it was only long afterward that there was any experimental verification of their truth. In fact, a great many attempts were made to test their truth by repetitions of the Morley Michelson tests, and they did not give the results required by Einstein's theory. Polanyi records that in a broadcast discussion with Bertrand Russell they both agreed that Einstein's theory was never likely to have any practical consequences. Only a few days later the first atomic bomb was exploded, and since that fateful date we have learned of many more practical consequences that have flowed from his theory. Yet the theory was held as true by scientists even in the absence of proof or of practical utility. This is an example of an important feature of scientific discovery. The theory was held to be true because of its intrinsic beauty, rationality, and comprehensiveness. These qualities were taken to indicate that it corresponded with reality, and that therefore it would open the way for new discoveries. The holding of the theory for truth is an act of faith in the rationality of the cosmos. The justification—if one may put it so—is by faith; only afterward, as a spin-off, does one find that it is also justified because it works. The analogy with Christian faith hardly needs to be pointed out.

A major paradigm shift, such as that from the Newtonian physics to that of Einstein, does not take place easily. Perhaps it will come mainly through the conversion of younger scientists to the new view. A similar long debate took place before the Copernican paradigm replaced the Ptolemaic. For such paradigms form the world within which scientists work for generations. They form the lenses through which things are perceived. They are not easily or lightly abandoned. I spoke in the last chapter about Polanyi's use of the example of a probe. In the act of using the probe we do not attend to the probe but to the lumps and cavities which are being explored by the tip of the probe. The probe becomes an extension of my hand. I indwell it, just as I indwell all the bodily functions—eyes, ears, fingers, and so on—through which I explore the world. I do not attend to them, but through them I attend to the world I am seeking to understand. My relation to them is a-critical. I may have to be told by a doctor that my eyes need attending to, and in that sense I have to take a critical attitude to them. But while I am using them to examine things—for example, to read a book—I do not and cannot take a critical attitude. I indwell them a-critically. Clearly the scientific tradition as a whole, and the many concepts, classifications of data, and theoretical models which are the working tools of science form as a whole a tradition *within* which scientists have to *dwell* in order to do their work. Without such an enduring tradition, science would collapse. At any moment in history several parts of the tradition may be under critical review and alternatives may be proposed; but this critical review would be impossible without the a-critical acceptance of the tradition as a whole. The progress of science depends, therefore, on the authority of this tradition.

The authority of this tradition is maintained by the community of scientists as a whole. This community is held together by the free acceptance by its members of the authority of the tradition. Attempts to organize science from a single center, such as those made at certain times in Russia, have failed and are bound to fail. The authority of the tradition is maintained by the free assent of its members. But it is, nonetheless, a powerful authority. It is exercised in practice by those who determine which articles will be accepted for publication in scientific journals and which rejected, and by those who determine appointments to teaching and research posts in universities and other institutions. There is no appeal within the scientific community against this authority, and any appeal outside falls on deaf ears. Polanyi in various writings has given a number of examples of theories put forward with a considerable body of evidence to support them but which have been rejected without examination or discussion by the scientific community. Among the many examples given I quote just one. In 1947 Lord Rayleigh, a distinguished member of the Royal Society, published an account of an experiment which demonstrated that a hydrogen atom impinging on a metal wire releases energies ranging up to a hundred electron volts. If this were true, it would have enormous implications for physics. But the article was ignored. No one attempted to repeat the experiment or to discuss it. It was simply implausible within the existing frame of understanding. And, says Polanyi, scientists were right to ignore it. If every experiment which purported to show novel results was followed up by detailed examination and debate, science would evaporate into futility. Great numbers of articles offered to scientific journals are rejected without discussion simply because they fall outside the accepted tradition. Without this careful protection of the tradition, science could not develop. Yet if the tradition did not make room for radical innovation, science would stagnate. The point to be made seems to be twofold: first, innovation can only be responsibly accepted from those who are already masters of the tradition, skilled practitioners of whom it could be said both that the tradition dwells fully in them and that they dwell fully in the tradition; and second, that one alleged new fact, or even a number of new facts, does not suffice to discredit an established paradigm. That can only happen when a new and more compelling paradigm is offered, a vision of reality which commends itself by its beauty, rationality, and comprehensiveness.

The acceptance of such a vision is a personal act, an act of personal judgment to which one commits oneself in the knowledge that others may disagree and that one may be proved wrong. It involves personal commitment. But it is not therefore merely subjective. The scientist who commits himself to the new vision does so—as Polanyi puts it—with universal intent. He believes it to be objectively true, and he therefore causes it to be widely published, invites discussion, and seeks to persuade his fellow scientists that it is a true account of reality. As I have already said, he may have to wait many years before there is convincing experimental verification of his vision. It is his personal belief to which he commits himself and on which he risks his scientific reputation. But at no stage is it merely a subjective opinion. It is held "with universal intent" as being a true account of reality which all people ought to accept and which will prove itself true both by experimental verification and also by opening the way to fresh discovery. It is offered not as private opinion but as public truth.

On what does the authority of this tradition rest? Obviously on nothing outside itself. Like all visions of ultimate truth, science is necessarily involved in a circular argument. It has to assume from the beginning the truth of that which it seeks to prove. It begins from the conviction that the universe is accessible to rational understanding, it refuses to accept as final evidence that which seems to contradict this faith, and it seeks with a passion which is one of the glories of human history to prove that the faith is true. It can only pursue this task within a tradition which is authoritative. The maintenance of the tradition depends on the mutual trust which scientists have in one another, in the integrity with which each does her work, for no one scientist can have direct knowledge of more than a tiny fraction of the whole. But the authority of the tradition is not something apart from the vision of truth which the tradition embodies. It would be a violation of the tradition if authority were to be substituted for the personal grasping of the truth. The scientist, from the pupil just beginning to study physics, to the pioneer on the frontiers of research, accepts the authority of the tradition not to replace personal grasp of the truth but as the necessary precondition for gaining this grasp. He accepts the authority of the tradition in order to reach the point where he can say, "I see for myself." In Augustine's phrase, his program is *Credo ut intelligam*—"I believe in order to understand." And if the scientist is a pioneer who has reached the point where he has to challenge the tradition and to propose a drastic innovation, it is not in order to undermine the authority of the tradition, but to strengthen it by making it more truly congruent with the truth. Insofar as his innovation proves acceptable to the scientific community, it will itself become part of the authoritative tradition.

Before I move on to consider the bearing of this discussion on the question of the authority of the Christian tradition, one further remark may be in order. I have emphasized the character of scientific knowledge as—in Polanyi's phrase—"personal knowledge." It is knowledge to which the scientist commits herself personally and on which she stakes her professional reputation. She accepts the risk that she might be wrong. If this is so, must we not say that it is part of the deep sickness of our culture that, ever since Descartes, we have been seduced by the idea of a kind of knowledge which could not be doubted, in which we would be absolutely secure from personal risk? And has not this seduction taken two forms which, even if they disclaim all relationship with each other, are really twin brothers? One is a biblical fundamentalism which supposes that adherence to the text of the Bible frees me from the risk of error and therefore gives me a security which does not depend on my own discernment of the truth. The other is a kind of scientism which supposes that science is simply a transcript of reality, of the "facts" which simply have to be accepted and call for no personal decision on my part, a kind of knowledge which is "objective" and free from all the bias of subjectivity. With that question I move to look briefly at the role of an authoritative tradition in Christian believing. Here I suggest only a few broad generalizations which will have to be developed in the later chapters.

When we are received into the Christian community, whether by baptism as infants or by conversion as adults, we enter into a tradition which claims authority. It is embodied in the Holy Scriptures and in the continuous history of the interpretation of these Scriptures as they have been translated into 1,500 languages and lived out under myriad different circumstances in different ages and places. This tradition, like the scientific tradition, embodies and carries forward certain ways of looking at things, certain models for interpreting experience. Unlike the scientific tradition, at least in its present form, this tradition is not confined to a limited set of questions about the rational structure of the cosmos. Specifically, unlike science, it concerns questions about the ultimate meaning and purpose of things and of human life—questions which modern science eliminates as a matter of methodology. The models, concepts, and paradigms through which the Christian tradition seeks to understand the world embrace these larger questions. They have the same presupposition about the rationality of the cosmos as the natural sciences do, but it is a more comprehensive rationality based on the faith that the author and sustainer of the cosmos has personally revealed his purpose.

Like the scientist, the Christian believer has to learn to indwell the tradition. Its models and concepts are things which he does not simply examine from the perspective of another set of models, but have to become the models through which he understands the world. He has to internalize them and to dwell in them. And, as in the case of the pupil learning physics or mathematics, this has to be in the beginning an exercise of faith. He has to trust the tradition and trust the teacher as an authorized interpreter of it. In an established Christian community the first teachers will be parents, followed perhaps by teachers in school and church. In the beginning the child has simply to accept what is told on the authority of parent or teacher. There is no alternative to this. But if the parents and teachers are wise, they know that their work is not truly done until the child has reached the point where he or she can say, "Now I see for myself. Now I know the Lord Jesus Christ as my personal Lord and Savior." And this "knowing" is of course not a matter only of the mind, but also of the heart and will. It is a personal and practical discipleship within the tradition.

But being personal does not mean that it is subjective. The faith is held with universal intent. It is held not as "my personal opinion," but as the truth which is true for all. It must therefore be publicly affirmed, and opened to public interrogation and debate. Specifically, as the command of Jesus tells us, it is to be made known to all the nations, to all human communites of whatever race or creed or culture. It is public truth. We commend it to all people in the hope that, by the witness of the Holy Spirit in the hearts of others, it will come to be seen by them for themselves as the truth.

The integrity and fruitfulness of this continuing learning and communicating will require (as in the case of science) the recognition and honoring of the authority of a tradition. There will be proposals which are simply so implausible within the tradition that they do not deserve serious attention. But, on the other hand, those who have learned to indwell the tradition and to become skilled interpreters of it will also be called from time to time to propose modifications in the tradition, modifications which must be submitted to the judgment of the Christian community as a whole, and which may be the subject of debate and dispute for many years. The purpose, however, should always be that the community as a whole should advance toward a more complete understanding of and living by the truth.

Thus far, I have suggested, there is a close parallel between the ways in which the authority of tradition works within the scientific community and within the Christian community. The parallel, however, is by no means complete. In the case of the scientific community, the tradition is one of human learning, writing, and speaking. In the case of the Christian community the tradition is that of witness to the action of God in history, action which reveals and effects the purpose of the Creator. These actions are themselves the reality which faith seeks to understand.

Thus the Christian understanding of the world is not only a matter of "dwelling in" a tradition of understanding; it is a matter of dwelling in a story of God's activity, activity which is still continuing. The knowledge which Christian faith seeks is knowledge of God who has acted and is acting. The special structure of this kind of knowing will be the subject of later chapters.

5. Reason, Revelation, and Experience

Reason and revelation have figured as two opposing principles in a long tradition of debate about the sources and the criteria for Christian believing. As we have seen, the eighteenth century was, above all, the time when the attempt was made to show that Christianity was acceptable within the limits of reason and without recourse to revelation. There is a long Anglican tradition which affirms Scripture, tradition, and reason as the three sources and criteria for the Church's faith. Contemporary theological debate has highlighted the role of experience as providing the contemporary context within which alone the message of Scripture and tradition has to be grasped. The contemporary experience of people, especially their experiences of oppression or alienation, are seen as the context without which the text cannot be rightly interpreted. How are we to understand the proper roles of and the interrelations between these three factors in seeking firm foundations for our belief?

In one respect we can claim that there has been an important clarification in the course of the last three decades. The relation between the first two of the Anglican triad—Scripture and tradition—has been a matter of dispute between Protestants and Roman Catholics ever since the Reformation. At the first session of the Second Vatican Council, when the first draft for the conciliar statement on revelation was presented to the bishops, it had as its title *The Two Sources of Revelation*. That draft was rejected. The document finally promulgated has as its title *Divine Revelation*. Its first two chapters are called "Revelation Itself" and "The Transmission of the Divine Revelation." Tradition is thus in no sense a distinct source for divine truth; it is that continuing activity in which, to quote the Council's text, "the Church's full canon of the sacred

books is known, and the sacred writings themselves are more profoundly understood and unceasingly made active in her" (*Verbum Dei*
II.8). Tradition is not a separate source of revelation from Scripture; it
is the continuing activity of the Church through the ages in seeking to
grasp and express under new conditions that which is given in Scripture. The study of Scripture takes place within the continuing tradition
of interpretation.

It would be equally inappropriate to speak of reason as though it
were a third source of true knowledge to be put alongside Scripture
and tradition as the third in a triad. No one can grasp and make sense
of what is given in Scripture except by the use of reason, and—similarly—reason does not operate except within a continuing tradition of
speech which is the speech of a community whose language embodies
a shared way of understanding. Reason is a faculty with which we seek
to grasp the different elements in our experience in an ordered way
so that, as we say, they make sense. It is not a separate source of information about what is the case. It can only function within a continuing linguistic and cultural tradition. What is very obvious when one
looks back—for instance—on the use of the word "reason" in the theological apologetics of the eighteenth century is that the word denoted
a set of assumptions about what is the case, assumptions derived from
the science and philosophy of the time. The sociology of knowledge
has taught us to recognize the fact, which is obvious once it is stated,
that in every human society there is what Peter Berger calls a "plausibility structure," a structure of assumptions and practices which determine what beliefs are plausible and what are not. It is easier to see the
working of the plausibility structure in a culture of a different time or
place than it is to recognize it in one's own. When "reason" is adduced
as a third source of truth, or a third element in a threefold criterion of
truth, it is obvious that what is happening is simply that the reigning
plausibility structure is being allowed to operate. Now that the Roman
Catholic duet of Scripture and tradition has been eliminated, it is to be
hoped that the Anglican trio of Scripture, tradition, and reason will
soon follow it. Let me try to spell out more fully why I think this should
happen.

What was said in the previous chapter about the role of tradition
in science helps us to recognize that all use of reasoning depends on
and is embodied in a tradition. First, and most obviously, we cannot
reason except by the use of language. Language embodies the ways in
which a continuing community has learned to grasp its experience in

53

a coherent way. It expresses the concepts which give shape to its understanding. And the language is only learned as, from early childhood, we use it in the way that our parents and teachers and older contemporaries use it. In learning a language we are being inducted into a tradition, and we have no way of developing our powers of reasoning except through the use of this language. Later we may also learn a second or third language, and that raises issues to which I will come in a moment.

Second, we learn to use our reasoning powers by entering into the experiences, the discoveries, the debates, and the disagreements of those who have gone before us. A tradition of reasoning is never static. It exists only through the continually renewed efforts of those who live in it to say what rationality is, what way of grasping things makes sense. This will involve debate and disagreement, sometimes passionate. To someone living in a totally different tradition, these debates may seem meaningless and futile.

It is customary for people living in the contemporary post-Enlightenment world to express mocking astonishment at the passion of the theological debates in the first centuries of the Church's history, or those among the scholastic theologians of the late Middle Ages. Certainly no one could say that they did not know how to reason: their reasoning was of a subtlety and power that has seldom been matched. But their reasonings do not make sense to one who is completely domesticated in a different plausibility structure.

Third, the development of a tradition of rationality is never unrelated to the social, political, economic, military, and cultural changes which the society in question is going through. The tradition is never a merely cerebral one. The rationality which is accepted is part of and is embodied in the total life of a community. It responds to the new experiences which that community is having—whether these come from outside or from within. The tradition of thought is not a disembodied ghost which has a life apart from the total life of the society which carries this tradition. The rationality is embodied in *this* society, with all its elements of contingency, particularity, and sheer happenedness. By this I do not mean to endorse the determinism of some Marxists and sociologists. I do not mean that the ideas about which a society argues are merely the products of its economic or military or other experiences. That way leads, of course, to logical absurdity. But neither is the rationality something developed apart from the actual experiences of the society in question. There is a continuing reciprocal relation of challenge and response in which a society whose tradition is alive and vigorous responds to and seeks to master its circumstances.

Fourth, it might be objected that this way of understanding the use of our rational powers leads to complete relativism. If all rationality is the exercise of the reasoning powers of a particular community, responding to particular historical happenings and using a particular language; if there is no such thing as a supracultural rationality which can judge between rival forms of rational discourse, do we then have to surrender the quest for truth? Is there no truth which is true for all, but only "truth-as-it-appears-to-us-in-our-culture"? Following (in part) the argument of Alasdair MacIntyre (*Whose Justice, Which Rationality?* chaps. 18 and 19), I suggest three lines of thought in response to this objection.

a. All traditions of rational discourse are continually changing in the effort to make sense of experience. Old formulations and concepts are called in question as not being adequate to the realities which the community is facing. Sometimes the tradition is strong and flexible enough to respond to the new situation without a radical break from the past. Sometimes this does not happen. The tradition faces a crisis. There are internal self-contradictions: there are experiences which cannot be understood in terms of the existing ways of thought. At this point another, rival tradition of rationality appears on the scene—perhaps one that was always present but muted by the success of the reigning tradition, perhaps a new arrival. It confronts the reigning tradition with a radical challenge. It offers another way of seeing things, another vision of the shape of things and of the human story, a paradigm shift. Some, perhaps many, adherents of the old tradition find the new one more adequate to the realities they face, and are converted to the new view. The fact that this happens demonstrates that while all exercise of rationality is within a social tradition, the tradition is not ultimate; it is subject to the test of adequacy to the realities which it seeks to grasp. Truth is grasped, can only be grasped, within a tradition, but traditions can be and are judged adequate or inadequate in respect of their perceived capacity to lead their adherents into the truth.

b. Traditions of rationality are embodied in languages. A rival tradition cannot become a serious threat to the adherents of an existing tradition unless these latter are able to learn the language in which the rival tradition is embodied. One may learn a language at two levels. It may be simply a second language: the learner continues to think and reason in the native language, but learns to find words and phrases in the second language which correspond as closely as possible to those of the first language. But one may acquire what MacIntyre calls a "second first language," a language which is learned in the same way that a child learns to use the native tongue. A missionary or an anthropologist who really hopes to understand and enter into the adopted culture will not do so by trying to learn the language in the way a tourist uses a phrasebook and a dictionary. It must be learned in the way a child learns to speak, not by finding words to match one's existing stock, but by learning to think and to speak in the way the people of the country do. A person who seeks to learn it in that way quickly discovers that the two languages are mutually translatable only to a very limited extent. Words used in the two languages to denote the same kinds of things have very different meanings because of the different roles that these things play in the two cultures. If I may take an example from Indian experience, anyone who has been nourished in the Saivite devotional poetry of the Tamil poets, and who is also as thoroughly at home in English as many Indians are, knows that the poetry is untranslatable into English. Of course the words can be rendered into English, but if the resulting English text were given for translation back into Tamil by someone who did not know the originals, the resulting translation would mean something quite different. There are many Indians for whom English is (in MacIntyre's phrase) a second first language, and some (alas few) English for whom Tamil is a second first language. Both of these will in some measure have come to be at home in both worlds. The English missionary can feel the force and beauty of the worldview embodied in the Tamil poetry. He can set it beside the worldview in which as an English person he has been trained and the biblical worldview into which he seeks to grow. There is thus an internal dialogue in which the question at stake is: "Which is more adequate for grasping and coping with reality with which all human beings are faced?" This is a dialogue about truth. In this dialogue the two traditions of rationality are compared with one another in respect of their adequacy to the realities with which all human beings have to deal. And, obviously, this internal dialogue is the necessary precondition for the external dialogue which is at the center of a missionary's proper concern. Although the two ways of reasoning are not mutually translatable except to a limited degree, that does not mean that they cannot be compared in respect of their adequacy to enable human beings to know and cope with reality.

c. If the relativist claims that, since all reasoning is embodied in a particular social context, no claim to know the truth can be sustained, one has to ask for the basis on which this claim is made. It is, after all, a claim to know something about reality—namely that reality is unknowable. What is the social context within which this claim can be formulated? The answer, MacIntyre suggests, is that the social context is that cosmopolitan world in which individuals live a rootless existence and are without a firm and stable social tradition. One element in this kind of cosmopolitan culture is the use of an international language such as English into which, it is supposed, all forms of human thought can be translated. Translations of the literature of a vast variety of human societies are in fact available. The person shaped by this culture will thus have the illusion of having an overview of all these different traditions without having had the actual experience of seeing the world through any of them.

For a person who dwells in the contemporary cosmopolitan culture, shaped by the reigning dichotomy between "facts" and "beliefs," it will be natural to relativize all the differing belief systems. And when, in this culture, "reason" is set against the specific, historically shaped tradition of Christian belief, it is obvious that what is happening is that the "plausibility structure" is performing its normal function. The Christian, on the other hand, will relativize the reigning plausibility structure in the light of the gospel. There is no disembodied "reason" which can act as impartial umpire between the rival claims.

The conclusion of the discussion so far is that when reason and tradition are opposed as separate or rival criteria of truth, then the nature of reason is being misunderstood. Every exercise of reason depends on a social and linguistic tradition which is, therefore, something which has the contingent, accidental character of all historical happenings. Lessing's great gulf which he confessed himself unable to jump, the gulf between accidental events of history and universal truths of reason, disappears on closer inspection. There are no "truths of reason" except those that have been developed in a historical tradition. The reasoning of Aristotle was developed in the actual context of the life of the Greek polis. The reasoning of John Locke was developed in the context of the rising property-owning citizenship of the England of that period. The reasoning which forms the texture of Christian theology arises out of the historical happenings which form the subject matter of the biblical record. It is the activity of a specific community among other human communities, namely that community which continually seeks to understand and cope with all experience in the light of what was disclosed to those who were participants in or witnesses of these happenings. The happenedness, the particularity, the contingency of these events, and the consequent particularity of the Christian Church as one community among the many human communities, do not invalidate the universal claim which its rational activities make and must make. It shares this particularity with every form of rationality. This social context of rationality becomes clear when we look at the use of the idea of "self-evident truths" which played such a large role in the eighteenth century. The famous statement of the American founding fathers, "we hold these truths to be self-evident. . . ," reads oddly now. It is obvious to us that the statements which follow these words are by no means self-evident. What we call "self-evident truths" are not the starting point for rational argument, but the product of a long history of rational argument. The mathematician John Puddefoot writes: "An axiom set is not the foundation of a system, but the product of generations of mathematical enquiry as it has eventually been formalised, or axiomatised" (*Logic and Affirmation,* p. 16).

Clearly, then, reason does not operate except within a continuing social tradition which cannot be understood as a purely cerebral operation unrelated to the ongoing experiences of the community which carries this tradition forward. The contemporary advocates of "contextual theology" wish to emphasize the role of contemporary experience in the formulation of theological truth. Theology, they affirm, cannot be a matter of timeless truths handed down from generation to generation in Bible and creeds; it must arise out of the experience which people are having now. It must be, as is often said, inductive rather than deductive. It does not start with dogmatic statements—the "axioms" of theology—and then argue deductively from them as to what is to be believed and done now; rather, it must begin with analysis of the present situation and discover, in this situation, what God is doing now. One must begin, as is often said, with the facts. This approach to theology is particularly congenial in the English scene with its strong tradition of empiricism. But, as the modern philosophers of science have so thoroughly taught us, "facts" are always theory laden. What we see depends on the conceptual framework formed by the tradition in which we stand. All experience is interpreted experience. The empiricist concept of experience as simply bare uninterpreted sense data was, says MacIntyre, a cultural invention of the late seventeenth and eighteenth centuries designed to bridge the gap which had opened up between "seems to be" and "is." It is a concept of experience which has had a short history and surely has no future. In the development of one particular form of contextual theology, namely the liberation theology of Latin America, it is clear that the "facts" are interpreted through Marxist theory. This may well be, probably is, a necessary corrective to the way of interpreting the facts through the concepts of post-Enlightenment economic theory as Christians in affluent circumstances have done. But it has to be asked whether it is intellectually coherent to use one conceptual framework for diagnosis and another for treatment.

In the third chapter, "Knowing and Believing," I said something about the way in which the data of experience function in the formation of overall theories and worldviews. I spoke of the role of intuition and imagination in the formation of new theoretical patterns. There is an intuition that a kind of rational coherence lies hidden behind apparently incoherent data. There is often a long period of brooding reflection. At some point there is an imaginative leap with a new vision of coherence, something which compels assent by its beauty, its simplicity, and its comprehensiveness. In the present chapter I have spoken of the Christian community as having a tradition of rationality which springs from what was disclosed to those who were witnesses of or participants in the events which are described in the Bible. There is, clearly, some analogy between this kind of disclosure and the imaginative leap that marks the birth of a new vision in scientific discovery. Events and experiences disclose a deeper meaning than first appeared. "Surely God is in this place, and I knew it not." A bush in the desert becomes the place where the lonely exile finds himself met and challenged by a living presence. "Who do you say that I am?" "You are the Christ." These moments of disclosure surely have something in common with the moments when great new visions of the coherence of nature flash into the mind of a scientist. There is something akin to these moments of disclosure in the experience of Kepler describing the discovery of his Third Law: "At last I have brought it to light and recognized its truth beyond all my hopes. . . . The pure Sun itself of the most marvellous contemplation has shone forth" (*Harmonices Mundi*, Book V, chap. 1, quoted by Polanyi, *Personal Knowledge*, p. 7).

Surely there is a likeness between these moments of disclosure in the work of science and the moments of revelation in the story of religion, but certainly there is also a difference. Kepler says, "I have brought it to light"; the prophet says, "God spoke to me." We begin to speak not of discovery but of revelation. What is at stake in this difference of language? Does the use of the word "revelation" mean that reason has been left behind? Obviously not. Both the discovery by Kepler of a new pattern in the movement of the heavenly bodies and the disclosure to Moses of a personal calling become the starting point of a tradition of reasoning in which the significance of these disclosures is explored, developed, tested against new experience, and extended into further areas of thought. There is a tradition of rational thought which takes the experience of Moses as its starting point and continues through the succeeding millennia into the present day in various forms, Jewish, Christian, and Islamic. Reason operates in this tradition no less rigorously than in the tradition of thought which has developed from the discoveries of Kepler. The difference between these two traditions is not that one relies on reason and the other on revelation. Both are inconceivable apart from their rationality. The difference lies at the point of contrast between the two ways of expressing the original experience: "I have discovered" and "God has spoken."

The difference lies at the point which was so unforgettably identified in the book of Martin Buber, *I and Thou*. Buber was the one who, at least for my generation, clarified the distinction between two kinds of experience, the experience of the world of I-it, and the experience of the world of I-You. The former is the world of the autonomous reason, the reason which is in control, which can say at the end, "I have discovered." In the world of I-it, I am in control. I decide what questions to ask, what tests to apply. I analyze and dissect. I formulate hypotheses. I force the world to answer the questions I put to it. I am sovereign. In the world of interpersonal relations the situation is different. It is, of course, true that it is possible to treat other persons in the way I have just described. I may try to force a person to answer the questions I put, but that person can refuse. I may set about analyzing the person's character, but I will not get far unless the person cooperates. I may perform operations to dissect and analyze the structure of his brain to find out how it works, but of course I can only do so by killing the person. In other words, I can gain a vast amount of knowledge about other people by the use of the autonomous reason and the tools which have been developed by psychology, neurology, sociology, and other sciences. The range of such investigation is unlimited. But it will never bring the knowledge of another person which is available to me if I will trust the other person as a free subject, listen to that person, answer the questions he or she puts to me, allow myself to be challenged, in other words abandon the role of sovereign autonomy and become a trusting and listening person. And it is obvious that if I move from the first attitude to the second, what has happened is not that I have abandoned the use of reason. I am still a rational person making rational judgments and drawing rational conclusions from data. The difference is in the role that reason is called to play. Reason has become the servant of a listening and trusting openness instead of being the servant of a masterful autonomy. The difference is not between the use of reason and its abandonment; it is the difference between two ways of understanding the world, one in which the self is sovereign and the other in which I understand myself only in a relation of mutuality with other selves.

It is thus surely clear that the traditional dichotomy, which has played such a large role in theology, between reason and revelation, rests on a serious misunderstanding. The real issue is, of course, between two different views of what is the case. If it is the case that the ultimate reality which lies behind all our experience is, in some sense, personal; if—that is to say—we approach an understanding of that ultimate reality most closely by following the clues which are given to us in personal relationship, then it will follow that personal knowledge of that reality will only be available in the way in which we come to know another person, or at least in a way which is more like this than the way in which we come to know the working of the electrical circuits in the human brain. Of course it is obvious that there *is* a kind of knowledge available through the ways of knowing which are appropriate to the "I-it" world. There *is* such a thing as "natural theology." If ultimate reality is best understood on the analogy of personal being, or, to put it in more familiar terms, if God has created all things and has made all human beings in his image, and has never left himself without witness in the mind and conscience of any people, then it will follow that data are available from which it is possible to arrive at the hypothesis that God exists. But between this kind of knowledge and the knowledge that we have of another person whom we know and trust personally, there is a radical discontinuity. The sort of analytical, psychological, sociological, or neurological knowledge of the working of another person's mind is not in any way a step toward the knowing of another person which we experience in love and friendship. By itself, it could only lead us away from such knowledge. That truly personal knowledge only becomes a possibility when I abandon the sovereign claim of autonomous reason, the claim to know the other person without that person's self-communication in speech and act and gesture; when I am ready to stop my investigations and listen, to be addressed, to be called in question, to be summoned to an adventure of trust. Natural theology, in other words, is in no way a step on the way toward the theology which takes God's self-revelation as its starting point. It is more likely, in fact, to lead in the opposite direction.

It is a misunderstanding of this position to say that the human person has no possibility of knowing God. The possibility is actualized in the fact that God does reveal himself and has revealed himself. As Karl Barth says, it is in the actual meeting of God with us that we come to know that "man is capable of perceiving the God who meets him and reveals himself to him; that he is capable of distinguishing him from himself and vice versa; that he can recognize his divine being as such and his word and his will" (*CD* III/2, p. 399). It is from this self-revealing of God that men and women can learn to discern the evidences of his presence and work through their daily experience of the created world. In doing so, we use our reason. The true opposition is not between reason and revelation as sources of and criteria for truth. It is between two uses to which reason is put. It may be put to the service of an autonomy which refuses to recognize any other personal reality except its own; which treats all reality as open to the kind of masterful exploration that is appropriate to the world of things, where the appropriate phrase is: "I discovered." But it may equally be put to the service of an openness which is ready to listen to, be challenged and questioned by another personal reality. In neither kind of activity can we engage except as rational beings. When reason is set against revelation, the terms of the debate have been radically confused. What is happening is not that reason is set against something which is unreasonable, but that another tradition of rational argument is being set against a tradition of rational argument which takes as its starting point a moment or moments of divine self-revelation and which will therefore naturally continue to say, not "We discovered," but "God spoke and acted." From another tradition of rational discourse it is of course possible to say that "God" does not exist and that the language of revelation has to be translated into the language of discovery. "God spoke to Moses" will perhaps be translated as "Moses had a religious experience." The lines are then laid down for a dialogue between two traditions of rationality, not between reason and revelation.

The argument so far leaves open a number of questions which have to be addressed in the next two chapters. Are we speaking about a general revelation available to all peoples, or about a special revelation to one people—the people of Israel? Is historicity, historical factuality, necessarily bound up with this revelation? If the revelation is to one people, how does this relate to God's purpose for his whole creation? We have to speak about revelation as history and about the logic of election. These will be the subjects of the following chapters.

The Christian tradition of rationality takes as its starting point not any alleged self-evident truths. Its starting point is events in which God made himself known to men and women in particular circumstances — to Abraham and Moses, to the long succession of prophets, and to the first apostles and witnesses who saw and heard and touched the incarnate Word of God himself, Jesus of Nazareth. These are all happenings within the world of secular events, the world which is investigated by the natural and human sciences. These revelations were always addressed to men and women in particular contexts and called for specific responses within and appropriate to those contexts. The community which responded to this call and challenge had to make sense of and cope with the ever changing circumstances of their ongoing history in the light of what had been revealed to them in the original events. The originally given revelation had to be continually reappropriated and reinterpreted in the light of new situations. It had to be tested to see whether it could continue to provide coherence and meaning for new experience. It was tested almost to the breaking point, especially in the experience of the destruction of the Jewish state and the long exile. That testing in turn provided the background through which the shattering experience which the first disciples had in the sequence of events leading up to Good Friday could be re-understood within the terms of the original revelation. Continually through the centuries the community seeks to find coherence, meaning, and hope in the events, sometimes apparently meaningless and chaotic events, through which it lives. As we have seen in looking at the work of science, so here the argument is necessarily circular. The believer starts from the faith that reality is rational, that a coherent purpose can be discerned in experience. The struggle is to prove that faith true in circumstances which seem to call it in question. The effort is always a rational effort, an effort to find rational meaning in apparently irrational events through the pattern given in the original revelation. So the tradition is being continually reshaped and reappropriated in the struggle to cope with ongoing experience.

Like every living tradition, it is always threatened with the possibility of disintegration. It has to be sustained in its integrity by the intellectual vigor and practical courage with which its members seek to be faithful to it—not by repeating past formulas but by courageously restating the tradition in the light of new experience. Like the tradition of rationality in the natural sciences, it has to be protected against aberrations. It cannot afford the luxury of chasing every maverick idea that turns up. It requires a discipline which has to be enforced not by any centralized authority but by the discernment of the whole body of its adherents. It makes universal claims, but coexists with other traditions of rational argument which make rival claims to universal validity. There is no neutral judgment seat from which these rival claims can be adjudicated. As I have said earlier, there is no form of rationality which is independent of all socially embodied traditions of rationality and which can therefore judge them all.

Clearly it is such a claim to universal judgment that is embodied in the often expressed idea that all claims to revealed truth must be judged by the canons of reason. There are no canons of reason which are not part of a socially embodied tradition of rational debate. It is especially important to say this because, as I said earlier, we who are Western Christians are also part of an international culture which uses the European languages as its medium of reasoning and which makes claims to universal validity—claims which are made more plausible by the success of this culture in establishing itself throughout the world as the standard of what is called "modernization." It is this way of understanding the world which provides the "plausibility structure" for most of the educated and urbanized peoples of the world. If we adhere to the Christian tradition we thus do so in conscious recognition of the fact that this is a personal decision. In contrast to the long period in which the plausibility structure of European society was shaped by the biblical tradition, and in which one could be a Christian without conscious decision because the existence of God was among the self-evident truths, we are now in a situation where we have to take personal responsibility for our beliefs. When we do so, we are immediately faced with the charge of subjectivity. In a consumer society where the freedom of every citizen to express his or her personal preference is taken as fundamental to human happiness—whether this personal preference is in respect of washing powder or sexual behavior—it will be natural to conclude that adherence to the Christian tradition is also simply an expression of personal preference. The implication will be that claims to universal truth are abandoned and that we are back again in a relativistic twilight. The only firmly established truth is the truth of the reigning plausibility structure, which is bound to deny the Christian's claim that God has acted in historic events to reveal and effect his purpose for all humankind.

In some situations it is possible to escape from this problem by withdrawing into a ghetto where, in a small community, the Christian tradition can function as the plausibility structure which is not questioned. There are places where that can happen, but they are few. How then do we deal with the threat of this relativism of a consumer-oriented society? In following the argument of MacIntyre I have suggested the answer. It is that one learns to live so fully within both traditions that the debate between them is internalized. As a Christian I seek so to live within the biblical tradition, using its language as my language, its models as the models through which I make sense of experience, its story as the clue to my story, that I help to strengthen and carry forward this tradition of rationality. But as a member of contemporary British society I am all the time living in, or at least sharing my life with, those who live in the other tradition. What they call self-evident truths are not self-evident to me, and vice versa. When they speak of reason they mean what is reasonable within their plausibility structure. I do not live in that plausibility, but I know what it feels like to live in it. Within my own mind there is a continuing dialogue between the two. Insofar as my own participation in the Christian tradition is healthy and vigorous, both in thought and in practice, I shall be equipped for the external dialogue with the other tradition. There is no external criterion above us both to which I and my opposite number can appeal for a decision. The immediate outcome is a matter of the comparative vigor and integrity of the two traditions; the ultimate outcome is at the end when the one who alone is judge sums up and gives the verdict.

6. *Revelation in History*

It is customary to make a sharp distinction between historical religions such as Judaism, Christianity, and Islam which depend crucially on events in the past which can be specified as to date and place, and—on the other hand—religions such as those which have their origins in the Indian subcontinent and which—while revering teachers in the past—depend not on the authority of these founding teachers, such as Gautama or Guru Nanak, but on what is held to be accessible to every human being apart from reference to any particular events in the past. Of course the distinction is not absolute. All the world religions have been developed through history in a continuing tradition of rational argument. No religion exists apart from such a historical tradition. And all religions appeal to the authority of great teachers in the past. Nevertheless the distinction is real. The truths which Buddhism teaches would (as Buddhists understand them) be true whether or not Gautama had discovered and promulgated them. But the whole of Christian teaching would fall to the ground if it were the case that the life, death, and resurrection of Jesus were not events in real history but stories told to illustrate truths which are valid apart from these happenings.

What is at stake in this distinction between a story which is a true story in the sense that it tells of something which happened at an ascertainable date and place in the past, and a story which is true in the sense that it communicates truth, truth which can be understood apart from the story? One may believe that Jesus' story of the prodigal son, his father, and his brother is true in the sense that it gives us a true picture of God and a true picture of two human possibilities; no Christian wants to claim that it is a true story in the other sense. Or, to come closer to the bone, it has often been pointed out that the story of the death and resurrection of Jesus has parallels in the myths of a dying and rising god, myths which are related to the recurring experience of winter and spring. What is at stake in the Christian insistence on the "happenedness" of the story told in the New Testament? Does it matter whether or not these things actually happened? Is it not much more important that we grasp for ourselves the meaning of the story? Is factuality a trivial matter compared to faith—as the Pietist rhyme suggests?

> Though Christ ten thousand times in Bethlehem were born,
> if he's not born in thee, thy soul's forlorn.

This couplet conveys exactly the Hindu reaction to the Christian's insistence on the "happenedness" of the gospel story. And his reasoning is powerful. What, after all, are we appealing to when we affirm this "happenedness." We have no direct contact with past events. We can only know of them at many removes through ancient documents, through traditions handed on by men and women whose fallible memories were at the service of strong personal and factional interests. In insisting on this element of factuality, do you not attach your eternal salvation to the very fallible and ever changing opinions of the students of history? What may or may not have happened in the past is of secondary importance: what matters is your living relationship with God now.

What, then, are the real issues involved in this debate? I suggest that they can be understood by looking at the phrase I have just put into the mouth of a Hindu or Pietist friend: "your living relationship with God now." The issue is this: Is this relationship with God something separate from your involvement in the ongoing life of the world, your family, your neighborhood, your nation in the family of nations? Do you have, or do you seek a relationship with God in which you can really turn your back on these other involvements? Or is your relationship with God necessarily bound up with your acceptance of the part God assigns for you in his purpose for his world? If the latter is the case, then your relationship with God cannot be separated from those acts in which God has revealed and effected his purpose for the world. Your life of devotion to God will be expressed in and through your involvement with history as you are now part of it. You will understand your own life as part of a story which is not a story made up by you, not just the story of your decisions and actions, but the story which is being enacted under God's creative and providential control in the events of contemporary history. It will be of the very essence of the matter that the events and places which you read in your Bible are part of the real world and the real history—the same world in which you live, and the same history as this in which you now participate and which is being chronicled with more or less understanding of its meaning in the daily bulletins in press and television.

How, then, shall I answer my Hindu or my Pietist friend who says: In that case you are handing yourself over to the tender mercy of the historical scholars? If everything depends on what really happened two or three thousand years ago, then it is the scholars who have been sharpening their historical-critical tools so assiduously for the past two hundred years who will have the last word. Go to the senior common room of a modern university and talk to the historians: they will certainly not accept your language about God's providential control of history. They will have, of course, varying views about the way history is to be studied, about their presuppositions, about the question whether or not one can properly talk about "meaning" in history. But they will certainly not respond favorably to your talk about God acting in history. What, then, becomes of your claim that Christianity is a historical religion, depending on the facts of history?

It is not only the historians who will be sceptical. If you move across the senior common room to where the theologians are sitting, you are likely to meet the same scepticism. There was a period, especially during the years following the Second World War, when the "Biblical Theology" movement was in the ascendant, and when much was said about the distinctiveness of the Old Testament way of understanding history as the form of God's self-revelation through his mighty acts. And in that period a secular historian who was also a believing Christian, such as Herbert Butterfield of Cambridge, could speak of God's providence "as a living and active agency both in ourselves and in its movement over the length and breadth of history" (*Christianity and History*, p. 112). Fifteen years later James Barr was delivering his lecture "The Concepts of History and Revelation," which was a comprehensive demolition of this whole way of thinking. The era of the so-called "Biblical Theology" was brought to an abrupt end, and today talk about God acting in history can be dismissed by the Bishop of Durham with his talk about laser-beam theology. Whatever may be the debates among the theologians, it is clear that divine providence is not a category normally used by secular historians in their work. From Augustine until the eighteenth century, European historians worked with a providential understanding of history. The past two centuries have seen great debates among historians as to what the method of their craft ought to be, and these debates continue. We shall look briefly at them in a moment. From the point of view of a theologian there is one question, perhaps a very simplistic one, which seems unavoidable. If God does not act in history, what meaning can there be in saying that God acts at all? And if there is no category in which we can speak of God acting, what meaning can we attach to the word "God"? Many of our contemporaries would, of course, answer "Exactly! The word 'God' stands for nothing real at all." The presupposition of most historical scholarship since the Enlightenment has been that God is not a factor in history.

Certainly any proposal to speak of God acting in history has to face intellectual difficulties of several kinds. An examination of them will be the best approach to a positive statement.

1. The first set of difficulties arises from the dominance of what we loosely call the modern scientific worldview. The sciences, both natural and human, have been so successful in uncovering the cause-effect links which lie behind all happenings that there seems to be no crack or cranny through which divine action could enter and influence them. "All causes are adequate to the effects which they produce" and all happenings are the result of sufficient causes. The door seems to be firmly shut against any intervention from outside this closed system. And yet everyone is conscious of exercising the power of personal decision expressed in action. All arguments designed to show that free will is an illusion break down into absurdity. The question *how* our consciousness of having the power to make personal choices is related to the operation of the cause-effect links which are studied by neurologists, physiologists, sociologists, and economists, of how the mind is related to the brain, is a matter of continuing debate. But no outcome of the debate can be accepted which simply denies our daily experience. Like every human being I know the difference between taking action as a personal decision, and being the victim of a force to which I did not consent. Perhaps the relation between them may be indicated in two ways. First, there is the difference between what we may call the inside and the outside of an action. From the inside I know that I did this because I decided to do it. A neurologist will describe my action in terms of the functioning of electrical impulses in the nervous system; a physiologist in terms of the movement of muscles, and a sociologist in terms of the conditioning I have received through my place in the class-structure of

the society in which I live. Neither type of description invalidates the other; both have a proper place in understanding the action.

Second, one may describe the difference in terms of future and past. From the inside, so to speak, I see an open future in which what is to happen is still undecided; the outsider, on the other hand, has no opportunity to see this; she can only see the completed event, which is no longer undecided and fixed. As a fixture in the structure of events he can describe the way it is related to previous events. Once the event has happened it can be brought into a deterministic pattern of natural law. If there were no point of view other than that of the outside *post-factum* observer, then it would seem absurd to say that something called a personal will could interrupt the operation of natural law, as absurd as to suggest that the will of God might be a factor in history.

But, continuing this picture, there can be two kinds of outsider. There can be the outsider who observes my action simply as an event in the world of things and happening to be accounted for in accordance with generally observable patterns of cause and effect. From the point of view of this observer I am merely a case for the medical or psychiatric textbook, a statistic for the sociologist or the economist. And their examination and classification of my action is a proper and necessary exercise. But there can also be the outsider who is a friend and shares, to some extent, my own insider view of the event. He knows me well enough to understand why I acted in that way. The action becomes one of the ways in which our mutual friendship grows, in which she comes to understand me better. Or perhaps at first she does not understand why I acted in that way. If she is a complete stranger, that will not bother her. She has no interest in understanding why I acted. But if she already has reason to think that I am a reasonable person, she will ask me why I so acted and I will try to explain. The word will be needed to illuminate the deed. In other cases it may be the other way around: some act of mine will show her that I really meant what I said. The deed will validate the word. Both will be reciprocally and necessarily involved in a developing friendship.

If this is a correct picture of a kind of experience which is normal in human life, it seems to invalidate the idea that it is irrational to speak of God acting in history. We do not require a special kind of "laser beam" to insure that the decisions we make of our own free will are faithfully executed by our bodies. We are aware of no contradiction in the fact that something purely spiritual (an intention) can change the course of events in the visible external world of happenings. Nor is it difficult to understand how there can be two different but perfectly valid ways of understanding events, one the "outsider" view and the other the view of the friend who can, at least in some measure, share the "insider" view of the agent and can find in the events further sources of understanding of his mind and purpose.

2. This line of reasoning seems to me to be valid as far as it goes, but of course it leads us to further difficulties. Everything that I do is an expression of my mind except insofar as I am compelled by outside forces to act against my will. If, by definition, God is not under compulsion by outside forces, it would seem that everything that happens in the world is an expression of God's mind. Plainly the Christian tradition affirms that some things which have happened express God's mind, but not all. God reveals himself in history, we would say, but not all history reveals God. How can these two things be affirmed? In part the answer lies in the subject of our next chapter, the logic of election. In part it lies in our belief about the relation of the world to God. In contrast to the monistic, pantheistic, and panentheistic thinking which is always present as an attractive option, we believe that in his creation of the world God gave it a measure of independence and to that extent limited his own freedom. Things therefore happen in history which are not in accordance with the will of God but represent a contradiction of his will. But in that case what becomes of providential history? What grounds are there for saying that in this event God was active and that something contrary to God's will was in action? How are we to understand history?

All writing of history involves selection among the vast mass of possible material. This selection has to be on the basis of what is significant from the point of view of the story which the historian has to tell. His data, of course, are not the happenings themselves, but the evidence for these happenings available in documents, archaeological finds, and oral traditions. These data are themselves the products of some decision about what was significant enough to be remembered or recorded. At every stage decisions have been made and are being made about what is significant. Historians debate endlessly the question of meaning in history, but it seems clear that no history could be written at all without some presuppositions about what is significant and therefore about the meaning of the story. From Augustine till the eighteenth century, history in Europe was written in the belief that divine providence was the key to understanding events. World history as well as local histories (such as Bede's *History of the Anglo-Saxons*) were written from this

71

perspective. From the time of the Enlightenment onward, history in Europe was mainly the history of nations, because the nation state was the bearer of the meaning of history as post-Enlightenment Europe saw it. When a move was made toward a universal history, the most prestigious example was that of Hegel, but it is very clear that his universal history culminates in the Prussian state. Arnold Toynbee endeavored to break from this tradition by taking civilizations as the unit of study, but in the story of the cyclical rise and fall of civilizations it is not clear that there is a criterion (which must necessarily lie beyond the stories themselves) of what is significant in the story of a particular civilization. As Eric Vogelin has written of Toynbee's study: "The wheels of civilization carry a vehicle that is not itself a civilization towards its goal" (Eric Vogelin, "The Intent of Toynbee's History," cited by Peter Russell in *Historian's Study Group*, July 1986). Histories have been written on the basis of the belief that God has acted in the rise of the British Empire, in the development of the Aryan race, in the opening up of a manifest destiny for the United States. It is impossible to write history without some vision of its meaning from which judgments of significance can be made. And if there is no meaning, why be a historian?

The Christian tradition affirms that God has made his mind and purpose known to some (not to all) people through events in history — not all events but some, the memory of which is treasured in the Christian tradition. This affirmation is a cause of scandal, what is sometimes called the scandal of particularity. Nowhere is it felt more acutely than in India with its incomparably rich and venerable history of religious experience and exploration. But there can be no rational human being who does not at some time feel the force of it. If God is God, the creator, sustainer, origin, and goal of all that exists, how can the knowledge of him be restricted to particular segments of the whole human race? If it is true that God reveals himself in history, how can it fail to be true that his presence is to be discerned in all history. On what rational grounds can one single out particular happenings from the whole seamless robe of history and say: Here God acted; here he revealed himself? These very natural questions involve two kinds of difficulty. There is the religious difficulty of believing in a God whose ways appear to be arbitrary and irrational; there is the philosophical difficulty of assigning meaning to the very idea of God acting in history if his actions are defined in this way. The former, religious difficulties will be the subject of the next chapter; here we must look at what I have called the philosophical difficulties.

3. I have used the experience of the personal will in its relation to the functioning of our physical organisms as a partial, though only partial, analogy for understanding the idea of God's action in history. Even if we take this limited analogy, we know that while all the words and behavior of a rational person convey something of that person's character, nevertheless not all her words and behavior are equally significant. If one is to enter into a deep understanding of his most enduring and overriding purposes and commitments, one will have to attend to particular words and actions which communicate these. One will not penetrate to an understanding of them merely by careful observation of her behavior over a period. And a person will not be able to communicate her purpose in such a way that I can really grasp it, until I am ready for the communication. She is always the same person, but not all her words and deeds communicate the secret of her deepest commitments.

One can accept this as a partial, only partial analogy for God's communication of his purposes. God is the same always and everywhere and to everyone. This is why it seems to be the case that wherever human beings are found there are always evidences of some kind of awareness of God, however faint and confused. It seems impossible to doubt that this is the case. But, from the point of view of a Christian believer, it would be necessary to say that this awareness, valid as it is and much to be respected as it ought to be, does not of itself communicate the full understanding of God's purpose for human beings. It is necessary also to attend to the particular events and words which communicate that purpose.

The analogy of the self-communication of the human person through the acts and words of his physical organism is, however, only a partial analogy. The created world has been given a degree of autonomy, of independence from God's will which is clearly other than the rapport which exists between the human mind and the body when the whole person is in proper health. Not only are there regularities of cause and effect within the natural world which appear to work autonomously, but—much more significant for our argument—human wills have an autonomy which enables them to act in rebellion against the purpose of their Creator. It follows, then, that no overview of the total human situation can provide authentic knowledge of the purpose of the Creator. If we may use the term "general revelation" for that awareness of God which seems to be part of human nature wherever it appears (even when it is suppressed), we have to add that this general revelation, valid as it is, cannot communicate the purpose of God for his creation. How could such communication take place?

Here we must refer to what was said in the previous chapter about the socially embodied character of every tradition of rationality. There is no way in which one could proceed from some sort of disembodied rationality to the answering of the question. We have no alternative but to begin with one specific community, and the tradition of rationality developed within that community. There can in principle be no *a priori* rational ground for saying that it must be one community rather than another, Japan rather than Israel, for example. But there is rational ground for saying that it must be a specific community, the community whose tradition of rationality has developed from those events in which it believes that God has so acted as to disclose his nature and effect his purpose. What I am calling "the logic of election," the rationality of this specificity, this particularity, will be spelled out in the next chapter. Here I simply affirm that the Christian tradition of rational discourse through which Christians seek to understand and cope with reality necessarily takes its rise (as every such tradition does) from a specific series of events in history. Within this tradition we remember, retell, and celebrate a story in which we believe that God was acting in a unique way to communicate and effect his purpose for the human race and the created world. Clearly we cannot justify this move by appealing to some tradition of rationality drawn from elsewhere. It must be justified, can only be justified at the end. Its acceptance is an act of faith which looks toward the end of history. But what one can do is to spell out what is involved in this move and so to clear away misunderstandings of it, and this—very briefly—is what we must try to do in the remainder of this chapter.

1. James Barr has attacked this "revelation in history" model on the ground that revelation implies the making known of something previously or otherwise unknown and that the biblical record itself shows that God is not unknown apart from this biblical story. How is it possible, he asks, to speak of the Torah as revealed when historians can show that it has large areas of overlap with other legal codes of the ancient world of West Asia? For the same reason he criticizes Karl Barth for making so sharp a dichotomy between religion and revelation and placing the Bible entirely on the revelation side of the line. There is, says Barr, much religion in the Old Testament, and of course he is right. The

use in the early books of the Pentateuch of ancient names for God, such as El Shaddai and El Elyon, and the identification of these as names for the God whom Israel knows as Yahweh, shows clearly that there is a continuity between the story which the Bible tells and the religious life of the peoples of the ancient world. Every missionary who seeks to proclaim the gospel in a new language has to rely on this continuity. He has to use one of the words which that language already had for God and which the people who speak that language used before they ever heard of the Bible. Without using that word the missionary cannot begin to communicate. In other words, what I have called general revelation is, in some way, presupposed. But it does not follow from this that the biblical story can be properly told simply as part of the history of religions in what Europeans call the Middle East. If there is a real continuity, as there is, there is also a discontinuity. God has done a new thing, but that does not mean that God was previously absent from the scene. The new thing is radically new and gives a new revelation of who God is and what his purposes are. In that sense Paul can say to his Gentile friends, "Formerly you did not know God." The fact that they had already a word, several words, for God means that they knew something, even if it is only the sense that "There is somebody here" which leads to the erection of an altar to an unknown god. But even an unknown god is not nothing.

It follows also that those who have been given God's self-revelation in Torah and prophecy can recognize the evidence of God's presence in nations and traditions outside Israel. Barr uses as one part of his attack on the concept of revelation in history the evidence of the Old Testament wisdom literature. Certainly this has much in common with material from other parts of the ancient world, and certainly it is not cast in story form. Yet it contains the repeated reminder that "The fear of Yahweh is the beginning of wisdom," and Yahweh has made himself known to Israel in his mighty acts. It is in the light of this knowledge which is Yahweh's gift to Israel that Israel can learn from and appropriate the wisdom which has been developed among the nations on the basis of that which God gives freely to all.

2. A second line along which James Barr mounted his attack on the Biblical Theology movement was directed to the distinction between events and words. The Biblical Theology movement emphasized the event character of God's mighty acts. Barr points out that much of what we may call revelation in the Old Testament is in the form of words, not events. From another angle there has frequently been an attempt to

drive a wedge between words and deeds by saying that the locus of revelation is not in the words of Scripture but in the events which Scripture records. The implication is that we are free, if we will, to go behind the biblical writers who were giving their own interpretation to the events and find out for ourselves "what really happened." The Bible, it is said, is not revelation but the record of revelation, a record shaped by the particular circumstances and interests of the various biblical writers. And plainly we have many examples in the Bible of differing interpretations of the same events. Obvious illustrations of this can be found in comparing the accounts of the life of Jesus in the four Gospels. Shall we say that it is the events which reveal God, or the words in which these events are told in the biblical writings?

I suggest again that there is no way in which we understand anything, whether we are talking about understanding the will of God or understanding physics or politics, except by being part of a continuing tradition of rational discourse. The work of historians is within such a tradition. The question "What really happened?" can only be answered within a tradition of rational discussion about what is "real." As I have already said, all understanding of history involves interpretation of the available "facts," and these "facts" are the written or oral records which are available because at some point they were judged to be significant in relation to some tradition of rational discourse. History is being rewritten in every new generation and in every culture, because all the available "facts of history" (that is, the available evidence) has to be understood in the light of a developing tradition of rational argument. If we ask "What really happened?" at the time of the events recorded in Exodus 14, we may say that there was a strong anticyclone over the Arabian peninsula, or we may say that God acted to deliver Israel from the Egyptian army. The answer to the question "What really happened?" depends on the tradition of rational discourse of which we are a part.

The biblical record as we have it comes from a community which (with wide diversities of interpretation at many points) understood history in terms of a purpose of God to bring salvation to the world through a particular people among all the peoples of the world. This understanding is expressed in the words through which the events have been made known to us. We have access to the knowledge of these events only through the words which embodied the understanding of those who witnessed them or participated in them, and which have been treasured and handed on by those who shared this understanding. As Christians we are part of that community and have the responsibility to seek to interpret contemporary history, the history which is now in the making, in terms of the same belief. But we are also part of another rational tradition, the one which controls our public educational system, which sees history in other terms. We do not have access to bare uninterpreted "facts" (if indeed such things exist), but we can undertake the exercise of relocating the events of the biblical story within this other tradition, so that they have their meaning through their place in this tradition. We inhabit both traditions, and there is an internal dialogue within each of us between the two. It is open to us to interpret the story which the Bible tells in terms of one or other version of the reigning public tradition—as one strand of the religious history of the Eastern Mediterranean, for example; or, in Marxist terms, as an early example of a proletarian revolutionary movement. In all cases we are interpreting the events. In no way do we have access to "what really happened" apart from any tradition of rational discourse, and there is no external criterion by which we can decide in advance which tradition is the one to be relied on. If I am committed to seeking to understand what happened from within this Christian tradition, that is a decision for which I am responsible. But this decision and commitment is delivered from mere subjectivity by being made—as Polanyi would say—with universal intent. In other words, I cannot treat it as simply a personal decision; I am bound to publish it, to commend it to others, and to seek to show in the practice of life today that it is the rational tradition which is capable of giving greater coherence and intelligibility to all experience than any other tradition.

3. But, third, these statements need to be further corrected. It is not just a matter of personal decision. There *is* a personal decision involved. I *am* responsible for my beliefs. But this decision is a response to a prior decision, to the decision of God who has chosen me to be part of that community which bears the secret of the meaning of history through history. Once again, we have to talk about the doctrine of election, which is the theme of the next chapter. At this point, and to complete the preceding argument, let me suggest one way of seeing how the particularity of those acts of God which we celebrate in the Christian tradition is related to the continuity of God's revelation of himself through all history, including the history of which we are now a part.

According to the Fourth Gospel, when Jesus was preparing his disciples both for his departure from them and for their mission to the world, he expounded to them the relation between that which had been revealed in his earthly ministry among them and that which they would still have to learn in the course of their mission among the nations. The essential elements in this Johannine passage can be expressed in seven points.

1. There has been a decisive and complete revelation of God in the particular event of Jesus' earthly ministry. "He who has seen me has seen the Father" (14:9).

2. Nevertheless there is much that they have still to learn. The Spirit of the Father himself will be their teacher, interpreting to them his revelation of the Father (14:16). This promise is to the Church and not for the world, for the world cannot receive the Spirit (14:17).

3. Nevertheless this gift is not for the private possession of the Church; the presence of the Spirit will constitute Christ's witness to the world (15:27).

4. This witness, however, will be in the form of a contradiction of the world's most fundamental beliefs (16:8-11). The work of the Spirit will thus continue through the witness of the Church that contradiction of the world's fundamental beliefs which was historically enacted in the cross.

5. To the Church, however, the work of the Spirit will be "to declare the things that are to come," to interpret coming events, to be the hermeneutic of the world's continuing history (16:13).

6. In doing so the Spirit will "glorify" Jesus. It will become clear through this teaching and guiding of the Spirit that the crucified Jesus is truly Lord of history (16:14).

7. The scope of this work of the Spirit is as wide as the universe itself, for "all that the Father has" belongs in truth to Jesus (16:15).

What is affirmed here is that a particular community in history, that community which bears the name of Jesus, will be given, through the active work of the Spirit of God, a true understanding of history—the ongoing history that continues through the centuries after Jesus, an understanding which is based on the particular events of whose memory they are the custodians. But this privileged position is not for their sake but for the sake of the world into which they are sent as the witnesses to Jesus in whom God's purpose for his entire creation has been disclosed. What I am affirming, in other words, is that, just as the experience of Israel is to be interpreted not merely as a chapter in the history of religions but as the self-revealing action of God, so the history of the Church is to be interpreted not merely as one among the varieties of religious experience but as the fruit of the promised work of the Spirit of God. Such a claim cannot, of course, be disproved by any compelling rational argument, but it may well be laughed out of court as a piece of absurd arrogance. Therefore, before proceeding to spell out more fully what this claim might mean, we must now look directly at the element in this picture which is most offensive to our natural minds, the element of privilege. We must look at the doctrine of election.

7. The Logic of Election

There is surely no part of Christian teaching which has been the subject of so much ridicule and indignant rejection as the doctrine of election. How absurd for intelligent, educated people to believe that almighty God should have his favorites, that he should pick out one small tribe among all the families of humankind to be the special objects of his attention. Is it not simply a piece of ignorant egotism? There can be few places where this is felt more keenly than in India, with its immensely ancient and venerable traditions of religious experience and sophisticated theological reflection. How can one believe that almighty God has hidden the secret of truth for all these centuries from the great saints and scholars of India, the men and women who were composing some of the greatest religious literature in the world at a time when the tribes of western Europe were wild barbarians, and that India should have to wait three thousand years to learn the secret of eternal salvation from the descendants of these barbarians? But the scandal is certainly not peculiar to India. It was Rousseau who said that he could not understand why, if God had something to say to Jean-Jacques Rousseau, he could not say it directly but had to go through Moses to say it.

And yet it is plain that the doctrine of election is central to any true exposition of the Bible. From the very beginning God chooses, calls, and sends particular people. God is always the initiator. The words of Jesus to his disciples, "You did not choose me; I chose you," are in line with everything in the Bible from beginning to end. We can, of course, if we wish, convert this language into the language of religion. We can say that the great figures of the Bible from Abraham to Peter and Paul had religious experiences which led them to think that God had called them in some special way. And one cannot say that these statements are untrue. But they leave open the question whether these religious experiences corresponded to any objective reality, whether in fact almighty God did choose and call and send them, or whether they merely thought that he had done so. Without question the point of view of the Bible is that God chose Abel and not Cain, Isaac and not Ishmael, Jacob and not Esau, David and not his elder brothers. Their religious experience, if we want to use that modern phrase, follows on the fact of the divine choosing and calling. But can we believe that almighty God, creator of heaven and earth, does act in this seemingly arbitrary way? Why Jacob, that sly, cunning, self-seeking man, and why not Esau—a man who is portrayed in Scripture as what we might call a perfect gentleman?

The first step toward an answer to these questions is to ask what assumptions lie behind them. What is implied in the complaint that I ought not to have to depend on another for that which is necessary for my salvation? One has only to pose this question to uncover a whole set of assumptions which have to be questioned, assumptions which go to the heart of what it is to be human. Some of these assumptions have a very long and venerable history, and here I am thinking of the Indian traditions which have taken it as self-evident that the knowledge of God and the path to salvation must be in the last analysis a matter for the individual soul. Of course the seeker may need the help of a spiritual guide, but in the end the journey must be made alone. Salvation, if we wish to use that word for that which is understood as the goal of human being, is in the end a matter of the relation between the individual soul and the Eternal. It is in accordance with this way of understanding matters that the initiative lies with the seeker: he must search for and find a spiritual guide, and he may well go from one to another until he finds the guru who can lead him. The guru is not sent out by God to seek and find lost souls. It is for others to seek him.

Modern Western culture has worked with analogous assumptions. Kant's famous slogan "Dare to Know," in which he summed up what was meant by enlightenment, was a summons to the autonomous human reason to trust its own powers and to dare to question the accepted traditions. Of course, as in the Indian tradition, one needs teachers on the way, but in the end it is for the individual, in the autonomy which is his right, to use his or her own reason to arrive at the truth and to hold it. Clearly the exercise of human reason is something which takes place not in a vacuum, but within a socially embodied tradition of rational discourse. No reasoning is possible except by the use of language, and language expresses the way in which a particular body of human beings has learned to grasp and cope with the world. In that sense human reason can never be totally autonomous. But the rationalism of modern culture has never accepted the idea that it was finally and irrevocably dependent on a particular tradition of human reasoning. The aim has been to subject every tradition to the scrutiny of reason, including every tradition which claimed to embody a particular divine revelation to one group of people. Yet, as Alasdair MacIntyre has shown *(Whose Justice? Which Rationality?)*, it is an illusion to suppose that there is available to us some kind of pure rationality existing in a disembodied state and therefore capable of passing judgment on all the various ways of grasping truth developed in particular socially embodied traditions of rational discourse. It is enough to remind ourselves once again that no critical act is possible except on the basis of a whole complex of beliefs which are assumed a-critically as the grounds on which one can criticize the belief under discussion. This complex of beliefs will itself be the product of a particular socially embodied tradition of reasoning.

We can only understand the biblical teaching about election if we see it as part of the whole way of understanding the human situation which is characteristic of the Bible. Here, in contrast to both the Indian and the modern Western views, there is no attempt to see the human person as an autonomous individual, and the human relation with God as the relation of the alone to the alone. From its very beginning the Bible sees human life in terms of relationships. There is no attempt to strip away the accidents of history in order to find the real essence of what it is to be human. Human life is seen in terms of mutual relationships: first, the most fundamental relation, between man and woman, then between parents and children, then between families and clans and nations. The Bible does not speak about "humanity" but about "all the families of the earth" or "all the nations." It follows that this mutual relatedness, this dependence of one on another, is not merely part of the journey toward the goal of salvation, but is intrinsic to the goal itself. For knowing God, for being in communion with him, we are dependent on the one whom he gives us to be the bearer of this relation, not just as a teacher and guide on the way but as the partner in the end. There is, there can be, no private salvation, no salvation which does not involve us with one another. Therefore, if I may venture to use a metaphor which I have used elsewhere, God's saving revelation of himself does not come to us straight down from above—through the skylight, as we might say. In order to receive God's saving revelation we have to open the door to the neighbor whom he sends as his appointed messenger, and—moreover—to receive that messenger not as a temporary teacher or guide whom we can dispense with when we ourselves have learned what is needed, but as one who will permanently share our home. There is no salvation except one in which we are saved together through the one whom God sends to be the bearer of his salvation.

What I have called the logic of election becomes very clear in that passage of the Letter to the Romans which has often been used as a basis for false teaching about election. I refer to Romans 9 through 11. For Paul it is axiomatic that God has chosen Israel uniquely among all the nations. And yet Israel has, as a nation, rejected God's chosen Messiah. How is this to be understood? Does it mean that God's purpose has been defeated? No. Does it mean that God has cast off his chosen people? No. How, then, are we to understand it? First, we must understand that God retains his freedom. Election does not give us claims against God. This has always been clear, for not all the descendants of Abraham are chosen. No one can find fault with God for this. Like the potter working with his clay, God has the freedom to dispose of his creation as he will. He *could* make some vessels for honor and some for destruction. Paul does not say that he has done so, but only that, if he did, we would have no ground for complaint. This is where false conclusions have been drawn from Paul. The whole passage makes clear that God has *not* done what he might have done. He has not made some for honor and some for destruction. What he has done is to consign *all* men to disobedience in order that he may have mercy on *all* (11:32).

How can this be so? Again we ask: what is the meaning of Israel's rejection of the Messiah? Paul's answer is an astonishing one, but it fits exactly what I call the logic of election. God, says Paul, has hardened the heart of Israel so that the gospel which they reject will—so to say—bounce off to the Gentiles. This is exactly what was happening in city after city where Paul was turned out of the synagogues and went to the Gentiles. So the apostasy of Israel has brought salvation to the Gentiles. Does this mean that Israel is lost? No! Impossible! God can never cast off his chosen people. As proof of this he has kept a remnant (as so often in the past) as pledge that Israel is not rejected. The small company of believing Jews is the pledge that Israel is not cast off. And how is it all to end? The answer is that this hardening of the heart of Israel is until the full number of the Gentiles come in, and so all Israel will be saved (11:25). In the end, therefore, it is through the Gentiles that Israel will be saved. So the logic of election is complete. I said earlier that in the biblical view there could be no salvation straight from above through the skylight, but only as we open the door to the neighbor whom God has appointed to be the bearer of salvation. It might have seemed that this was not quite true, since Israel, in the person of Abraham, received the message direct and not through any human messenger. Yes indeed, but we learn that it is not enough to be descendants of Abraham. They have no privileged status. In the end the chosen people, the elect, will have to receive salvation through the nonelect—the Gentiles. The logic of election is complete. Not just at the beginning but all the way until the end, salvation involves us with the neighbor whom God chooses to be the bearer of salvation, and there is no salvation otherwise.

In the light of this crucial passage we can expose the false ideas which have gathered around the doctrine of election and which have made it unacceptable to many Christians as well as to others. In the first place, and most obviously, there is the idea that election is election to privileged status before God. This false belief is something against which the prophets of Israel had constantly to contend. It is indeed true that in many moving passages of the Old Testament we are told of God's undying love for Israel, of his commitment to its cause. Yet this love and commitment are to Israel as the instrument of God's purpose of love for all the nations, and when Israel interprets God's love as a license to do as it pleases chastisement follows. In a classic passage Amos says in the name of God, "You only have I known of all the families of the earth; therefore I will punish you for all your sins" (Amos 3:2). As the story unfolds, it becomes clear that to be God's chosen people means not privilege but suffering, reproach, humiliation. Israel is called to embody in her own life God's agony over his disobedient world. And in the New Testament this comes to its final manifestation in that God's chosen one is called to suffer the ultimate agony of a death which carries God's curse, on behalf of all peoples. We know that this disastrous misunderstanding of what God's election means has persisted right through the history of the Church and to the present day, so that Christians believe that as Christians they have a claim on God's love which others do not have. The trenchant words of Paul have been quietly ignored in the history of the Church: "There is no distinction between Jew and Greek; the same Lord is Lord of all and bestows his riches upon all who call upon him" (Rom. 10:12). But that recognition, so far from eliminating the doctrine of election, becomes for Paul the very basis for that doctrine, for how shall they call on him of whom they have not heard, and how shall they hear without a preacher, and how can they preach unless they are sent? It is the universality of God's saving love which is the ground of his choosing and calling a community to be the messengers of his truth and bearers of his love for all peoples. Once again we have to remember that neither truth nor love can be communicated except as they are embodied in a community which reasons and loves.

But there is also a second, perhaps more subtle way in which the doctrine of election is misunderstood. Granted, it may be said, that election confers no special privilege but rather great responsibility, must one not agree, nevertheless, that where those who are chosen and called do what is commanded, they have a claim on God which others do not? Again Paul's argument precludes such a conclusion. God's grace is free and unconditional. We cannot turn the covenant of grace into a contract. No one, whoever he or she be, can establish claims on God's grace which exclude others. God's electing grace calls into being a people charged with the responsibility of being the bearers of his universal salvation. He commits himself to them. But they can never establish exclusive claims on him. His grace is free and his covenant cannot be converted into a contract.

There is a particular form of this misunderstanding which is also exposed in this Pauline argument. Let it be agreed that our obedience to God's command, our good works, do not entitle us to make claims on God by which others are excluded. Let it be agreed that we are, in Paul's favorite phrase, justified (put right with God) by grace through faith alone. Is it not clear, then, that those who have this faith have a claim on God which unbelievers do not have? This seems to be the assumption against which Paul is warning the Roman Christians. To those who evidently were tempted to a certain self-satisfaction because they were believers and the majority of the Jews were unbelievers, Paul writes: "If some of the branches were broken off, and you, a wild olive shoot, were grafted in their place to share the richness of the olive tree, do not boast over the branches. . . . Do not become proud but stand in awe. For if God did not spare the natural branches, neither will he spare you" (Rom. 11:17-21). God's electing grace, his choosing of some to be the bearers of his salvation for all, is a matter for awe and wonder and thankfulness: it can never become the ground for making claims against God which exclude others. God does not choose to save some and to destroy others. (He has consigned all to disobedience in order that he may have mercy upon all.) His grace is free and sovereign, and there is no place for an exclusive claim on his grace, a claim by which others are excluded. This obviously has great importance when we come to consider the relation of the gospel to the world religions.

Fourth, there is a way in which the doctrine of election has been distorted by separating it from the doctrine of Christ. We surely go far astray if we begin from a doctrine of divine decrees based on an abstract concept of divine omnipotence (a concept which all too obviously falls into Feuerbach's description of theism as the projection of our human ego onto the heavens). We have to take as our starting point, and as the controlling reality for all our thinking on this as on every theological topic, what God has actually done in Jesus Christ. It is in Jesus Christ that, as Paul says, we are elect from the foundation of the world. Jesus is not a latecomer into the world. He is the one in whom and through whom and for whom we and all things exist. And the things that happened when he took our human nature and came among us as a man make clear what the meaning of God's election is. It is, as Paul says in the passage we have been looking at, that God has consigned all to disobedience that he may have mercy on all. The cross of Jesus is the place where all human beings without exception are exposed as enemies of God, and the place where all human beings without exception are accepted as beloved of God, objects of his forgiving grace. No one is excluded from the scope of that prayer: "Father, forgive them, for they know not what they do." It is for all. And yet just as the universal and unbounded grace of God could only be made known through this historic deed wrought out at one place in the world and at one point in history; just as it could only be the action of God's grace by having the concreteness, the particularity, and therefore the limitedness of one particular happening which can only become known to others if it is told by one person to another; so also it is made known not by some cosmic spiritual illumination but by being communicated to certain specific men and women who had been chosen as witnesses and prepared beforehand for that role. The risen Jesus did not appear to everyone. He did not appear (as is often foolishly asserted) to the believers; there were no believers before he appeared to them. He appeared, as the Scripture makes clear, to those who had been chosen beforehand as witnesses. They are chosen not for themselves, not to be the exclusive beneficiaries of God's saving work, but to be the bearers of the secret of his saving work for the sake of all. They are chosen to go and bear fruit.

To be chosen, to be elect, therefore does not mean that the elect are the saved and the rest are the lost. To be elect in Christ Jesus, and there is no other election, means to be incorporated into his mission to the world, to be the bearer of God's saving purpose for his whole world, to be the sign and the agent and the firstfruit of his blessed kingdom which is for all. It means therefore, as the New Testament makes abundantly clear, to take our share in his suffering, to bear the scars of the passion. It means, as Paul says elsewhere, to bear in the body the dying of Jesus so that the life of the risen Jesus may be manifest and made available for others. It means that this particular body of people who bear the name of Jesus through history, this strange and often absurd company of people so feeble, so foolish, so often fatally compromised with the world, this body with all its contingency and particularity, is the body which has the responsibility of bearing the secret of God's reign through world history. The logic of election is all of one piece with the logic of the gospel. God's purpose of salvation is not that we should be taken out of history and related to him in some way which bypasses the specificities and particularities of history. His purpose is that in and through history there should be brought into being that which is symbolized in the vision with which the Bible ends—the Holy City into which all the glory of the nations will finally be gathered. But— and of course this is the crux of the matter—that consummation can only lie on the other side of death and resurrection. It is the calling of the Church to bear through history to its end the secret of the lordship of the crucified.

Before leaving the subject I must append two matters which may have been suggested by this discussion. One is this. It will be obvious that there is a logical connection between what I have been saying about election and the point about the nature of rational argument which I have been quoting from MacIntyre. I referred earlier to what MacIntyre calls one of the characteristic illusions of our culture, the idea that there is some sort of rationality which exists apart from any particular human society and which can therefore provide criteria for passing judgment on all the traditions which different human communities have developed and cherished. This is an illusion. There is no rationality except a socially embodied rationality. That rationality which can lead to a true understanding of reality as a whole will necessarily be a rationality embodied in a particular society. The Christian community, the universal Church, embracing more and more fully all the cultural traditions of humankind, is called to be that community in which a tradition of rational discourse is developed which leads to a true understanding of reality, because it takes as its starting point and as its permanent criterion of truth the self-revelation of God in Jesus Christ. It is necessarily a particular community among all the human communities. It cannot pretend to be otherwise. But it has a universal mission, for it is the community chosen and sent by God for this purpose. This particularity, however scandalous it may seem to a certain kind of cosmopolitan mind, is inescapable.

The other point is of a quite different kind. Does the argument so far point to universalism, that is to say, to the doctrine that as God wills all to be saved, all will in the end infallibly be saved? Certainly the passage we studied in Romans has a universalist ring. "The full number of the Gentiles will be gathered in and all Israel will be saved." Paul's vision is truly cosmic and universal. His earlier description of Jesus as the new Adam also points in that direction. "As one man's trespass led to condemnation for all, so one man's act of righteousness leads to acquittal and life for all" (Rom. 5:18). And yet the same Paul can say of himself that he must exercise the strictest self-discipline "lest after preaching to others I myself should be disqualified" (1 Cor. 9:27). It seems to me that the whole nature of the gospel requires us to maintain this tension and not to try to resolve it either by a rationalistic universalism which denies the possibility of finally missing the mark, or by increasingly fruitless arguments about who will and who will not be saved. When Jesus was asked the question about whether few or many would be saved he declined to answer it but sternly warned the questioner to strive to enter the narrow door that leads to life. His often repeated words about the reversal of expectations (the first shall be last and the last first) and the parables which suggest that those who are confident will find themselves excluded and those who never expected it find themselves welcomed, all point in the same direction. There is a kind of confidence which leads to complacency, and there is a kind of anxiety which leads to selfish efforts to save oneself. It seems to me clear from the whole New Testament that the Christian life has room both for a godly confidence and for a godly fear. The contrast between these is not a contradiction. If I know that God in his limitless grace and kindness has chosen and called me to be a bearer of his grace for others, my trust in him will not exclude the awareness that I could betray his trust in me, and that very awareness will drive me closer to him. This is a deeply personal relationship. It excludes, I think, the kind of rationalistic universalism which I have referred to. It also excludes, I think, any temptation to set limits to God's grace, or to write off any human being as beyond God's redeeming love.

8. *The Bible as Universal History*

A learned Hindu friend has several times complained to me that we Christians have misrepresented the Bible. He has said to me something like this: "As I read the Bible I find in it a quite unique interpretation of universal history and, therefore, a unique understanding of the human person as a responsible actor in history. You Christian missionaries have talked of the Bible as it were simply another book of religion. We have plenty of these already in India and we do not need another to add to our supply."

Surely this complaint has some justice. Certainly the Bible is sharply differentiated from the sacred books of the East at exactly this point. Unlike them, it sets out to speak of human life in the context of a vision of universal, cosmic history. Although, of course, it contains a great variety of material—legal codes, prayers, wise sayings, and moral instruction—it is, in its overall plan and in a great part of its content, history. It sets before us a vision of cosmic history from the creation of the world to its consummation, of the nations which make up the one human family, and—of course—of one nation chosen to be the bearer of the meaning of history for the sake of all, and of one man called to be the bearer of that meaning for that nation. The Bible *is* universal history.

How, then, are we to assess it in relation to the other visions of history which are offered in our culture, whether world history as taught in the schools and universities, or natural history as it is deciphered by the biologists, palaeontologists, and cosmologists? To try to answer that question fully would require a much deeper consideration than I am capable of. But one can begin by asking another question: What does it mean to write or to tell history? It cannot mean the recording of all the uncounted millions of things which have happened in the past. It involves selection. And this means selection on the basis of what is significant. But, significant for what? The answer depends on one's belief about the point of the story. If it is the history of a small society, a school or a college for example, the things selected for inclusion will be those that contributed to the growth and development of the school, but even here historians will differ about what is important according to their different views of what the college should be. Probably most of the history taught in European schools in the past two or three centuries has been national history—the history of one's own nation and of others insofar as they impinged on ours. World history, when it is taught, is usually taught as the history of civilization; the significant facts are those which have had a bearing on the development of the kind of society which we now regard as modern. But is this in fact the point of the story? Many people in many cultures have denied that world history in this sense can be written. If human affairs are, like the rest of nature, essentially cyclical in character, moving endlessly through the cycle of birth, growth, maturity, decay, and death, then events are hardly worth recording, and if there is to be a history it will not be of "civilization" but of the rise and fall of civilizations in a series which does not lead to any significant end.

World history as it was taught in European schools for more than 1,000 years from Augustine was based on his vision embodied in *Civitas Dei*, which in turn was based on the biblical vision. In the seventeenth century the millenarian element in the biblical vision was reaffirmed by several Christian thinkers and, in the following century under the influence of the Enlightenment, this became secularized in the doctrine of inevitable progress, a doctrine which lasted perhaps up to the First World War. After that shattering event, it became increasingly difficult to believe that the whole point of the cosmic story was to produce the civilized society of Europe in the twentieth century. The doctrine survived in an apocalyptic form in Marxism, which was strongly attractive to Europeans between the wars, but it also has lost its power as a key for explaining the whole human story. In the closing decades of this century it is difficult to find Europeans who have any belief in a significant future which is worth working for and investing in. A society which believes in a worthwhile future saves in the present so as to invest in the future. Contemporary Western society spends in the present and piles up debts for the future, ravages the environment, and leaves its grandchildren to cope with the results as best they can. One searches contemporary European literature in vain for evidence of hope for the future; rather, in Jürgen Moltmann's words, it is characterized by cold despair, loss of vision, resignation, and cynicism.

My Hindu friend saw in the Bible a unique vision of universal history and of the place of the human person as a responsible actor in history. The two belong together. You cannot have hopeful and responsible action without some vision of a possible future. To put it in another way, if there is no point in the story as a whole, there is no point in my own action. If the story is meaningless, any action of mine is meaningless. The loss of a vision for the future necessarily produces that typical phenomenon of our society which the sociologists call *anomie,* a state in which publicly accepted norms and values have disappeared.

But does the story have a point? Normally you cannot be sure what is the point of the story until you have reached the end. There can always be surprises at the end, and in the best stories there are. How then can we, who are still in the middle of the cosmic story, know what the point of the story is, or whether it has any point at all? Only if the author of the story has let us into the secret while we are still in the middle. There can be no other possibility. And here of course, when we speak of "the author letting us into the secret," we are talking the language of revelation. There is no escape from this language if this is our situation, and to pose "reason" against revelation at this point is simply unreasonable. When reason is set against revelation as an alternative or supplementary way of reaching an understanding of our situation, it is obvious that there is confused thinking. If, in this argument, "reason" means the use of inductive methods to discover the truth about our situation by observing all the "facts" and drawing conclusions from them, then it is clear that this kind of inductive process is not applicable to the question of the meaning of the human story as a whole, for the reason that the data for a valid induction are not available until cosmic history has reached its end. There is, of course, a science called futurology which, with the help of the new tools of artificial intelligence, seeks to make forecasts for the future on the basis of existing trends. No one need doubt its usefulness, but certainly no one should pretend that it is other than a very limited exercise. The failures of the futurologists are far more obvious than their achievements, whether one is thinking of the statistical forecasts used by government departments or of the more romantic exercises such as those of Alvin Toffler which have been proved wrong almost before the ink was dry on the pages.

91

And there are vast areas of human life where the predictive power of the most sophisticated computers is exactly nil. No computer in 1900 could have predicted quantum mechanics, for to have predicted it would have been to have achieved it. The universe, as physicist John Polkinghorne has recently said, is nothing like a clock with fixed and predictable movements. It is full of surprises and will continue to surprise us. If it has any coherent purpose, if the story of which we are part has any real point and is leading to any worthwhile end, then there is no alternative way of knowing it other than that its author should let us into the secret. There can be, in strict logic, no other way.

The Bible, as my Hindu friend rightly saw, is the communication of that secret by those who have been chosen to be entrusted with it as bearers of it, agents of it, witnesses of it. I have tried to show in the previous chapter why it is appropriate that it should be entrusted to a chosen few for the sake of all, why there is a logic in the way of election. Let me now suggest some of the implications of this for those who are so chosen.

1. The first is that the communication of the secret calls for faith. It can be disbelieved. Those who believe stake their lives on their belief. There can be no coercive proof that they are right. If there could be, revelation would be unnecessary. In the light of the Bible as a whole one may say that those who believe will probably always be a minority. Certainly the Bible has many warnings that they must expect to be a persecuted minority if they are faithful. As I said earlier, one of the elements of sickness in our society is the belief that there is, or there ought to be, available to us a body of knowledge which cannot be doubted, in respect of which we do not have to take the risk of committing ourselves to that which cannot be coercively demonstrated. Because the secret is the secret of the author's intention, it can only be communicated through those means by which mutual understanding between persons is achieved—that is to say, by acts of trust. In this sense it is a personal belief, a belief for which I am personally accountable. But it is not therefore merely subjective: it is belief about what is true and is therefore true for everyone and for all time. It is the truth about the meaning of the whole human story. Therefore the belief is held, as Polanyi would say, with universal intent, and the proof of this is that I seek to share it with all human beings in all times and places, irrespective of their race, creed, or culture, and to test it against every situation that confronts me. Only if I am so committed is it genuine belief.

2. The secret is communicated through happenings in the course of the history of one nation, Israel. At this point a person lecturing in a university classroom will be expected to say something like: "The Israelites believed that in the things that happened to them God was revealing his purpose for them and for the world." I resist the temptation to speak that way, because that is immediately to distance myself from this Israelite faith. It is to take up a standpoint outside that faith, the standpoint of a historian of religions. The faith of Moses and the prophets and the apostles is thus safely sterilized, stuffed, and mounted like a specimen in a museum. I must state the facts as I believe them. God communicated the secret to his chosen people Israel through events in their history. A person called upon to conduct biblical studies in the academic world of our contemporary culture will be expected to use what is called "objective" language in describing the events of the Bible. What is called "confessional" language is regarded as inappropriate to a university context, fitted rather for a denominational seminary. By using this "objective" language, the lecturer is supposed to protect himself from the charge of explaining historical events by invoking the idea of divine action. But this protection is illusory, for two quite distinct reasons. In the first place, it is obviously inadmissible to suppose that while God can act in the minds of people to alter their beliefs, he cannot intervene in the world of nature to alter the course of events. There are no human beliefs apart from events in the natural world, such as electrical impulses in the cerebral cortex. You cannot divide the natural world into two parts, one open to divine influence and the other not. And, in the second place, it is obviously an illusion to suppose that one way of interpreted history—namely without reference to divine action—is simply objective truth, whereas another way, which incorporates the idea of divine action, is not objective truth but part of a confessional stance. The truth is, of course, that all history is interpreted history, and the question, "What is the frame within which history is interpreted?" requires an answer which can only be a matter of faith. Indubitable knowledge of the meaning and goal of history will only be available when history has reached its terminus. The difference between the two ways of telling the biblical story, the way of *Religionsgeschichte* and the confessional way, is, in terms of the sociology of knowledge, simply that one represents the reigning plausibility structure and the other calls it in question. There is therefore no need to apologize for the forthright affirmation that God chose to communicate the secret to the people whom he had chosen to be the bearers of it for all the nations, namely the people of Israel.

3. I said that this communication of the secret was in the course of the events of Israel's history. I referred previously to James Barr's attack on the so-called Biblical Theology movement on the ground that according to the biblical record the communication is as much a matter of words as it is of happenings. I have tried to meet this criticism already. Obviously the happenings are understood and recorded in words; there is no other way. But the words refer, directly or indirectly, to the happenings. God is always "the LORD who brought you up out of the land of Egypt," or "the Father of our Lord Jesus Christ." The words do not hang in the air; they refer to things that have happened. And of course these things are interpreted by reference to the activity of God, or else—as often in the Psalms—to his apparent failure to act. The interpretation (namely that God is at work) is not something added to the experience of the event; it is the context for understanding the event. There is thus a circularity which is characteristic of all fundamental faith-commitments and which we noted already in the work of science. The scientist starts with the conviction that the world is rational and that events at different times and places in the natural world can be related to one another in a coherent way. Without this conviction, which is a matter of faith, he could not begin his work. But the goal of his work is to prove the truth of the faith from which he began, to prove it in ever new situations. So also the biblical writers take for granted the reality of God's presence and activity in all things and struggle to find it true in ever new situations, situations which seem to contradict it such as the endless disasters that afflicted Israel and that reached their climax in the crucifixion of the Messiah. This circularity is, as I have said, the mark of all fundamental thinking. One can stand outside the circle, declining to accept the starting point. But then, if one is to make any sense of things at all, one has to work in another circle.

4. Although event and interpretation are thus indissolubly linked, this does not mean that there is only one interpretation. Evidently not. The work of critical scholarship on the documents of both testaments has helped us to see how the same events were reinterpreted by successive generations in the light of new experiences. This is true of the exodus from Egypt and of the experience of exile and return. It is very clearly true of the events of Jesus' ministry, death, and resurrection. There is no single interpretation of these events. It is therefore of great positive significance that Jesus did not write a book to record in unchangeable form the revelation which he brought. It is not an unfortunate accident, but of the very heart of the gospel, that we do not

know exactly what Jesus said and did. It is of the essence of the matter that he did not provide us with such a record, but communicated the secret to a community which was then sent out into the world to carry the secret into the life of the world, always reappropriating and reinterpreting it in the light of new circumstances. This means that from the very beginning there has been in the Church debate and struggle and difference of opinion about how to interpret the secret in new situations. The New Testament itself gives us ample evidence of this. The understanding of God's action in history, in other words, remains always a matter of faith and never of indubitable knowledge. We are required in each generation afresh, guided by the original witnesses, to interpret the events of our time in the light of what has been disclosed in those particular events through which God chose to reveal and effect his purpose.

5. What are the implications of this for our understanding of the role of the Bible in the life of the Church? The question of biblical authority is at the very heart of our task as bearers of the gospel in our contemporary Western culture. During the long centuries in which the Bible was the main controlling element in the "plausibility structure" of Western society, the question hardly arose. History was understood as providential history from Augustine until the eighteenth century. Arguments about God's providence and his purposes were as natural in a debate in the House of Commons as they would be astonishing today. There could of course be fierce debates about how we are to interpret God's providential dealings at any particular moment, but no argument about the fact that that is what needs interpreting. Today there can be vigorous debates among scientists about what is the case, but there are very few to question the authority of science as such. Now the biblical interpretation has to justify itself before the bar of reason as it is understood within the reigning plausibility structure. It is hardly necessary to document the fact that a great deal of contemporary theology attempts to do just that. In the oft-repeated phrase, the attempt is made to understand the biblical message in the light of modern thought. Yet no believer can really be content with this, since it assigns the final authority to what is called modern thought. What we are required to attempt is the much more difficult enterprise of trying to understand modern thought in the light of the biblical story.

But is this possible? Many would deny that it is. In a recent review article in the journal *Theology* the writer said that trying to criticize one's own culture is like trying to push a bus while you are sitting in it. Modern thought is not something outside me as a Christian. My whole education and even my theological training has shaped me into a person who shares the ways of thinking that are roughly covered by the phrase "the modern scientific worldview." Is there any escape from this? Can I get off the bus? Can I stand outside myself and look at my way of thinking as a critic of it? More specifically can this book, one among millions of books which we call *the* book, the Bible, call into question the whole way in which I, as a member of this society, understand the world?

This is a point at which the experience of a foreign missionary has something to contribute. A missionary in India learns to realize that there are certain ways of understanding the world that are so fundamental that they have never been questioned in all the revolutions of Indian thought from the Buddha to the Mahatma, from Gautama to Gandhi. I mean, for example, the doctrines of *karma* and *samsara* which see human life in terms of the wheel of nature, the endless cycles of birth, growth, maturity, decay, death, and then a new birth. That is, strictly speaking, the "natural" way to understand human life—the life of the individual and the life of nations. Within this view it is therefore inconceivable that the life of one man at a particular point in history could permanently alter the state of things. Jesus can illustrate the truth about the human condition, but he cannot change it. And so, as I have mentioned earlier, a portrait of Jesus can be happily accommodated in the premises of a Hindu missionary establishment, because Jesus has been painlessly incorporated into the Hindu worldview. The foreign missionary knows that this is not the conversion of India but the co-option of Jesus, the domestication of the gospel into the Hindu worldview. He only slowly begins to realize that the same thing has happened in the West. Jesus is understood in the light of the assumptions which control our culture. When "reason" is invoked as a parallel or supplementary authority to "Scripture" and "tradition," what is happening is that Jesus is being co-opted into the reigning plausibility structure. But the business of the missionary, and the business of the Christian Church in any situation, is to challenge the plausibility structure in the light of God's revelation of the real meaning of history. How is this to be done? Archimedes said, "Give me a lever and a fulcrum outside the earth, and I will move the earth." Where can we find that Archimedean point outside our culture? Are we compelled to sit tight in the bus, even if it is headed for a precipice? Or can we appeal to the Bible to call our culture in question?

One group of people who say "Yes" are the people usually called "fundamentalists." Obviously that term can be used in a wide variety of ways. Fundamentalists are often dismissed as obscurantist or crazy fanatics, and some may be. Whatever their defects, they recognize the problem. If we cannot speak with confidence about biblical authority, what ground have we for challenging the reigning plausibility structure? But the fundamentalist case has been flawed. If the Bible is treated as a compendium of factually inerrant propositions about everything in heaven and earth, then it is impossible to explain both the contradictions between parts of the Bible and things we certainly know as the results of the work of science, and also the obvious inconsistencies within the Bible itself on factual matters. Even the most convinced fundamentalist who lives in the modern world has to rely at innumerable points on knowledge provided by science and not by the Bible. In fact this way of looking at the Bible is nearer to the Muslim way of looking at the Qur'an and prompts the question: "Why, then, did Jesus not write a book as the Prophet did?"

Nor can the Bible provide the Archimedean point that we need if we treat it as the record of unique religious experiences. Anyone who is familiar with the religious literature of the world knows that the religious experiences of the biblical writers are not unique. There is a large amount of devotional literature in the worlds of Hinduism and Islam which can be used without incongruity by a Christian. What is unique about the Bible is the story which it tells, with its climax in the story of the incarnation, ministry, death, and resurrection of the Son of God. If that story is true, then it is unique and also universal in its implications for all human history. It is in fact the true outline of world history, as my Hindu friend rightly saw. This story is, quite simply, unique. In many cultures stories are told about dying and rising gods, stories which are clearly rooted in the universal human experience of death and birth, but these stories make no claim to be actual history. They have no dates and places attached to them. They illustrate the unchanging human condition but make no claim to change it irreversibly. The biblical story is unique. But how does the telling of it challenge the reigning worldview?

6. The answer is that it can do so through the witness of a community which, in unbroken continuity with the biblical actors and witnesses, indwells the story the Bible tells. Here I have used the word "indwells," one of the key words in the epistemology of Michael Polanyi which I have referred to earlier.

To make the point as clearly as possible, I would like to refer to a saying of one of the Latin American liberation theologians to the effect that the important thing in the use of the Bible is not to understand the text but to understand the world *through* the text. What I understand him to be saying is something like this: it is possible to undertake the most exhaustive and penetrating examination of the biblical text in a way which leaves one, so to say, outside it. The text is an object for examination, dissection, analysis, and interpretation from the standpoint of the scholar. This standpoint is normally that of the plausibility structure which reigns in her society. From this point of view she examines the text, but the text does not examine her. Of course that can happen, as it did for Karl Barth as he sat under his apple tree in Safenwil, when he discovered to his astonishment that the apostle Paul was not only addressing his contemporaries in Rome but was actually addressing Karl Barth, and that an answer was required. But most biblical study as currently conducted is protected from that interruption. The text is examined, so to say, from outside.

What is required, according to the Latin American writer, is that one lives in the text and from that position tries to understand what is happening in the world now. This concept of "living in" or "indwelling" is connected in Polanyi's writing with the concepts of tacit and focal awareness. The simplest example of what is meant is to be found in my relation to my body. It is only through my body that I make contact with and obtain knowledge of the world. The five senses all operate through physical organs of my body. If I use my hands to feel something in the dark, I am only tacitly aware of my hands: I am focusing my attention on the surface I am exploring. I indwell my body and am tacitly aware of it and relying on it. But I do not focus attention on my bodily organs unless something has gone wrong. I am focally aware of the things out there which I want to understand. And, as Polanyi says, we are all the time using means to extend our understanding of what is out there—tools, instruments of all kinds, and—very fundamentally—the language we use and the concepts we develop (often very abstract concepts) to grasp and cope with our experience. All of these are, as it were, extensions of our hands and eyes and ears. While we are using words we are only tacitly aware of the words we are using: we are focally aware of the thing they refer to. We *indwell* our language, our concepts, our whole plausibility structure. That is why no one is conscious of the plausibility structure unless something happens to show that it is failing to cope with reality as it is being experienced.

What the quotation from Latin America suggests is that our proper relation to the Bible is not that we examine it from the outside, but that we *indwell* it and from within it seek to understand and cope with what is out there. In other words, the Bible furnishes us with our plausibility structure. This structure is in the form of a story. In Hans Frei's phrase, it is realistic narrative which "renders" the character which it portrays. What is involved in this phrase "realistic narrative"? Consider what it means to get to know a person. One can read an account of his character and career such as might be embodied in an obituary notice. But in order to know the person one must see how she meets situations, relates to other people, acts in times of crisis and in times of peace. It is in narrative that character is revealed, and there is no substitute for this.

If we follow these suggestions we get a picture of the Christian life as one in which we live *in* the biblical story as part of the community whose story it is, find in the story the clues to knowing God as his character becomes manifest in the story, and from within that indwelling try to understand and cope with the events of our time and the world about us and so carry the story forward. At the heart of the story, as the key to the whole, is the incarnation of the Word, the life, ministry, death, and resurrection of Jesus. In the Fourth Gospel Jesus defines for his disciples what is to be their relation to him. They are to "dwell in" him. He is not to be the object of their observation, but the body of which they are a part. As they "indwell" him in his body, they will both be led into fuller and fuller apprehension of the truth and also become the means through which God's will is done in the life of the world. Very briefly let me suggest six implications of this way of looking at the matter:

a. I am suggesting that to live in this way means to inhabit an alternative plausibility structure to the one in which our society lives. A plausibility structure is not just a body of ideas but is necessarily embodied in an actual community. It cannot exist otherwise. In this case the community is that company of people who have been chosen and called by God in continuity with those who have gone before from the very beginning of the story. A plausibility structure is embodied in an actual historical community among all human communities, one which carries forward a tradition of rational discourse and argument as ever new situations have to be met and coped with, and it is therefore something which is always changing and developing.

b. The structure is essentially narrative. An actual history, enacted at the specific times and places which form the background of the Bible, provides the clue for understanding contemporary history. As we face new opportunities and new dangers, we are the people who know what it is to cross the Red Sea on dry land, to be fed with manna in the wilderness, to return with singing from Babylon, to stand before the cross, and to meet the risen Lord in the breaking of bread. This is our story, and it defines who we are. Just as character can only be truly rendered in narrative form, so the answer to the question "Who am I?" can only be given if we ask "What is my story?" and that can only be answered if there is an answer to the further question, "What is the whole story of which my story is a part?" To indwell the Bible is to live with an answer to those questions, to know who I am and who is the One to whom I am finally accountable.

c. To say this does not mean that I am relieved of the responsibility for making day-by-day and moment-by-moment decisions about what to do. The Bible does not provide answers to my questions of a kind which could relieve me of this responsibility. The character which is rendered in the biblical story is the character of the One who as creator and Lord of all calls his people into a responsible relationship of love and obedience. The story is therefore, from the beginning, the story of human decisions which are sometimes, indeed often, wrong. The biblical characters are no more infallible than we are. A central part of the character that is rendered in the narrative is the infinite patience of God, both his wrathful correction of the erring and his loving wooing of them back to himself. The story is carried forward in the same way by men and women who must take responsibility for their decisions about how to act here and now in situations which are always new, but who can also trust in the infinite resources of the one who has called them.

d. If I am asked what grounds I can show for choosing to live in this community and to share this plausibility structure rather than the one which rules public life, my answer must be twofold. First, that a plausibility structure is by definition the frame within which one makes all decisions; one does not decide for it on the basis of some more ultimate framework of belief. Like the scientist's faith in the rationality of the cosmos it is the starting point for exploration, not the conclusion of reasonings based on some other premises. Second, that I do not choose this, but that I am chosen. If I am pressed to answer the question, this is the only final answer. God in his mysterious providence has chosen and called me, through means which are only partly known to me, to be part of this community of faith for the sake of sharing his secret with the whole world.

e. The distinguishing mark of this community will be hope. I have spoken repeatedly about meaning in history, but that is a phrase which is perhaps of doubtful clarity. No one knows the meaning of history in the sense of having a full understanding of everything that happens. I shall speak in the next chapter about the sense in which Christ is the meaning of history. But it is perhaps better to speak of the goal of history, for action is only meaningful when it is directed to some goal which is at least conceivable. Within the community whose plausibility structure is shaped by the biblical story there is a clear vision of the goal of history—namely the reconciliation of all things with Christ as Head—and the assurance that this goal will be reached. This is what gives its distinctive character to the Christian hope. In most ordinary speech "hope" means little more than desire for a better future. When I was learning to read and speak the Tamil language I slowly came to realize that it had no word for "hope." When I questioned my Hindu teacher about this, he asked me in turn what I meant by hope. Does hope mean anything? Things will be what they will be. I may wish that they turn out better than likely, but why should I wish to be deceived by my desires? This conversation helped me to realize that in English also the word "hope" often stands for nothing more than a desire for what may or may not be. In contrast to this, the New Testament speaks of hope among the great enduring realities—an anchor of the soul entering in beyond the curtain which hides the future from us, something utterly reliable. I suggested earlier that the absence of any sense of a worthwhile future was one of the marks of our present culture. By contrast one of the marks of the biblical counterculture will be a confident hope that makes hopeful action possible even in situations which are, humanly speaking, hopeless. That hope is reliable, because the crucified Lord of history has risen from the dead and will come in glory.

f. Hopeful action means having something to which one can confidently look forward. It means having a horizon. As I said earlier, apart from what has been done in the ministry, death, and resurrection of Jesus, we are shut up to only two possibilities. One possible horizon for our action is a vision for the future of the human race, a future in which we shall have no part. The other possible horizon is a personal future for me beyond death. From that future the world in which I now seek to serve God is absent. Its future is not part of my future. The one possibility gives meaning to my participation in the public life of neighborhood, nation, and world at the cost of marginalizing the human person. The other provides meaning for the individual human person at the cost of marginalizing our shared public life. What is made possible through the gospel is a life looking toward a horizon which is different from either of these. That horizon is defined in the words "He shall come again." For a Christian the horizon for all action is this. It is advent rather than future. He is coming to meet us, and whatever we do—whether it is our most private prayers or our most public political action—is simply offered to him for whatever place it may have in his blessed kingdom. Here is the clue to meaningful action in a meaningful history: it is the translation into action of the prayer: "Your kingdom come, your will be done, as in heaven so on earth."

9. Christ, the Clue to History

Can one speak of "meaning" in history? Only if there is some sense in which history moves toward a goal which is worth achieving. The historicist school of historians claimed that the meaning—in the sense of worthwhileness—of history is particular to each nation or culture. As Ranke said, each period of history is equally near to God. If this is so, history as a whole does not move toward a goal and human unity is an impossible dream. Humankind may come from one origin, but the different peoples go their separate ways. We have seen the bitter fruit of this in the nationalist wars of Europe. James Barr attacks the Biblical Theology movement for its alleged exaggeration of the distinctiveness of the Hebrew view as against the Greek, saying that the Greeks were better historians than the Hebrews. Perhaps Herodotus was a better chronicler of events than the authors of the Pentateuch, but what is distinctive in the Hebrew understanding of history is the belief that it has a goal. For Greek thought this was impossible since the essence of perfection is changelessness, and perfection cannot arise from the changes of human history. By contrast the Old Testament writers look forward to a glorious and terrible consummation of history. History has meaning in the sense that it has a goal. This is not, of course, an evolutionary view. History does not reach its goal by the development of the forces immanent within it. Human existence is not to be understood in these terms. On the contrary, all human life is a gift from God and all things exist by his will. History, therefore, is not the story of the development of forces immanent within history; it is a matter of the promise of God. History has a goal only in the sense that God has promised it.

One could say that the theme of promise and fulfillment runs like a thread through the whole Bible. There is the mysterious promise to Adam that humankind will crush the power of evil (Gen. 3:15), the promise to Noah that the world of nature will be sustained for all time (Gen. 8:22), the promise to Abraham that in him and in his posterity all the nations will be blessed, the promise to the patriarchs of the gift of the land of Canaan, the promises in the Psalms that God shall reign over all that opposes him, and the many specific promises in the prophetic writings regarding the events of their immediate future. And all these lead up to and find their culmination in those writings which we call "apocalyptic," which speak of a final consummation of all history, both human and cosmic. As Berkhof has emphasized, there is no sharp line to be drawn between prophecy and apocalyptic; they form parts together of one unbroken movement (H. Berkhof, *Christ, the Meaning of History*, p. 54). And of course Jesus, with his fundamental message that the kingdom of God is at hand, speaks as a representative, rather the final representative, of the apocalyptic tradition. In him the end has come. In him, therefore, history finds its meaning.

Since the publication of Schweitzer's famous book *The Quest of the Historical Jesus*, which demonstrated that Jesus stood firmly within this tradition of apocalyptic writing, there has been a belief, something constantly repeated and hardly questioned, which can be summarized as follows. Jesus and the early church believed that the end of the world was about to happen. Everything in the New Testament is to be understood from this point of view. But in fact the end of the world did not happen. Jesus was mistaken. The Church had to adjust its thinking to this reality and so learn to settle down, live like sensible people in this world as it is, and put away wild ideas about the end of the world.

Let us begin by granting an element of truth in this picture. It is true that the Church did come to settle down and become part of the established order, even though there have always been groups on the fringes of the Church which have retained and still cherish vivid hopes of a coming new age. Such groups are normally also on the fringes of society—the poor and the marginalized. These are facts. The question, however, is whether the received opinion is a correct reading of the New Testament and of the teaching of Jesus. It is indeed difficult to believe, on the face of it, that the Church in its first two or three decades of existence had managed to come to terms with the fact that Jesus was completely mistaken in the very heart of his message, that in spite of this the early Church could speak of him in the terms they did, and that this enormous volte-face could be accomplished without leaving any larger traces of the convulsion in the pages of the New Testament. That is indeed difficult to believe. But the main business is to look at the teaching of Jesus as we have it in the four Gospels, and to ask whether it corresponds to this scenario.

1. In Mark's version of the story, the primary statement of the message of Jesus is in the words: "The kingdom of God has come near" (Mark 1:15). From the predominant use of the verb *engiko* in the New Testament it seems clear that "near" is to be interpreted spatially rather than temporally. The reign of God is now confronting you as a present reality. It is "among you" (Luke 17:21). Its powers are now at work in your midst (Matt. 12:28). This is so because in fact the reign of God, his kingly power, is present in the man Jesus.

2. But at the same time this presence is veiled. It is not obvious to the naked eye of unconverted men and women. They cannot see because they face the wrong way and look for something which is not in truth the power of God. They must make a mental and spiritual U-turn, be converted, in order to believe (not see) that the good news is true: the reign of God is present.

3. It follows from this that this hidden presence creates crisis and conflict. The powers that be, both in their outward form as the established religious and cultural and political structures, and in their inward reality as the principalities and powers of this age, are challenged and fight back. The presence of Jesus precipitates the hour of the power of darkness (Luke 22:53). This conflict with the powers is portrayed in the Synoptic Gospels as gradually intensifying until it comes to its climax on the cross. In the Fourth Gospel it is present throughout. The presence of Jesus strips the masks of righteousness and piety from the face of the powers. It does so precisely because in him the kingship of God is veiled, hidden in a humble and powerless man. The power of God is not of the same kind as the powers of this dark age.

4. Those who are in the thick of this conflict as disciples of Jesus are therefore taught to pray for the day when what is hidden will be revealed, uncovered (the strict sense of apocalypse), when the rule of God will be manifest on earth as it is now in heaven. The key to the seeming contradiction between the statements which speak of the kingdom as present and those which speak of it as future is to be found here. It is not the difference between the incomplete and the complete; it is the difference between the hidden and the manifest. This is expressed in

105

the frequent use by New Testament writers of the words of Psalm 110: "The LORD says to my Lord, 'Sit at my right hand till I make your enemies your footstool.'" Jesus does now reign at God's right hand, but this reign is hidden in heaven. It will become manifest. What is now hidden will be revealed: this is the exact meaning of apocalypse. Jesus who has come will come again. In Mark 14:62, Jesus before the supreme court conflates words from this psalm with words from Daniel: "You will see the Son of God seated at the right hand of power and coming with the clouds of glory." In Daniel the Son of Man comes *to* the throne of God with the clouds of heaven and is given dominion over the nations (Dan. 7:13). In Jesus' reinterpretation of this prophecy, as the New Testament writers understand it, a time is given during which the Son of Man, Jesus, is at God's right hand until the nations come to accept his dominion, and he comes to reign in manifest glory.

5. Thus there is a precise meaning to this gap which opens up between the coming of the kingdom veiled in the vulnerable and powerless Jesus, and the coming of the kingdom in manifest power. That meaning is to be found in the mission of the Church to the nations. It is in the mercy of God that the final unveiling of his power is held back so that all the nations may have the same opportunity that was given to the first hearers in Galilee, the opportunity to repent, to be converted, and to believe and recognize the presence of the reign of God in the crucified Jesus. "The gospel of the kingdom will be preached throughout the whole world as a testimony to all the nations; and then the end will come" (Matt. 24:14). And this preaching of the kingdom will be accompanied, as Jesus' preaching was, by the signs of the kingdom. There will be evidence of the power of the kingdom at work, even in this age. The authority which is given to Jesus as he sits at the right hand of God will be shown in the fulfillment of the mission to all the nations (Matt. 28:18ff.). Because Jesus goes to the Father, the disciples will do even greater works than he did (John 14:19). When the Spirit (the *arrabōn* of the kingdom) comes upon the disciples, they will receive the powers of the kingdom and thus become Jesus' witnesses (Acts 1:6-8). In this sense some of those who heard Jesus speak will live to see the kingdom of God coming with power (Mark 9:1).

6. There is therefore great need for patience. The disciples do not and cannot know how long is the time given for this witnessing and repenting. A great deal of the teaching of Jesus is about this watchful patience. Patience is needed because "you know not the day or the hour." Watchfulness is needed because that hour is certainly coming.

Be warned. Do not sleep. Do not say to yourself, there will always be time. There will not. A day will come when you will hear those terrible words: too late. The two elements in this teaching are not contradictory: they belong together—the sense of immediacy which calls for the alertness and readiness of the good watchman, and the call for patience because no one—not even Jesus himself—can know the times and seasons which the Father has kept in his own authority, the Father who alone knows what possibilities remain for human history. To see a contradiction between the sayings which speak of an immediate unveiling and those which speak of long waiting is to miss the central message of the gospel. It is the same message which is found in St. Paul, who can tell his friends to rejoice because the Lord is at hand and also remind them of the need for patience and forbearance. The two elements are brought together in exemplary fashion in Romans 8, where we are told that it is precisely those who have received the firstfruit of the kingdom, namely the Spirit, who also suffer and groan as they wait for redemption, who are saved in hope and who therefore wait with patience for that which is promised.

7. I have said that it is clear from the New Testament that the early Church saw itself as living in the time between the times, the time when Jesus, having exposed and disarmed the powers of darkness (Col. 2:15), is seated at the right hand of God until the time when his reign shall be unveiled in all its glory among all the nations. The character of this time is given to it by the character of the earthly ministry of Jesus. It is marked by suffering, and by the presence of the signs of the kingdom. That is why the Fourth Gospel, in its portrayal of the missionary commission, says that when Jesus said, "As the Father sent me, so I send you," he showed them his hands and his side—the scars of his passion—and he breathed into them the Spirit who is the foretaste of the kingdom (John 20:19-23). The Church in its journey through history will therefore have this double character insofar as it is faithful to its commission. On the one hand it will be a suffering church, because the powers of darkness, though disarmed and robbed of final authority, are still powerful. As Jesus in his earthly ministry unmasked the powers and so drew their hostility on himself, so the Spirit working through the life and witness of the missionary Church will overturn the world's most fundamental beliefs, proving the world wrong in respect of sin, of righteousness, and of judgment (John 16:8). Consequently the world will hate the Church as it hated its Lord. But, on the other hand, just as the ministry of Jesus was marked by mighty works which, for those with

107

eyes to see and ears to hear, were signs of the presence of the kingdom of God in power, so in the life of the Church there will be mighty works which have the same function. They are not—so to say—steps on the way to the kingdom, but unveilings of, glimpses of that kingdom which is already a reality, but a reality known only to those who have been converted, have been turned from false gods to the living God. These negative and positive elements in the life of the Church will be related to each other in the same way as cross and resurrection were related to each other in the ministry of Jesus (cf. 2 Cor. 4:10). The cross was a public execution visible to all—believers and unbelievers alike. The resurrection was as much a fact of history as the crucifixion, but it was made known only to the chosen few who were called to be the witnesses of the hidden kingdom.

8. This hiddenness is what makes possible the conversion of the nations. The unveiling of the glory of God's kingdom in all its terrible majesty could leave no further room for the free acceptance in faith which Jesus called for. Only when that glory was veiled in the lowliness of the incarnation could it call out freely given repentance and faith. When the Church tries to embody the rule of God in the forms of earthly power it may achieve that power, but it is no longer a sign of the kingdom. But when it goes the way the Master went, unmasking and challenging the powers of darkness and bearing in its own life the cost of their onslaught, then there are given to the Church signs of the kingdom, powers of healing and blessing which, to eyes of faith, are recognizable as true signs that Jesus reigns. All of this is portrayed in the New Testament as forming the substance of the mission to the nations. The mission is an expression of the authority Jesus has on earth and in heaven as he sits at God's right hand. It is manifest in the powers which the presence of the Spirit confers on the Church so that it becomes— both in its words and in its deeds—a witness to the reign of Jesus. And mighty works are promised as part of the fulfillment of the mission.

9. It follows that the Church will always be tempted to deviate from this path either to the one side or to the other. On the one side is the temptation to look for an immediate end to history. It is the temptation to ask, as the disciples are represented as asking Jesus after they had come to believe in his resurrection, "Lord, will you at this time restore the kingdom to Israel?" (Acts 1:6). It is the temptation of those referred to in the Gospel who supposed that "the kingdom of God was to appear immediately" (Luke 19:11). It is the temptation of those who, when things fall apart, think that this is the end of the world and do not

recognize that it is "but the beginning of the sufferings" (Mark 13:8). The material in the Synoptic Gospels which is often referred to as the Little Apocalypse is full of these warnings. There will be many happenings which some will interpret as signs of the end. There will be false Christs claiming to bring in the final kingdom. But the end is not yet. God's patience is not exhausted, and as long as God is patient, the Church must be so also. The gospel must first be preached to all the nations. All must have the opportunity to repent and believe in the hidden reality of the kingdom. The other temptation is the one which has most constantly beset the comfortably established churches. It is the temptation to say, "Where is the promise of his coming? For ever since the fathers fell asleep all things continue as they were from the beginning" (2 Pet. 3:4). It is the temptation of the lazy servant who says, "My master is not coming back and I can do what I want with his household." In its more dignified theological form it goes by the name of realized eschatology: we have already had everything that there is and we cannot look forward to anything radically new. The confident hope expressed in the words "He shall come again in glory to judge the living and the dead" drops out of our working creed. The future will be nothing more than an extension of the past. We must make do with the world as it is. Against both of these temptations the New Testament warns us with its insistent call for a patient hope, a hope which is—on the one hand—confident and sure, an anchor of the soul, and on the other hand patient and enduring. These are two sides of the same thing. Impatience is a sign of unbelief. Firm belief in the one who has promised will lead to patient endurance. That, I suggest, is the central thrust of the New Testament's teaching about what we can look forward to.

Does this New Testament teaching about the kingdom of God enable us to speak of "meaning" in history? Can history be said to have a goal? Once again we must remember that responsible human action is not possible without some vision of the future. In Scott's account of his tragic journey to the South Pole there is an incident which poignantly illustrates the point I want to make. On one occasion the weather conditions were such that a white haze blended with the unbroken whiteness of the snow and no horizon was visible. Wherever they looked there was simply one unbroken whiteness. There was no point on which they could direct their course as they drove their sledges forward. Before long they were coming upon their own tracks. Thinking that they were going forward, they were in fact only going around in a great circle. To solve the problem they began throwing snowballs ahead of them in the direction of true south so that they had something to fix their eyes on. Without some vision of the future, how is it possible to direct one's course in a rational way? In practice we do what Scott did; we have projects, literally things we throw forward, long- or short-term projects, and we measure our progress by the degree of success we have in reaching our self-set targets. But where do these projects lead in the end? Scott had a compass to tell him in which direction to throw the snowballs. Without a compass, how do we know whether our success in reaching our targets is in fact progress or regress? When we look back we can easily see that a great many of our "successes" were in fact disasters. Does our journey have, in fact, a definable goal? That is a question which at some time or other has to be answered if we are to live a rational life.

The New Testament evidently envisages a goal, one toward which we can make progress. "Now is salvation nearer than when we first believed," says Paul (Rom. 13:11). The eager expectation of a real end is vibrant on almost every page. The Bible ends with the vision of the city of God from which all that is evil will have been excluded and into which all the nations will bring their treasures. Even the Johannine texts which are often quoted as evidence for what is called "realized eschatology" nevertheless speak emphatically of a future consummation, of a "last day" in which believers will be raised up (John 6:39) and unbelievers judged (John 12:48), and in which "we shall be like him, for we shall see him as he is" (1 John 3:2). This vision of a real horizon, a real goal toward which we move, is what gives to the whole New Testament its most distinctive character, the character of a hope which is both alert and patient. The last day to which all the prophets had looked forward has dawned. The resurrection of the crucified Messiah is the breaking in of the last day. It is the day of the Lord, the Lord's Day. But here a parable from Karl Barth is illuminating. The Bernese Oberland seen from Berne looks like a single ridge; when you reach it, you find that it is not one ridge but a whole world of mountains and valleys and lakes and forests. The day of the Lord seen from afar looked like a single day. Now that it has dawned we find that it is not just a single day but a new age, an age in which the powers of the kingdom, the powers of the new day, are at work alongside and among the still continuing powers of the old. We have seen why this is so. It is so that there may be time for the mission to all the nations and for the calling of all peoples to repentance and faith. The extending of the Day into an age is the work of God's mercy. He

110

holds back the final unveiling in order that there may be time for repentance. Therefore we who live in the new day and rejoice in it, knowing that Jesus already reigns, yet knowing that this reign is hidden from the world, are not impatient but patient and watchful, redeeming the time and using it to set forward until its completion the work of bearing witness to that hidden reign. Yet this patience must never deteriorate into sloth, into a lazy acceptance of things as they are. The unveiling of the hidden kingdom is not going to be delayed forever. To think that would be to make nonsense of all that Jesus is and has done. The time given to the world to repent will not last forever. The new age is defined by the threefold affirmation in which we declare the mystery of faith:

- Christ has died, once for all disarming the principalities and powers.
- Christ has risen, and now reigns at the Father's side until all his enemies submit.
- Christ will come again, and the glory of his reign will be manifest to all.

And if that final day is delayed it will not be a cause for impatient complaining on our part. We will recognize the delay as a sign of God's patience. In the words of Berkhof, "the joy of the great beginning removes all alarm about the delay in the end" (*Christ, the Meaning of History*, p. 77).

I have tried to indicate what seems to me to be the way in which the New Testament writers understand the meaning of the history of which we are now a part. It does not seem to be the way in which contemporary Christians see it. I said earlier that it seemed to me to be one of the marks of contemporary society that there was a widespread loss of any sense of meaning in history at all. The nineteenth-century beliefs in progress have largely disappeared. It is hard to find people in our society who have any strong sense of a worthwhile future. One becomes aware of this when one contrasts our society with some others, and particularly some Third World countries, where there is a strong sense of commitment to a specific goal for the future, whether in terms of "modernization" in China, or in terms of "nation-building" in Africa, or in terms of "liberation" in Latin America. Whatever may be our opinion of the validity of these goals, there is no doubt that they provide the context for responsible and hopeful action. By contrast Jürgen Moltmann is surely right when he says that over the developed and affluent Western societies there seems to hang the banner: "No Future." He is not referring only to the fact that millions of people in these affluent societies are not able to articulate any vision of a worthwhile future; not only to the widespread sense that we may all face annihilation in a nuclear catastrophe, not only to the mindless violence and vandalism which is a growing mark of "developed" societies, but also to the fact that our societies appear to be intent on immediate consumption rather than on investment for the future. We are piling up enormous debts and exploiting the natural environment in a manner which suggests that we have no real sense of any worthwhile future. Just as a society which believes in the future saves in the present in order to invest in the future, so a society without that belief spends everything now and piles up debts for future generations to settle. "Spend now and someone else will pay later."

The period in which the wealth and power of the nations now called "developed" were generated was marked by a strong belief in the idea of progress. From the middle of the eighteenth century until the First World War Europe and its cultural offshoots lived largely by and with the faith that progress is the meaning of history. In the strength of that belief they achieved prodigies of scientific, industrial, technical, and political development. It was no accident that this belief developed within the society shaped by Christian teaching. Its roots are in the biblical vision of a meaningful history. The first beginnings of the doctrine can be traced to the revival of millenarian beliefs in the sixteenth and seventeenth centuries. In terms of the theological analysis which I am following, one could say that it was a one-sided development of the New Testament hope—one-sided in that it was an attempt to reproduce in history the power of the resurrection without the marks of the cross. It had an optimistic view of the possibilities of human history and failed to recognize the enduring power of that which works to destroy human life. Its most daring development has been in Marxism, which undertakes to deliver humankind finally and completely from that which alienates and enslaves us, so that humanity can at last take control of its own destiny. It is not an accident, but a matter of inner necessity, that this project has led to the most terrible mass destruction of human beings that history has known. For if the meaning of history is to be found in a state of society which will exist only after all those now living are dead—and this is what the doctrine of progress implies—then those now living are expendable. Their lives have no meaning other than their contribution to the total project. But Marxism is by no means the only form in which the idea of progress has reached its nemesis. National-isms of various hues have pursued the same path, sacrificing millions of human beings to a national project. And even in some Christian circles one finds voices decrying the traditional forms of compassionate service to the suffering because these will only delay the revolution after which everything will be put right. This combination of moral cynicism with political naivete demonstrates the way in which a doctrine of prog-ress which seeks to give meaning to history by fixing attention on a fu-ture earthly utopia can operate to deny meaning to the life of the human person now suffering the wrongs that society inflicts. The doctrine of progress which sustained Western society through its great period of expansion is now dead. It perhaps only survives among those Marxists who live under non-Marxist governments, and few of those living under Marxist governments are now Marxists.

With the collapse of the belief in progress, Christians in the af-fluent societies have tended to lapse into a purely privatized eschatology, which pins any hope that it has to the vision of personal blessedness for the soul after death. This naturally diminishes the sense of responsi-bility for public affairs. It encourages the old to withdraw from involve-ment in these public responsibilities, to see them as simply a training ground for the virtues that may fit the soul for eternity. The sense that in their work in and for the common life of the nation and the world they are being given a share in God's project for his world disappears. One expression of this, at least in Protestant circles, is the lack of inter-est in the communion of saints. In the vision which the Letter to the Hebrews gives of the faithful departed as a great cloud of witnesses sur-rounding us and encouraging us in our journey of faith, and looking with us toward the coming of Jesus to consummate the whole story, we have the impression that they are still concerned about the doing of God's will on earth as in heaven. And if they share the life of God, how could it be otherwise? But a privatized eschatology encourages us as we grow older to turn our back on the struggle and conflict of public life and to withdraw into a purely private kind of piety.

Why should it be that we are apparently shut up to these two al-ternatives—meaning for the public life of the world at the cost of margi-nalizing the human person, or meaning for the life of the human per-son at the cost of losing the meaning of history as a whole? It is, of course, because of the fact of death. Death removes each of us from the story before it reaches its goal. And death, as the Bible teaches us, is not merely a biological fact. Like every fact of existence it has meaning. Its

113

meaning is that all human life is so flawed and marred that it cannot lead straight to the perfect consummation of history which God has promised. Flesh and blood, unredeemed human nature, is not fit for the kingdom of God (1 Cor. 15:50). Then what place can there be for hope in a meaningful future and a meaningful history? None, unless sin and death have been dealt with. None, unless the goal is beyond the reach of death and yet not in such a manner as to destroy the significance of all that lies this side of death.

Meaningful action in history is possible only when there is some vision of the future goal. But the future is hidden from us—our own personal future and the future of the world. The curtain of death lies across the path. The good news is that Jesus has opened a way through the curtain and has come to lead us on the way which he has opened and which he is, the way which consists in abiding in him, sharing his passion so that we may share his victory over death. Our life is still lived as his incarnate life was lived, in a world in which the power of darkness is still at work. The more actively we challenge these powers in the name of Jesus, the more violently will they attack. But exactly when this attack is most violent and exactly when we are at our most vulnerable, signs will be given of the presence of the kingdom, the power of the Spirit to speak the word that bears witness to Christ's kingly power and assures us that the victory is to him and not to the powers of darkness. Eventually we ourselves must die and much of what we have labored to create may decay and be forgotten. But because Jesus, the one who was rejected, crucified, dead, and buried, has risen from the dead and now lives and reigns, we know that what appears to be lost is not lost but is safely kept against the day of resurrection. The New Testament contains several metaphors to convey both the continuity and the discontinuity between what we now do and what we now are on this side of death, and what we shall see and know in the end. There is the metaphor of the grain of wheat which is buried in the ground and apparently lost, but which brings a harvest of fresh grain. There is the metaphor of childbirth: the travail of the mother is forgotten in the joy of the birth of a child. And there is the metaphor of the building in which the worthless materials are destroyed by fire but what is fit to survive the fire will be preserved.

This faith enables us to be at the same time realistic and hopeful. We can be realistic, knowing that no human project can eliminate the powers of darkness as they operate in human life. This realism delivers us from the utopian fanaticisms which have condemned millions of people to misery and death in the cause of an imagined future. But at the same time we can be hopeful, acting hopefully in apparently hopeless situations, not dreaming of an absolute perfection on this side of death, but doing resolutely that relative good which is possible now, doing it as an offering to the Lord who is able to take it and keep it for the perfect kingdom which is promised. In this sense, to use a phrase of Schweitzer, our actions in the public life of the world are acted prayers for the kingdom. They do not themselves lead directly to the kingdom. They are acted prayers for its coming and as such they act as signs of its reality and so enable others to act in hope.

When the disciples were perplexed and could not understand why Jesus was to leave them and go alone to his death, he told them that he was himself the way by which they were to follow (John 14:1-6). One can always travel hopefully if there is a reliable track and good ground for believing that it leads to the destination. The track on which we walk is one that disappears from sight before it reaches the destination. We may have a vision of the peak we are aiming for, but we do not see the track all the way to it. It goes down into the dark valley of death, and we, with all our works, go that way. We can go forward with confidence because Jesus has gone that way before us and has come back from the deep valley. If he is himself the track, we can go forward confidently even when the future is hidden. We are not lost. We have a reliable track.

What is promised as the goal of history, that which makes possible responsible action in history, is something which heals the dichotomy between the private and the public worlds which death creates. The Holy City as John portrays it in the final book of our Bible is in one sense the consummation of all public history. It represents the goal of the whole story of civilization, which is the creation of the true city. It is perfect in beauty and unity. And into it all the nations of the earth will bring their treasures. The great sculptured panels beside the long flight of steps leading up to the central throne at Persepolis portray all the nations bringing their distinctive gifts to the feet of the Emperor Darius. Perhaps some such picture inspired the writer of the apocalypse. The achievements of human civilization, art, technology, and culture are not obliterated. All that is unclean is excluded, but all that is worthy will find its place as an offering to the King of kings. That is the vision which these words suggest. But at the same time the Holy City is the place where the journey of each soul finds at last its goal. "The throne of the Lamb shall be in it, and his servants shall worship him; they shall see his face, and his name shall be on their foreheads" (Rev. 22:3-4).

10. The Logic of Mission

Perhaps my title, "The Logic of Mission," may seem an odd one, but I am concerned to explore the question how the mission of the Church is rooted in the gospel itself. There has been a long tradition which sees the mission of the Church primarily as obedience to a command. It has been customary to speak of "the missionary mandate." This way of putting the matter is certainly not without justification, and yet it seems to me that it misses the point. It tends to make mission a burden rather than a joy, to make it part of the law rather than part of the gospel. If one looks at the New Testament evidence one gets another impression. Mission begins with a kind of explosion of joy. The news that the rejected and crucified Jesus is alive is something that cannot possibly be suppressed. It must be told. Who could be silent about such a fact? The mission of the Church in the pages of the New Testament is more like the fallout from a vast explosion, a radioactive fallout which is not lethal but life-giving. One searches in vain through the letters of St. Paul to find any suggestion that he anywhere lays it on the conscience of his readers that they ought to be active in mission. For himself it is inconceivable that he should keep silent. "Woe to me if I do not preach the gospel!" (1 Cor. 9:16). But nowhere do we find him telling his readers that they have a duty to do so.

It is a striking fact, moreover, that almost all the proclamations of the gospel which are described in Acts are in response to questions asked by those outside the Church. This is so in the case of Peter's sermon on the day of Pentecost, of the testimonies given by the apostles and by Stephen under interrogation, of the encounter of Philip with the Ethiopian, of Peter's meeting with the household of Cornelius, and of the preaching of Paul in the synagogue at Antioch of Pisidia. In every case there is something present, a new reality, which calls for explanation and so prompts the question to which the preaching of the gospel is the answer. This is clearly so in the first of the cases I have cited, the sermon of Peter on the day of Pentecost. Something is happening which prompts the crowd to come together and ask, "What is going on?" The answer of Peter is in effect a statement that what is going on is that the last day has arrived and the powers of the new age are already at work, and that this is so because of the life, ministry, death, resurrection, and ascension of Jesus. The sermon leads up to a climax in the citing of the Psalm 110 (Acts 2:34). Jesus, whom they had crucified, is now seated at the right hand of God until all things are put under his feet. This has to be told to all who will hear simply because it is the truth. This is the reality which all human beings must henceforth take into account. The real government of the universe, the final reality which in the end confronts every human being, is the crucified and risen Jesus. And to the question "What, then, are we to do?" the answer is "Repent and be baptized in the name of Jesus." To repent is to do the U-turn of the mind which enables you to believe what is hidden from sight, the reality of the presence of the reign of God in the crucified Jesus. To be baptized is to be identified with, incorporated into that which Jesus did when he went down into the waters of Jordan as one of a company of sin-burdened men and women and so inaugurated a mission which would lead him through his great encounter with the principalities and powers to its victorious climax in the cross. To be baptized is to be incorporated into the dying of Jesus so as to become a participant in his risen life, and so to share his ongoing mission to the world. It is to be baptized into his mission.

His mission. It is of the greatest importance to recognize that it remains his mission. One of the dangers of emphasizing the concept of mission as a mandate given to the Church is that it tempts us to do what we are always tempted to do, namely to see the work of mission as a good work and to seek to justify ourselves by our works. On this view, it is *we* who must save the unbelievers from perishing. The emphasis of the New Testament, it seems to me, is otherwise. Even Jesus himself speaks of his words and works as not his own but those of the Father. His teaching is the teaching of the Father, and his mighty works are the work of the Father. So also in the Synoptic Gospels, the mighty works of Jesus are the work of God's kingly power, of his Spirit. So also with the disciples. It is the Spirit who will give them power and the Spirit

117

who will bear witness. It is not that they must speak and act, asking the help of the Spirit to do so. It is rather that in their faithfulness to Jesus they become the place where the Spirit speaks and acts.

This means that their mission will not only be a matter of preaching and teaching but also of learning. When he sends them out on their mission, Jesus tells the disciples that there is much for them yet to learn and he promises that the Spirit who will convict the world will also lead them into the truth in its fullness (John 16:12-15). What does it mean that Jesus is at the right hand of God until all his enemies submit? To believe it is not to arrive at an end of all learning but to arrive at a starting point for learning. All history and all experience have now to be understood in terms of this faith and this promise. But this "understanding" is something the Church has to be learning in the course of its mission. Even the incarnate Lord, according to the Scriptures, had to learn obedience by the things which he suffered (Heb. 5:8). Like its Lord, the Church has to renounce any claim to a masterful control of history. By following the way her Lord went, the way of suffering witness, she unmasks the powers which claim this masterful control and confronts each succeeding generation with the ultimate goal of history. What Christ's lordship over the world means, what it means that all authority is given to him, is something which the Church has to learn in her journey. The Spirit, the foretaste of the kingdom, who performs the works of power in the midst of human weakness and thus convicts the world in respect of its most fundamental ideas, by the same token leads the Church into the fullness of the truth, a fullness which will be complete only when Christ's lordship is no longer hidden but manifest to all.

The mission of the Church is to be understood, can only be rightly understood, in terms of the trinitarian model. It is the Father who holds all things in his hand, whose providence upholds all things, whose tender mercies are over all his works, where he is acknowledged and where he is denied, and who has never left himself without witness to the heart and conscience and reason of any human being. In the incarnation of the Son he has made known his nature and purpose fully and completely, for in Jesus "all the fullness of God was pleased to dwell" (Col. 1:19). But this presence was a veiled presence in order that there might be the possibility of repentance and freely given faith. In the Church the mission of Jesus is continued in the same veiled form. It is continued through the presence and active working of the Holy Spirit, who is the presence of the reign of God in foretaste. The mission of the Church to all the nations, to all human communities in all their diversity and in all their particularity, is itself the mighty work of God, the sign of the inbreaking of the kingdom. The Church is not so much the agent of the mission as the locus of the mission. It is God who acts in the power of his Spirit, doing mighty works, creating signs of a new age, working secretly in the hearts of men and women to draw them to Christ. When they are so drawn, they become part of a community which claims no masterful control of history, but continues to bear witness to the real meaning and goal of history by a life which—in Paul's words—by always bearing about in the body the dying of Jesus becomes the place where the risen life of Jesus is made available for others (2 Cor. 4:10).

It is impossible to stress too strongly that the beginning of mission is not an action of ours, but the presence of a new reality, the presence of the Spirit of God in power. The whole New Testament bears witness to this, and so does the missionary experience of the Church through the ages. Perhaps this has been made especially clear to us in the present century through the experience of the Church in the Soviet Union and in China. In both these vast countries we have seen the Church crushed to a point where no kind of explicit public witness, in spoken or written word, or in service to the public, was permitted. And in exactly these situations, we have seen the marvelous growth of the Church through the active power of the Spirit drawing men and women to recognize in this human weakness the presence and power of God. This corresponds to what we have seen in the New Testament, not only in the explicit linking of the mission with the presence of the Spirit, but also in the fact that the great missionary proclamations in Acts are not given on the unilateral initiative of the apostles but in response to questions asked by others, questions prompted by the presence of something which calls for explanation. In discussions about the contemporary mission of the Church it is often said that the Church ought to address itself to the real questions which people are asking. That is to misunderstand the mission of Jesus and the mission of the Church. The world's questions are not the questions which lead to life. What really needs to be said is that where the Church is faithful to its Lord, there the powers of the kingdom are present and people begin to ask the question to which the gospel is the answer. And that, I suppose, is why the letters of St. Paul contain so many exhortations to faithfulness but no exhortations to be active in mission.

The presence of the kingdom in the Church is the presence of its foretaste, its firstfruit, its pledge *(arrabōn)* in the Spirit. It is the presence of power veiled in weakness. It is a presence which leads us to speak, with the New Testament, both of having and of hoping. "We ourselves," says St. Paul, "who have received the firstfruit, namely the Spirit, groan inwardly as we wait for adoption as sons, the redemption of our bodies. For in this hope we were saved" (Rom. 8:23-24). It is this indissoluble unity of having and hoping, this presence now of something which is a pledge of the future, this *arrabōn* which is both a reality now and at the same time a pledge of something far greater to come, it is this which constitutes the Church as witness. But the Church is not the source of the witness; rather, it is the locus of witness. The light cast by the first rays of the morning sun shining on the face of a company of travelers will be evidence that a new day is coming. The travelers are not the source of that witness but only the locus of it. To see for oneself that it is true, that a new day is really coming, one must turn around, face the opposite way, be converted. And then one's own face will share the same brightness and become part of the evidence.

This presence of a new reality, the presence in the shared life of the Church of the Spirit who is the *arrabōn* of the kingdom, has become possible because of what Jesus has done, because of his incarnation, his ministry as the obedient child of his Father, his suffering and death, his resurrection, his ascension into heaven, and his session at the right hand of God. When the apostles are asked to explain the new reality, the new power to find joy in tribulation, healing in sickness, freedom in bondage, life in death, this is the explanation they give. It follows that the visible embodiment of this new reality is not a movement which will take control of history and shape the future according to its own vision, not a new imperialism, not a victorious crusade. Its visible embodiment will be a community that lives by this story, a community whose existence is visibly defined in the regular rehearsing and reenactment of the story which has given it birth, the story of the self-emptying of God in the ministry, life, death, and resurrection of Jesus. Its visible center as a continuing social entity is that weekly repeated event in which believers share bread and wine as Jesus commanded, as his pledge to them and their pledge to him that they are one with him in his passion and one with him in his victory. Instead of the celebration of the sabbath as the end of God's old creation, they celebrate the first day of the week, the Lord's Day, as the beginning of the new creation. In this they find enacted and affirmed the meaning and goal of their lives as part of the life of the cosmos, their stories as part of the universal story. This story does indeed lead to a glorious end and is therefore filled with meaning, but the end is not at some far distant date in terrestrial history. The end is the day when Jesus shall come again, when his hidden rule will become manifest and all things will be seen as they truly are. That is why we repeat at each celebration of the Supper the words which encapsulate the whole mystery of faith: "Christ has died. Christ is risen: Christ shall come again."

It is in this light that we must understand the purpose and goal of missions. I am here using the word "missions" in distinction from the more all-embracing word "mission." This latter word I take to mean the entire task for which the Church is sent into the world. By "missions" I mean those specific activities which are undertaken by human decision to bring the gospel to places or situations where it is not heard, to create a Christian presence in a place or situation where there is no such presence or no effective presence. The goal of such a missionary action has been defined in different ways. Sometimes the emphasis is on the conversion of the greatest possible number of individuals and their incorporation into the Church. The success of the mission is to be evaluated in terms of church growth. Sometimes the emphasis is on the humanization of society, the eradication of social ills, the provision of education, healing, and economic development. Success in either of these aims is hailed as success for the mission. By contrast St. Paul's criterion seems to be different. He can tell the Christians in Rome that he has completed his work in the whole vast region from Jerusalem to the Adriatic and has "no longer any room for work in these regions" (Rom. 15:23). What, exactly, has he done? Certainly not converted all the populations of these regions. Certainly not solved their social and economic problems. He has, in his own words, "fully preached the gospel" and left behind communities of men and women who believe the gospel and live by it. So his work as a missionary is done. It is striking, for a modern reader, that he does not agonize about all the multitudes in those regions who have not yet heard the gospel or who have not accepted it. He does indeed, in the same letter, agonize over the fact that the Jews, to whom the gospel primarily belongs, have rejected it. But he is certain that in the end "the fullness of the Gentiles will be gathered in" and "all Israel will be saved" (Rom. 11:25-26). We shall have to consider in a later chapter what to make of this confidence of the apostle. The point here is that he has completed his missionary task in the creation of believing communities in all the regions through which he has passed. These communities are, as he says to the Corinthians, composed

121

mostly of people whom the world despises. They do not look like the wave of the future. They are ignored by contemporary historians. They do not pretend to take control of the destiny of the Roman Empire, let alone of the whole world. What, then, is their significance?

One could answer most simply by saying that their significance is that they continue the mission of Jesus in accordance with his words: "As the Father sent me, so I send you." They share his weakness, and as they do so, they share in the powers of the new age which he brings. They thus perform, as he did, a critical function. They confront men and women with the ultimate issues of human existence. They therefore share, in their measure, his passion. "A servant is not greater than his master, nor a messenger [apostle] greater than the one who sends him" (John 13:16). All this is spelled out in the apocalyptic passages of the first three Gospels and the corresponding sayings in the fourth. As the coming of Jesus precipitated a crisis for Israel, so the coming of the Church will precipitate a crisis for the world. The coming of light into darkness must necessarily have this effect. In the darkness things can be hidden; when the light comes people have to choose. If Jesus was rejected, so will his messengers. Not only so, there will be false Christs. The coming into the world of the promise of total salvation, of a radically new age, precipitates at the same time the appearing of those who offer salvation on other terms. Therefore it will not only be the old paganisms that fight against the Church, but also the new messianisms. Wherever the gospel is preached, new ideologies appear—secular humanism, nationalism, Marxism—movements which offer the vision of a new age, an age freed from all the ills that beset human life, freed from hunger and disease and war— on other terms. It is no accident that the only areas of India where Marxism has become a real power are areas of vigorous Christian missionary activity, or that those who led the Marxist revolution in China were the products of Christian schools and colleges. Once the gospel is preached and there is a community which lives by the gospel, then the question of the ultimate meaning of history is posed and other messiahs appear. So the crisis of history is deepened. Even more significant as an example of this development than the rise of Marxism is the rise of Islam. Islam, which means simply submission, is the mightiest of all the post-Christian movements which claim to offer the kingdom of God without the cross. The denial of the crucifixion is and must always be central to Islamic teaching. But Islam and Marxism are only the most powerful illustrations of something which must necessarily mark the progress of the Christian mission to the nations. Once the real end of history has been disclosed, and once the invitation is given to live by it in the fellowship of a crucified and risen messiah, then the old static and cyclical patterns are broken and can never be restored. If Jesus is not acknowledged as the Christ, then other christs, other saviors will appear. But the gospel must first be preached to all the nations. Every human community must have the opportunity to hear, believe, and freely accept the true goal. That goal lies beyond history. Kingdoms will pass away. The earth itself and the visible cosmos will pass away. In the end Jesus Christ will be seen as the one to whom authority is given. And so the call is for patient endurance.

What I have been saying seeks to reflect the material of the synoptic apocalypse. The corresponding Johannine teaching is to be found in chapters 14–16 of the Fourth Gospel. Here, too, the disciples are warned that they will be rejected and cast out (John 15:18ff.). They are promised the presence of the Spirit, who will himself be the witness and by whose presence they also will be witnesses (John 15:26-27). This same Spirit will bring the world under judgment, exercising the same power that had been present in Jesus to overturn accepted ideas of sin and righteousness and judgment (John 16:8-9). The Spirit will call for the same radical conversion to which Jesus called men and women. The Spirit is the Spirit of truth, in contrast to the many spirits of this age which lead mean and women into falsehood. The Holy Spirit will lead the Church into ever fuller understanding of the truth—beyond what it was possible for the incarnate Lord to communicate to that group of disciples limited to one time and place and culture (John 16:12-15). The work of the Spirit will be to manifest the glory of Jesus by taking what belongs to him (which is in fact everything, because "all that the Father has is mine") and showing it to the Church. By the work of the Spirit the Church will be able to understand "the things that are to come" and to learn that all that exists belongs to Christ. As it lives in the power of the Spirit, and as it shares in the suffering and rejection of Jesus, the Church will learn more and more fully what it means that Jesus is the clue to history, its source and its goal. But clearly this learning process is part of and cannot be detached from the Church's missionary journey to all the nations. There is already in the life of the Church a foretaste of what is promised for the end, namely that the nations shall walk in the light of the Lamb and their kings shall bring their glory into the Holy City (Rev. 21:24). In this sense, as the mission goes its way to the ends of the earth new treasures are brought into the life of the Church,

123

and Christianity itself grows and changes until it becomes more credible as a foretaste of the unity of all humankind. The first steps of this journey are chronicled in the New Testament, where we see the struggles which were required before the Church could accept that the Gentiles, as Gentiles and not as Jewish proselytes, were to be part of the new community.

The fulfillment of the mission of the Church thus requires that the Church itself be changed and learn new things. Very clearly the Church had to learn something new as a result of the conversion of Cornelius and his household. And, once again, the point must be made: this is not an achievement of the Church but a work of the Spirit. In that story we see Peter's extreme reluctance to mix with the household of a pagan Roman officer. He tells the story of Jesus in that Roman house because he is directly questioned. The fruit of the telling is an action of the Spirit which takes matters out of Peter's hands. He can only confess with astonishment that these uncircumcised pagans have been made part of God's household. So the Church is moved one step on the road toward becoming a home for people of all nations and a sign of the unity of all. The last two centuries have seen giant steps along that road. The Church is now recognizable as a universal community in which all human cultures can be welcomed. But still we are only on the way, and the Church has to continue to learn new things as new peoples are brought to Christ. Only at the end shall we know what it means that Jesus is Lord of all. Till then our confession can only be partial, culture-bound, and thus incomplete. The whole world needs to know what Jesus' lordship means. The writer to the Hebrews, speaking of the saints of the previous generations, says that apart from us they could not be made perfect, because God had prepared some better thing for us (Heb. 11:39-40). The same logic leads us to look into the future and say that we cannot be made perfect without those who are to come after. God's perfect reign cannot be made manifest to all until the mission of the Church to all nations is complete.

In this sketch of the logic of mission, it is obvious that the center of the picture is not occupied by the question of the saving, or the failure to save, individual souls from perdition. That question has dominated Protestant missionary thinking at many times and places. Clearly it cannot be left out of the picture, but I do not find that in the New Testament it occupies the center. If this were the central question, St. Paul could not have said that his work in the Eastern Roman world was finished. However many local churches had come into being through his ministry, only a tiny minority of those who had died during the years of his ministry had died as Christian believers. If this is the criterion by which missions are to be judged, then plainly they have been and still are a colossal failure. Not only today, but through all the centuries, the great majority of human beings who have died have died without faith in Christ. The missionary calling has sometimes been interpreted as a calling to stem this fearful cataract of souls going to eternal perdition. But I do not find this in the center of the New Testament representation of the missionary calling. Certainly Jesus tells us that God seeks the last lost sheep, and Paul is ready to be all things to all people in order that he may by all means save some (1 Cor. 9:22). And he goes on to say, "I do it all for the sake of the gospel, that I may share in its blessings." I shall return to this verse. But meanwhile we must also consider the important passage in Romans 9–11 where Paul gives his most fully developed theology of mission, and here the center of the picture is the eschatological event in which the fullness of the Gentiles will have been gathered in and all Israel will be saved. This is in spite of the fact that the vast majority of Jews have rejected the gospel, and that the event to which Paul looks forward will certainly occur long after the death of the unbelieving Jews. Plainly Paul is not thinking in terms of the individual but in terms of the interpretation of universal history. The center of the picture is the eschatological event in which the fathomless depths of God's wisdom and grace will be revealed. His ways are inscrutable and his judgments unsearchable. He has consigned all men to disobedience in order that he may have mercy on all (Rom. 11:32-36). Until that day none can share in God's perfection. Until that day, we are all on the way. There is no room either for anxiety about our failure or for boasting about our success. There is room only for faithful witness to the one in whom the whole purpose of God for cosmic history has been revealed and effected, the crucified, risen, and regnant Christ.

So the logic of mission is this: the true meaning of the human story has been disclosed. Because it is the truth, it must be shared universally. It cannot be private opinion. When we share it with all peoples, we give them the opportunity to know the truth about themselves, to know who they are because they can know the true story of which their lives are a part. Wherever the gospel is preached the question of the meaning of the human story—the universal story and the personal story of each human being—is posed. Thereafter the situation can never be the same. It can never revert to the old harmonies, the old securities, the old static or cyclical patterns of the past. Now decisions have to be made for or against Christ, for Christ as the clue to history or for some other clue. There will always be the temptation, even for those within the Christian community, to find the clue in the success of some project of our own, to see our program (whether of church growth or of human development) as the success story which is going to give meaning to our lives. The gospel calls us back again and again to the real clue, the crucified and risen Jesus, so that we learn that the meaning of history is not immanent in history itself, that history cannot find its meaning at the end of a process of development, but that history is given its meaning by what God has done in Jesus Christ and by what he has promised to do; and that the true horizon is not at the successful end of our projects but in his coming to reign.

One may say, therefore, that missions are the test of our faith. In earlier chapters I have emphasized the fact that the Christian gospel cannot be validated by reference to some more ultimate commitment. The Christian faith is itself an ultimate faith-commitment which can be validated only in its exercise. As such it is open to the charge of subjectivity. In drawing on the epistemological work of Polanyi I referred to his insistence on the importance of the subjective pole in all our knowing. All knowing is an exercise of a knowing subject which involves personal commitment. How, then, is it saved from pure subjectivity? This is a vital question in our present cultural situation where Christian faith is widely regarded as belonging to the world of subjective values rather than to the world of objective facts, and as being therefore merely a matter of personal choice about which the words "true" and "false" cannot be used. How is this charge to be refuted? Not by seeking some more ultimate ground on which faith could rest. There is nothing more ultimate than Jesus Christ, through whom all things came to be and in whom all things will find their consummation. Polanyi's answer to the charge of subjectivism is that while we hold our beliefs as personally committed subjects, we hold them with universal intent, and we express that intent by publishing them and inviting all people to consider and accept them. To be willing so to publish them is the test of our real belief. In this sense missions are the test of our faith. We believe that the truth about the human story has been disclosed in the events which form the substance of the gospel. We believe, therefore, that these events are the real clue to the story of every person, for every human life is part of the whole human story and cannot be understood apart from that story. It follows that the test of our real belief is our readiness to share it with all peoples.

I do not say that that is the only way to speak of missions. Missions are also an expression of our hope: they express our belief that there is a real future for us and for the world and that there are therefore solid grounds for hope. Missions are also an expression of love. As Paul says, the love of Christ constrains us. We have been reconciled to God through the atoning love of Christ, and therefore we have an obligation to share that love with all for whom he died. We have a ministry of reconciliation entrusted to us because God has reconciled us to himself. But clearly both of these motives depend on the truth of what we believe. If it is not true, then there are no grounds for hope. And if it is not true, then to persuade men and women to follow Jesus is not an act of love. Missions are the test of our faith that the gospel is true.

It will be clear from what I have said about Paul's eschatological vision of salvation that I am not placing at the center of the argument the question of the salvation or perdition of the individual. Clearly that is part of what is involved, but my contention is that the biblical picture is distorted if this is put in the center. But it may be asked: if it is true that those who die without faith in Christ are not necessarily lost, and if it is also true that those who are baptized Christians are not necessarily saved, what is the point of missions? Why not leave events to take their course? In answer to that question, I would refer again to the word of Paul which I quoted earlier, "I do it all for the sake of the gospel, that I may share in its blessings" (1 Cor. 9:23). Jesus said as he was on his way to the cross, "Where I am, there shall my servant be" (John 12:26). The one who has been called and loved by the Lord, the one who wishes to love and serve the Lord, will want to be where he is. And where he is is on that frontier which runs between the kingdom of God and the usurped power of the evil one. When Jesus sent out his disciples on his mission, he showed them his hands and his side. They will share in his mission as they share in his passion, as they follow him in challenging and unmasking the powers of evil. There is no other way to be with him. At the heart of mission is simply the desire to be with him and to give him the service of our lives. At the heart of mission is thanksgiving and praise. We distort matters when we make mission an enterprise of our own in which we can justify ourselves by our works. I said at the beginning of this chapter that the Church's mission began as the radioactive fallout from an explosion of joy. When it is true to its nature, it is so to the end. Mission is an acted out doxology. That is its deepest secret. Its purpose is that God may be glorified.

11. Mission: Word, Deed, and New Being

Throughout these chapters I am suggesting that the gospel is to be understood as the clue to history, to universal history and therefore to the history of each person, and therefore the answer that every person must give to the question, Who am I? In distinction from a great deal of Christian writing which takes the individual person as its starting point for the understanding of salvation and then extrapolates from that to the wider issues of social, political, and economic life, I am suggesting that, with the Bible as our guide, we should proceed in the opposite direction, that we begin with the Bible as the unique interpretation of human and cosmic history and move from that starting point to an understanding of what the Bible shows us of the meaning of personal life. And, more specifically, I have suggested that we are to understand the mission of the Church in the light of the fact that the meaning of contemporary history is that it is the history of the time between Christ's ascension and his coming again, the time when his reign at the right hand of God is a hidden reality, the time in which signs are granted of that hidden reign but in which the full revelation of its power and glory is held back in order that all the nations—all the human communities—may have the opportunity to repent and believe in freedom. One could therefore say that the Christian world mission is the clue to history in a double sense, which one might characterize as proclaiming and propelling.

On the one hand, by proclaiming Christ the Christian world mission offers to all people the possibility of understanding what God is

doing in history. By its witness—in word and deed and common life—
to the centrality of the work of Jesus in his ministry, death, and resurrection it offers to all people the possibility of understanding that the
meaning and goal of history are not to be found in any of the projects,
programs, ideologies, and utopias which offer themselves in competi-
tion with one another; the rise and decline one after another of movements promising happiness in the future; movements which sweep forward for a time and then falter and fall back like the ceaseless movement
of the waves on an ocean shore; but that it is to be found in a person
and a history which breaks decisively through this endless succession
by breaching the final barrier of death and opening a new horizon for
human affairs, a hope which on the one hand affirms and energizes all
those human hopes which correspond to God's purpose as revealed in
Christ, but yet on the other hand transcends them all. The Church, reaching out to every human community, living a life which is centered in
the continual remembrance and reenactment of that central revelation,
offers to all peoples a vision of the goal of human history in which its
good is affirmed and its evil is forgiven and taken away, a vision which
makes it possible to act hopefully when there is no earthly hope, and
to find the way when everything is dark and there are no earthly land-
marks. This is what I have called the proclaiming aspect of the Church's
world mission as it relates to universal history.

On the other hand, the mission has what I must call a propelling
role. It presses events toward their true end. This is the abiding significance of the apocalyptic teachings of the New Testament. The coming of
the gospel changes the course of events. It awakens people out of the
age-long slumber of what Arendt van Leeuwen called the ontocratic
society, the way of life which exists in societies where it is taken for
granted that all things are governed by what is and not by what shall be.

J. L. Myres in his book *The Dawn of History* has an opening chapter entitled "The People Who Have No History." It is a reminder to the
reader that vast numbers of human beings have lived and died without
leaving any history. They have lived (as millions still do) in the belief
that things are what they are and will not be fundamentally changed;
that hope for a different future is a delusion born of desire, a delusion
which the wise will avoid because they know that what will be will be
and no desire of ours can change it. In such societies there may be a
story to be told about small units—the family, the city, the school—because in these one can trace movement toward significant goals. But for
human affairs as a whole there is no history. The coming of the gospel

129

into such a society introduces the vision of a new world, a different world, a world for which it is legitimate to hope. It creates, as we say, a revolution of expectations. The point of van Leeuwen's book (Arendt van Leeuwen, *Christianity in World History*, 1964) was that even the secularized forms of the Christian hope which have fueled the European idea of progress and have made possible the explosive growth of modern science and technology have had the same effect on the old ontocratic societies. They have created an explosion of expectations and therefore a deepening crisis when these expectations are not met.

This can be illustrated from almost any page of the missionary history of the past hundred years, and nowhere more vividly than in China. It was the young graduates of the Christian schools and colleges who made the break with the old China, who had a glowing vision of a new China communicated to them by the kind of teaching they had received from missionary teachers, and who became convinced that Christianity could not deliver what it promised, who turned to Marxism with its promise of a new world tomorrow. I have listened to young Indians who said, "Christianity taught me to believe in the possibility of a different world; Marxism showed me how to get it." It does not take more than a generation to discover that Marxism necessarily betrays the hopes by which it lives. I am told that it is only some of the old in China who are still Marxists. But the point is that neither China nor India nor any other society can go back to where it was before this vision of a different world was brought to it. Burma has tried to do it by isolating itself from the West, but the attempt is doomed to failure. Once the old ontocratic mold is broken it can never be restored. History is propelled inexorably toward the future.

I have suggested that the apocalyptic passages in the New Testament are the clue for our understanding of this. The coming of Jesus precipitates the crisis of history. Once a vision has been given of the new age, there will be prophets offering the blessings of the new age on terms other than those offered in the story of Jesus. The question of the meaning and goal of history can no longer be evaded. The conflict between rival visions of that goal rages. There is war and tumult. This is among the signs of the fact that the end—the real goal of history—has come near in Jesus. All of this is brought before us in the last book of the Bible in a series of vivid pictures. The ascended Jesus has a sharp two-edged sword coming from his mouth, for the word of the gospel has that sharpness to divide truth from falsehood. He is the slain Lamb who alone can unseal the scroll of history and declare its meaning and

130

end. We are shown a series of catastrophes in each of which there is both destruction and restraint of destruction. We are shown the appearing of the power that wars against the Lamb, the antichrist, embodied (as all spiritual powers are embodied) and taking the form of Roman imperialism with its apparatus of propaganda. We are shown in the figure of the rider on the white horse the preaching of the gospel through all the world. We are given a vision of the thousand-year reign of the saints to encourage us that it is proper to work for goals within history. But finally we are shown the end of history, the creation of a new heaven and a new earth and the coming down of the Holy City as a gift of God's grace and as the consummation of history. It is the slain Lamb who opens the seals and unleashes the woes on the earth. His weapon is the word of testimony. He is followed by the company of those who have shed their blood for the testimony of Jesus. It is he who leads history to its true end, through the faithfulness of those who follow him in his testimony. The mission of the Church is not merely an interpretation of history; it is—in Berkhof's phrase—a history-making force. It is that through which God brings history to its goal, and only because this is so does it provide the place where the goal of history can be understood. It is not only declaratory; it is performatory. It can be the first because it is the second.

There has been a long tradition which has isolated the declaratory element in the Church's mission and insisted that it must have priority. Evangelism, the direct preaching of the gospel, it is often said, must be the first priority. Everything else is secondary or—at best—auxiliary. The missionary movement at the present time suffers from the running battle between those who make this emphasis on the primacy of evangelism, of the declaratory function of the Church, and those who insist that the first priority must be given to action for challenging injustice, prejudice, and oppression, action for justice and peace. For how, it may be asked, is a Christian message to be credible if its meaning is not being illustrated in patterns of action which correspond to it? And yet the New Testament has many passages which speak of the power of the word. It is the seed that, small and vulnerable as it is, can bring forth immense fruit. It is the sword by which the ascended Lord destroys his enemies. It is the power of God for salvation. Is there not good biblical ground for affirming the priority of preaching over any other kind of action in the mission of the Church?

If we turn to the Gospels we are bound to note the indissoluble nexus between deeds and words. A very large part of the first three

131

Gospels is occupied with the acts of Jesus—acts of healing, of exorcism, of feeding the hungry. And while in the Fourth Gospel there is a larger proportion of teaching, yet most of this teaching is explanatory of something Jesus has done: the healing of a paralytic, the feeding of a multitude, the giving of sight to a blind man, and the raising of a man from death. These four mighty works of Jesus form the context of the long passages of teaching from chapter 5 through chapter 11, and the discourse with Nicodemus is explicitly stated to have arisen from Jesus' mighty works. The intimate link between acts and words is made very clear in the mission charge to the twelve as it is given in the tenth chapter of Matthew. At the outset this is simply a mandate to heal and exorcise. "He called to him his twelve disciples and gave them authority over unclean spirits, to cast them out, and to heal every disease and every infirmity." Then follow the names of the Twelve. Nothing is said here about preaching. Only in verse 7 do we read: "Preach as you go, saying 'The kingdom of heaven is at hand.'" Clearly, therefore, the preaching is an explanation of the healings. On the one hand, the healings—marvelous as they are—do not explain themselves. They could be misinterpreted—as in fact they were by Jesus' enemies, who attributed his healing works to Satanic power. The works by themselves did not communicate the new fact. That had to be stated in plain words: "The kingdom of God has drawn near." That means that there is a call for radical decision, for repentance and faith. The healings by themselves, uninterpreted, do not make such a demand. They could be fitted into the existing order. After all, there were other healers and exorcists in Galilee and Judea. Healings, even the most wonderful, do not call this present world radically into question; the gospel does, and this has to be made explicit.

On the other hand, the preaching is meaningless without the healings. They are the true explanation of what is happening, but if nothing is happening no explanation is called for and the words are empty words. They do not answer any real question. They can be brushed aside as mere talk. They are only meaningful in the context of the mighty works. They presuppose that something is happening which calls for explanation. Here I may refer again to the point to which I drew attention earlier, namely that almost all the great Christian preachings in Acts are made in response to a question. Something has happened which makes people aware of a new reality, and therefore the question arises: What is this reality? The communication of the gospel is the answering of that question. The world has a thousand other questions which it is eager to ask. The Church does not necessarily have an answer to any of them. In any case, the answering of the world's questions is not the Church's business. But the answering of *this* question is the Church's first business. And the question is only asked if there is some evidence that the new reality is present. What is this new reality?

In the Gospels the new reality is the presence of Jesus himself. He is here. In him the kingdom of God has come near so that it now confronts men and women with its reality and requires them either to be so radically turned around that they recognize the truth and believe, or else to continue on their way facing in the wrong direction and pursuing that which is not God's kingdom. The presence of that new reality is attested by the mighty works of Jesus, which in turn call for the explanation which is the preaching of the gospel of the kingdom. But does that presence come to an end with the ending of the story of the incarnation? There are those who in effect say, "Yes." Jesus, they say, did not intend to found a church. He preached the kingdom of God and called men and women to seek it. Those who came after (and of course St. Paul is the primary villain) substituted the Church for the kingdom and thus subverted the intention of Jesus. If we are to be true to the intention of Jesus today we must put in the center of our vision not the Church but the kingdom. Now one can see the grain of truth which has produced this belief. The Church is not an end in itself. The growth and prosperity of the Church is not the goal of history. The Church is not the kingdom of God. This is the truth, but it does not warrant the conclusion drawn from it. Jesus manifestly did not intend to leave behind him simply a body of teaching. If that had been his intention he would surely have written a book and we should have something like the Qur'an instead of the book we have. What he did was to prepare a community chosen to be the bearer of the secret of the kingdom. This community is his legacy. The Fourth Gospel makes this very clear, both in its interpretation of the prayer of Jesus on the night of his passion and in its interpretation of his commission to the apostles after his resurrection. In the great consecration prayer Jesus, facing his death on the cross, says, "As thou didst send me into the world, so I have sent them into the world. And for their sake I consecrate myself, that they also may be consecrated in truth" (John 17:18-19). After the resurrection Jesus is represented as saying to the disciples, "As the Father sent me, so I send you"; and the word was accompanied by the gesture which showed what the manner of the sending was to be: "He showed them his hands and his side" (John 20:19-20). The intention of Jesus was not to leave behind a disembodied teaching. It was that through his total consecration to the Father in his passion there should be created a community which would continue that which he came from the Father to be and to do—namely to embody and to announce the presence of the reign of God. And the authenticating marks of that body, when it is true to its nature and calling, will be that it shares the passion of Jesus. The Church is not authorized to represent the reign of God, his justice and his peace, in any other way than that in which Jesus represented it, namely by being partners with him in challenging the powers of evil and bearing in its own life the cost of the challenge. When Church and kingdom are set against each other, then the language of the kingdom can be used, and is constantly used, to sacralize whatever is the contemporary program for justice and peace. The message of the kingdom then becomes again a form of the law. It is a corpus of ethical demands. It has the effect which law divorced from gospel always has, of hardening the conscience and mightily increasing the power of evil. The new thing which has dawned with the coming of Jesus is twofold: first, that the kingdom of God is no longer a formal concept into which we are free to pour our own content in accordance with the spirit of the age. The kingdom of God now has a name and a face: the name and the face of Jesus. When we pray, "Your kingdom come," we are praying, or we ought to be praying, as the early Church did, "Maranatha: Come, Lord Jesus." The fact that liberal Protestantism separated these two, was willing to talk about the coming of the kingdom but not about the coming of Jesus, is a sign of betrayal. Second, the new thing is that we have already been given a foretaste of the kingdom in the gift of the Spirit to the believing and committed community. It is the presence of this foretaste, this *arrabōn,* this gift already of a true measure of the justice and peace of the kingdom, that makes the Church a witness to the gospel and that makes its preaching gospel and not law. It is the presence of this new reality which (when the Church is faithful) prompts the questions to which the preaching of the gospel is the answer. The true missionary dialogue, in other words, is not initiated by the Church. In a secondary sense it is initiated by the outsider who is drawn to ask: What is the secret of this new reality, this life of praise, of justice, and of peace? In the primary sense, however, it is initiated by the presence of the Spirit who is the *arrabōn* of the kingdom, and whose presence leads people (perhaps without the prior knowledge of any missionary or evangelist) to make this inquiry.

It seems to me to be of great importance to insist that mission is not first of all an action of ours. It is an action of God, the triune God—of God the Father who is ceaselessly at work in all creation and in the hearts and minds of all human beings whether they acknowledge him or not, graciously guiding history toward its true end; of God the Son who has become part of this created history in the incarnation; and of God the Holy Spirit who is given as a foretaste of the end to empower and teach the Church and to convict the world of sin and righteousness and judgment. Before we speak about our role, the role of our words and deeds in mission, we need to have firmly in the center of our thinking this action of God. This is the primal reality in mission; the rest is derivative. I am aware that this doctrine of the *missio Dei* has sometimes been used to support concepts of mission which bypass the Church and even bypass the name of Jesus. That is a radical misuse of the concept, of which I shall say something in a moment. But here let me say that if we place in the center of our thinking the reality of God's mission, we shall be saved from two wrong concepts of mission which are at present deeply dividing the Christian community.

On the one hand, there are those who place exclusive emphasis on the winning of individuals to conversion, baptism, and church membership. The numerical growth of the Church becomes the central goal of mission. Action for justice and peace in the world is a secondary matter. It is not the heart of mission. The gospel, it is said, is about changing people, not about changing structures. (I shall try in a later chapter to show how this neglects the very important biblical teaching about the principalities and powers, but I leave that aside for the moment.) The emphasis here is exclusively on the salvation of the individual soul and the growth of the Church. The primary task is evangelism, the direct preaching of the gospel in words—spoken or written. Action for social justice and peace may be a way of drawing people to hear the gospel, but it is not an intrinsic part of the gospel itself. The preaching of the gospel of salvation from sin and of the offer of eternal life is the primary business of the Church.

On the other hand, there are those who condemn this as irrelevant or wrong. The gospel, they will say, is about God's kingdom, God's reign over all nations and all things. At the heart of Jesus' teaching is the prayer: "Your kingdom come; your will be done, as in heaven so on earth." The central responsibility of the Church is indicated by that prayer. It is to seek the doing of God's will of righteousness and peace in this world. A Christian community which makes its own self-enlargement its primary task may be acting against God's will. In societies such as India where good men and women seek to overcome interreligious strife and to build up the common life, the Church's program of aggressive evangelism is threatening. What is needed—it will be said—is not evangelistic preaching but action by Christians along with all people of goodwill to tackle the terrible problems of the nation, to free the oppressed, heal the sick, and bring hope to the hopeless.

If I am not mistaken, the conflict between these two ways of understanding mission is profoundly weakening the Church's witness. The conflict continues because both parties have hold of important truth. And I am suggesting that both parties are inadequately aware of the central reality, namely that mission is not primarily our work—whether of preaching or of social action—but primarily the mighty work of God. What is true in the affirmation of the evangelical side of this debate is that it does matter supremely that every human being should have the opportunity to know Jesus as Lord and Savior, that without a living Church where this witness is borne neither evangelism nor Christian social action is possible, and that the gospel can never be identified with any particular project for justice and peace however laudable and promising. What is true in the position of the social activists is that a Church which exists only for itself and its own enlargement is a witness against the gospel, that the Church exists not for itself and not for its members but as a sign and agent and foretaste of the kingdom of God, and that it is impossible to give faithful witness to the gospel while being indifferent to the situation of the hungry, the sick, the victims of human inhumanity.

I am suggesting that both parties to this dispute need to recover a fuller sense of the prior reality, the givenness, the ontological priority of the new reality which the work of Christ has brought into being. Because Jesus has met and mastered the powers that enslave the world, because he now sits at God's right hand, and because there has been given to those who believe the gift of a real foretaste, pledge, *arrabōn* of the kingdom, namely the mighty Spirit of God, the third person of the Trinity, therefore this new reality, this new presence creates a moment of crisis wherever it appears. It provokes questions which call for an answer and which, if the true answer is not accepted, lead to false answers. This happens where there is a community whose members are deeply rooted in Christ as their absolute Lord and Savior. Where there is such a community, there will be a challenge by word and behavior to the ruling powers. As a result there will be conflict and suffering for the Church. Out of that conflict and suffering will arise the questioning which the world puts to the Church. This is why St. Paul in his letters does not find it necessary to urge his readers to be active in evangelism but does find it necessary to warn them against any compromise with the rulers of this age. That is why it was not superiority of the Church's preaching which finally disarmed the Roman imperial power, but the faithfulness of its martyrs. That is why the risen Jesus, according to the Fourth Gospel, when he sent out his disciples to continue his work, showed them his hands and his side. That is why, according to Luke's account, he told them that it would be the coming of the Holy Spirit that would make them witnesses, because the Spirit *is* the presence in foretaste of the kingdom. When the mission of the Church is seen in this way, several things become clear.

1. First, it is clear that to set word and deed, preaching and action, against each other is absurd. The central reality is neither word nor act, but the total life of a community enabled by the Spirit to live in Christ, sharing his passion and the power of his resurrection. Both the words and the acts of that community may at any time provide the occasion through which the living Christ challenges the ruling powers. Sometimes it is a word that pierces through layers of custom and opens up a new vision. Sometimes it is a deed which shakes a whole traditional plausibility structure. They mutually reinforce and interpret one another. The words explain the deeds, and the deeds validate the words. Not that every deed must have a word attached to explain it, but that the total life of the community whose members have different gifts and are involved in the secular life of the society in which they share, will provide these occasions of challenge. But no one will know exactly when and where and how this happens. It is always a work of the Holy Spirit. It is always mysterious. The ways by which the truth of the gospel comes home to the heart and conscience of this or that person are always mysterious. They cannot be programs and they cannot be calculated. But where a community is living in alert faithfulness, they happen.

2. Second, it is clear that action for justice and peace in the world is not something which is secondary, marginal to the central task of evangelism. It belongs to the heart of the matter. Jesus' action in challenging the powers that ruled the world was not marginal to his ministry; it was central to it. Without it there would be no gospel. But Jesus' challenge was not in the name of an alternative way of exercising power. He did not offer an alternative government. He did not repeat the story of which history has so many illustrations, the story of the victim of op-

pression who, in the name of justice, dethrones the oppressor and takes his seat on the same throne with the same instruments of oppression. The manner of Jesus' challenge, the way that led through his own death to resurrection and the sharing of a new life with the community he formed to go the same way through history to its end, opened up a new route through history along which every human rule would stand under both the judgment and the mercy of God.

3. And so, third, it is made clear that action for justice and peace can never mean total commitment to a particular project identified unambiguously as God's will. The concept of *missio Dei* has sometimes been interpreted so as to suggest that action for justice and peace as the possibilities are discerned within a given historical situation *is* the fulfillment of God's mission, and that the questions of baptism and church membership are marginal or irrelevant. That way leads very quickly to disillusion and often to cynical despair. No human project however splendid is free from the corrupting power of sin. To invest one's ultimate commitment in such proximate goals is to end in despair. The history of the Church furnishes plenty of illustrations of the point I am making. At various times and places loyalty to the Church has been identified as invoking the defense of feudalism against capitalism, the defense of aristocracy against democracy, the defense of the free market against Marxism, and the support of movements of liberation based on a Marxist analysis of the human situation. Adrian Hastings in his history of English Christianity in the present century has reminded us that for the first two decades of this period the Christianity of the English Free Churches was interpreted as almost necessarily involving support for the Liberal Party. When the Liberal Party destroyed itself, the Free Churches suffered a blow, a loss of identity, from which they have hardly begun to recover (*A History of English Christianity: 1920-1985,* 1986). It does not require much knowledge of history to recognize that, with all its grievous sins of compromise, cowardice, and apostasy, the Church outlasts all these movements in which so much passionate faith has been invested. In their time each of these movements seems to provide a sense of direction, a credible goal for the human project. The slogans of these movements become sacred words which glow with ultimate authority. But they do not endure. None of them in fact embodies the true end, the real goal of history. That has been embodied once for all in the events which form the substance of the gospel and which—remembered, rehearsed, and reenacted in teaching and liturgy—form the inner core of the Church's being. To commend this gospel to all people

in all circumstances, to witness to it as the ultimate clue to the whole human story and therefore to every human story, can never be unnecessary and never irrelevant, however much it may be misunderstood, ignored, or condemned.

4. But, fourth, it is immediately necessary to say that this fundamental truth can become a source of disastrous error if it is used to withdraw those who believe the gospel from responsible engagements in the immediacies, the relativities of the political and cultural life of their times. The vision of the ultimate goal of the human story must not be used to withdraw attention from the immediate possibilities which the Lord of history offers. As those who understand the whole human story in the light of the biblical story, we have the responsibility to discern by faith the duties of this particular moment. We have no guarantee of infallibility in our judgments. If history teaches anything it is that the most faithful believers may judge wrongly. But at the heart of faith is the assurance that God is able to forgive our errors and even to turn our wrong choices to good ends. The fact that we may be mistaken must not be supposed to excuse us from action, for inaction is itself a fateful choice. As Reinhold Niebuhr has taught us, we have an absolute duty to choose the relatively better among possibilities none of which is the absolutely good. We shall differ from one another but only while carefully listening to one another, respecting one another's choices, and remaining one body because we know that what we do in the liturgy and life of the Church has an ontological priority and an enduring reality far beyond these choices that we make.

5. Fifth, it follows that the major role of the Church in relation to the great issues of justice and peace will not be in its formal pronouncements but in its continually nourishing and sustaining men and women who will act responsibly as believers in the course of their secular duties as citizens. There will indeed be occasions when the Church acting corporately through its appointed leaders will have to remind those who hold power that they are responsible for all their actions to the one who sits at the right hand of God, and to warn them when they pursue policies manifestly contrary to his revealed nature and will. But these pronouncements will lack authority if they are not reflected in the activities of believers from day to day in their secular involvement.

6. Finally, there will always be the need to point explicitly to the central reality by which the Church exists, to the central verities of the gospel, to Christ incarnate, crucified, risen, regnant at God's right hand and to the promise of his coming to judge the living and the dead. This

preaching of the gospel can never be irrelevant. But if the Church which preaches it is not living corporately a life which corresponds with it, is living in comfortable cohabitation with the powers of this age, is failing to challenge the powers of darkness and to manifest in its life the power of the living Lord to help and to heal, then by its life it closes the doors which its preaching would open. That does not mean that the preaching is void, because there is no limit to the power of the word of God. But it means that the Church comes under severe judgment from him who will ask of us not about our confession but about our commitment to doing his will.

12. *Contextualization: True and False*

The gospel is addressed to human beings, to their minds and hearts and consciences, and calls for their response. Human beings only exist as members of communities which share a common language, customs, ways of ordering economic and social life, ways of understanding and coping with their world. If the gospel is to be understood, if it is to be received as something which communicates truth about the real human situation, if it is, as we say, to "make sense," it has to be communicated in the language of those to whom it is addressed and has to be clothed in symbols which are meaningful to them. And since the gospel does not come as a disembodied message, but as the message of a community which claims to live by it and which invites others to adhere to it, the community's life must be so ordered that it "makes sense" to those who are so invited. It must, as we say, "come alive." Those to whom it is addressed must be able to say, "Yes, I see. This is true for me, for my situation." But if the gospel is truly to be communicated, the subject in that sentence is as important as the predicate. What comes home to the heart of the hearer must really be the gospel, and not a product shaped by the mind of the hearer. It has often been said that during the period of liberal Protestantism, when innumerable "lives of Jesus" were written, designed to help educated middle-class Europeans and Americans to respond to the gospel, the portraits that resulted were very obviously self-portraits. They told you more about the writer than about Jesus. But that criticism has much wider application. If one looks at the long history of Christian art one can see in successive portraits of Jesus the self-portrait of the age—the Byzantine picture of Jesus as the supreme Emperor, the Pantocrator; the medieval picture of the pain-drenched figure on the cross, the blond, fair-haired boy of the Anglo-Saxon Protestant ideal, and the Liberator Christ modeled on Che Guevara. In each case the figure of Jesus has been so painted as to fit the reigning cultural ideal, but what does this gallery of portraits have to do with the real Jesus? How can the gospel "come alive" in all these different cultural contexts, and still be the same authentic gospel? That is the problem of contextualization.

The debate about contextualization has been carried on mainly among those engaged in cross-cultural missions, what used to be called foreign missions. The reasons for this are obvious; when we seek to translate the Christian message into the language and culture of a people which has lived outside the range of Christian influence, the problem has to be faced. As we shall see later, it is in fact a problem involved in every communication of the gospel, whether in one's own neighborhood or at the ends of the earth, but it will be helpful to begin by looking at the problem as it has presented itself to those engaged in cross-cultural mission. The actual word "contextualization" is of recent coinage. Older discussions used such terms as indigenization, adaptation, and accommodation. The reasons for dissatisfaction with these words are twofold. In the first place they have tended to relate the gospel to past traditions and to underestimate the forces in every society which are making for change. In the second place they have sometimes seemed to imply that what the missionary brought with him was the pure, unadapted gospel, and that "adaptation" was thus a kind of concession to those who had not the advantage of having a Christian culture. But of course the truth is that every communication of the gospel is already culturally conditioned. The word "contextualization" seeks to avoid both these dangers and to direct attention to the need so to communicate the gospel that it speaks God's word to the total context in which people are now living and in which they now have to make their decisions.

Some of the most famous debates about true and false contextualization have raged around the daring efforts of the Jesuit missionaries to India and China in the seventeenth century, especially Mattheo Ricci at the imperial court of China and Roberto de Nobili in South India. Earlier Portuguese missionaries in India had required of their converts a total break with traditional Hindu customs, including caste, with the result that Christian converts were automatically excluded from Indian social and cultural life and were reckoned among the untouchables. De Nobili, by contrast, lived the life of a high-caste Indian in respect of food, clothing, and such customs as the wearing of the sacred thread. He encouraged his converts to remain within their caste affiliations, treating caste as a purely social institution which, from the point of view of the gospel, did not raise any fundamental issue of faith. While the converts gathered by the Portuguese missionaries remained outside the Hindu world, following Western customs and dependent on Western missionaries, the converts of the Jesuit mission became a rapidly growing group within the world of Hindu culture. The Jesuits were furiously attacked by the other missionary orders, and the battle, which lasted for more than a century, led to repudiation of De Nobili's methods by Rome. But, more importantly, later Indian Christian sentiment has also rejected his acceptance of caste. For him caste was a matter of social organization and did not raise a question of faith. For later generations this was unacceptable. Caste was seen as something fundamentally incompatible with the gospel. A daring effort at contextualization has, in this later view, betrayed the gospel. Yet customs which the Franciscan missionaries had condemned as heathen have been accepted by later generations of Indian Christians as harmless.

The discussion of these questions at the present time is made difficult because of the emotional hangovers from the colonial period, both among the former colonial powers and among their former colonies. The churches of the Third World belong to societies which are struggling to achieve authentic nationhood after a period in which their cultures were overshadowed by the Western invasion. Churches in these countries, or at least some of their Western-educated leaders, are eager to shed the remaining cultural trappings inherited from the Western missionaries, and to prove their truly national character. Churches in the old colonial powers, ridden by feelings of guilt, are eager to apologize for the fact that their presentation of the gospel was so much colored by their culture, that they presented a European or American gospel instead of the pure, unadulterated article, and—for the same reason—are eager to welcome and applaud any expression of Christianity which is authentically Asian or African. Sometimes it seems that it is acceptable, however bizarre, as long as it is clearly not European. Thus we applaud in the younger churches a synthesis of nationalism and Christianity which we deplore in our missionary grandparents. And the irony is still more complex. In many cases the thing which made Christianity attractive to the younger generation of Asians and Africans was precisely that it brought with it access to the skills, the learning, and the technology of the West. Thus contemporary Indian and Chinese writers are often found praising the work of missions just because they opened the way

143

for what is called "modernization"—that is to say, the acceptance of the science and technology of the West. This is a reminder of the fact that cultures are never monochrome and static; they are always complex and changing. Within any community there will be cultural conservatives and cultural radicals. The former will resist the invasion of foreign ideas, while the latter will welcome them just because they are different from the tradition. Thus the Western missionary, often a traditionalist in her own culture, becomes the ally of the radicals in the country to which she goes, while the conservatives in that culture will find a welcome among the radicals in the Western world just because the culture— Asian or African—which they are clinging to is different from that of Europe. The great movement of foreign missions in the 150 years from 1800, and the ecumenical movement which developed out of this, opened the eyes of European Christians to the extent to which Christianity had become domesticated within Western culture. The rise of various forms of Third World theologies has challenged this domestication. And since it is the Europeans who are now the accused, it is difficult for a European Christian to draw attention to the danger that Asian and African Christianity might suffer from the same kind of domestication. The question therefore must be addressed as objectively as possible, with as much freedom as possible from the emotional effects of guilt on the one side and resentment on the other. How far should the gospel be "at home" in a culture, and how far should it resist domestication. What is true contextualization?

We must start with the basic fact that there is no such thing as a pure gospel if by that is meant something which is not embodied in a culture. The simplest verbal statement of the gospel, "Jesus is Lord," depends for its meaning on the content which that culture gives to the word "Lord." What kind of thing is "lordship" in the culture in question? The gospel always comes as the testimony of a community which, if it is faithful, is trying to live out the meaning of the gospel in a certain style of life, certain ways of holding property, of maintaining law and order, of carrying on production and consumption, and so on. Every interpretation of the gospel is embodied in some cultural form. The missionary does not come with the pure gospel and then adapt it to the culture where she serves: she comes with a gospel which is already embodied in the culture by which the missionary was formed. And this is so from the very beginning. The Bible is a book which is very obviously in a specific cultural setting. Its language is Hebrew and Greek, not Chinese or Sanskrit. All the events it records, all the teachings it embodies, are shaped by specific human cultures. And, of course, it could not possibly be otherwise. Something which is not expressible in any human language, which is not embodied in any human way of living, which is not located in any specific time or place, can have no impact on human affairs. Here we are back again with the doctrine of election. I have tried already to suggest what I have called the logic of election. God's universal purpose of blessing has to be wrought out through specific acts at specific times and places and involving particular people. It is wrought out in history, and history is a matter of these specific and particular places, times, and people.

Would this mean, then, that Hebrew culture has to become the world's culture? Is this, in fact, just one more version of the familiar imperial story, the conviction of one human culture that it is the way for all? That is, indeed, what is explicit in the universal claim of Islam. God's will as it is communicated in the untranslatable Arabic of the Qur'an is that to which every human society must conform. There can be no adaptation. There can be no translation of the Qur'an, for translation is always adaptation. If it were true, as the Qur'an affirms, that Jesus was not crucified, then indeed he would simply be one of the messengers in the series that culminates in Muhammad. But the earthly mission of Jesus ended on a cross. The corn of wheat had to fall onto the ground and die. The new reality born of that dying, the new creation of which the risen body of Jesus is the foretaste, is of a different nature. It is not simply a prolongation of the life of Jesus. It is the beginning of a new epoch in human history in which the guiding clue is held in trust for all by that community which lives by the life of the crucified and risen Jesus.

Would this mean, then, that this new community would be simply an extension of Israel, of that particular cultural community which can be spoken of as "Israel after the flesh"? So it seemed at first. It seemed obvious that all who were "in Christ" would be bound to keep the whole law, including that foundation pillar of the law which Jesus himself had never questioned, namely circumcision. The words of Scripture seemed unequivocal: "Any uncircumcised male who is not circumcised in the flesh of his foreskin shall be cut off from his people; he has broken my covenant" (Gen. 17:14). But it was made clear to the first Christians—not by their own unaided reason but by the fact that the Holy Spirit was freely given to uncircumcised believers—that this was not so. What, then, are the essentials in the way the community lives which cannot be changed? Is all the long schooling of Israel in the Torah,

145

the loving instruction of God, now to be thrown overboard? Do we say, "In Christ, anything goes"? If "culture" is rightly defined as the whole way in which a community lives together, then surely Christ must have something to do with culture. But exactly what? The decrees sent to the Gentile churches by the elders in Jerusalem laid on them the obligation to keep certain of the Jewish dietary laws which later Christian centuries have judged unnecessary. If even such fundamental things as circumcision, the sabbath, and the laws about food are thrown overboard, what remains? If one of the ten commandments can be scrapped, what justification is there for insisting on the others? What is required, in any culture wherever it may be, by Christian obedience?

Many have answered, and still answer, that question by invoking some highly general concept. *Jesus Means Freedom* is the title of a widely read book. Jesus is the liberator, and whatever liberates men and women is authentic following of Jesus. Or, perhaps, "Jesus means justice," and whatever serves to overturn injustice is authentic discipleship. Or, perhaps more common, "Jesus means love." Following Jesus means living a life of universal and unconditional love. The effect of these moves, of course, is that the gospel is replaced by a moral law or a political program, or—more often—a combination of the two in which a particular program is invested with a degree of moral passion which raises it above the level of merely pragmatic argument. The other effect is that the Church is bypassed, since it is obvious that many people who are committed to the practice of freedom, justice, and love have nothing to do with the Church.

But if the gospel is not to be identified on the one hand with a particular pattern of behavior bound to one of the many cultures of humankind, nor on the other hand with abstract moral or political principles, how exactly is it embodied? To put the question as it arises in cross-cultural mission, what are the conditions for saying that the gospel has been truly communicated? When can the missionary say, "Mission accomplished"? Here let me call as witness one of the most penetrating and provocative of recent writers on missiology, the China missionary Roland Allen. Allen, who served in China in the early years of this century, carried on a sustained polemic against the missionary methods of his time and contrasted them with those of St. Paul. St. Paul, he argued, never stayed in one place for more than a few months, or at most a couple of years. He did not establish what we call a "mission station," and he certainly did not build himself a mission bungalow. On the contrary, as soon as there was an established congregation of Christian believers, he chose from among them elders, laid his hands on them, entrusted to them the care of the church, and left. By contrast the nineteenth-century missionary considered it necessary to stay not merely for a lifetime, but for the lifetime of several generations of missionaries. Why? Because he did not think his work was done until the local church had developed a leadership which had mastered and internalized the culture of Europe, its theological doctrines, its administrative machinery, its architecture, its music, until there was a complete replica of the "home church" equipped with everything from archdeacons to harmoniums. The young church was to be a carbon copy of the old church in England, Scotland, or Germany. In rejecting this, and in answering the question, What must have been done if the gospel is to be truly communicated? Allen answered: there must be a congregation furnished with the Bible, the sacraments, and the apostolic ministry. When these conditions are fulfilled, the missionary has done her job. The young church is then free to learn, as it goes and grows, how to embody the gospel in its own culture.

I believe that Allen was right, and that his argument has a wider relevance. If one takes the argument out of the particular context in which he was writing, that of cross-cultural mission, and asks, How is the life of Christ, the life which is a true foretaste of the kingdom, continued in the period between the ascension and the parousia? the answer must be somewhat as follows. It will not be by the universal application of an unchanging pattern of personal and social behavior as laid down in the faith and practice of Islam. It will not be in a series of abstract moral and political principles. It will be in the life of a community which remembers, rehearses, and lives by the story which the Bible tells and of which the central focus is the story told in the New Testament. This remembering and rehearsing will be through the continual reading of and reflection on the Bible and the continual repetition of the sacraments of baptism and the eucharist. And it will maintain its link with, its continuity with the body of men to whom Jesus said, "As the Father sent me, so I send you," through a ministry in which the personal call of Jesus, "Follow me," is continued through the generations, not in abstract moral or political principles but in the actual personal encounters in which men and women who have themselves been called, call others to follow. It is this actual body, this community which as a matter of historical fact has existed through the centuries from the first apostles, which is the prior reality, having ontological primacy over the particular styles of life and ethical codes and political principles which

147

it may develop as it seeks to be faithful in its situation. Once again we have to insist that since the response to the gospel has to be made in freedom, and since all human beings are fallible, there will not be unanimity in the ways in which the Church in any time and place seeks to "contextualize" the gospel, seeks, that is to say, so to proclaim and to embody the life of Jesus that his power both to sustain and to judge every human culture is manifest. The New Testament itself makes it clear that there have been from the very beginning sharp differences among Christians about how to relate to the surrounding culture. The passages in the epistles to the Romans and to the Corinthians referring to controversies about food offered to idols are ample evidence of this. One must expect that this will be so to the end. If Christian obedience were to be exhaustively defined in terms of following one or other "line" in respect of all these controversies, the Church would have splintered into fragments long before the end of the first century. That it did not do so is, I am sure, the central clue to answering our question about true and false contextualization. Where there is a believing community whose life is centered in the biblical story through its worshipping, teaching, and sacramental and apostolic life, there will certainly be differences of opinion on specific issues, certainly mistakes, certainly false starts. But it is part of my faith in the authenticity of the story itself that this community will not be finally betrayed. The gates of hell shall not prevail against it. But where something else is put at the center, a moral code, a set of principles, or the alleged need to meet some criterion imposed from outside the story, one is adrift in the ever changing tides of history, and the community which commits itself to these things becomes one more piece of driftwood on the current.

I have been speaking about the question of contextualization as it has arisen in the practice of cross-cultural mission. But at the present time the question is very widely raised in situations where the crossing of cultural boundaries is not involved. There is at the present time a growing number of particular styles of theological development under the broad rubric of theologies of liberation. There is the Latin American liberation theology, which may be regarded as the mother of them all, arising from the experience of extreme oppression in that continent. There is black theology in various forms arising out of the black experience. There is feminist theology which has as its context the experience of male domination. Most recently there is the Indian Dalit Theology which already boasts a professional chair in Madras, and which arises from the experience of the communities to which Gandhi gave the name "Harijan" (people of God) but for which an older name is now felt to be more appropriate—the crushed people. All these theologies take as their starting point the experience of domination and oppression. They interpret the Bible story as the story of liberation from oppression. They see Jesus as one who identified himself with the oppressed. For them, therefore, true contextualization is the identification of the Church with the oppressed and with their struggle to find liberation. The heart of Christian discipleship is this "struggle." The struggle is of course something which goes on far beyond the boundaries of the Church, and which in many cases bypasses the Church altogether because the Church is frequently on the side of the oppressors and not of the victims. It follows that the first step in a true theology is the "option for the poor." Sound theology, we are frequently told, must begin with the aspirations of the people. Both theology and ecclesiology must be done "from below." The idea that we can do it "from above" is the illusion of traditional theology. All theology, and all biblical interpretation, is done from a specific historical situation. It is not done in heaven, in a sphere above the battle. It is done on earth by people who are part of the battle, on one side or the other. Most theology has been done from within the establishment. It is done by the oppressors. We require, as is often said, a hermeneutic of suspicion. We do not take statements at their face value, even the statements of Scripture. We ask, Who wrote this? What were his interests? What position was he defending? There is no position above the conflict between the oppressors and the oppressed; there is only a position on one side or the other. Biblical interpretation, and the theology developed from it, is either part of the oppression, or it is part of the struggle of the oppressed—whether the oppressed be dwellers in the Brazilian slums, Dalits in Madras, blacks in Harlem, or women everywhere.

Can this be accepted? Clearly the questions asked by the practitioners of the "hermeneutic of suspicion" are legitimate questions. Everyone is influenced by self-interest of one kind or another. The practitioners of the hermeneutic of suspicion are not exempt from its procedures. Their hermeneutic is also interest-governed. Must we, then, abandon all hope of reaching beyond our various interests to the truth? The answer, if I understand these writers correctly, is that we need not despair, because the way the oppressed see things is the way they really are. To understand how things really are, one must stand with the oppressed. The oppressed have an epistemological privilege. Their vision is not distorted by the bias which must always incline those who benefit from the status quo to defend that status. One must therefore go on to press the question: "On what grounds do we know that the oppressed have this epistemological privilege?" In the case of some writers it is fairly clear that the belief in question is part of the Marxist interpretation of history, derived in turn from the Hegelian dialectic, in accordance with which, at the present stage of history, the proletariat are the bearers of truth and of right. They are the messianic people. In the case of other writers the option for the poor rests on the belief that God as he is revealed in Scripture and in the ministry of Jesus is on the side of the poor. These two different positions call for two distinct comments.

In the first case belief in the epistemological privilege of the oppressed is prior to and independent of belief in the authority of Scripture. In many writings of liberation theology it is made clear that the analysis of the human situation in terms of the model of oppression is prior to the appeal to Scripture. It is accepted as axiomatic that the clue to understanding the human situation is found in this model: everywhere there are oppressors and there are oppressed. Justice requires that we stand by the oppressed. Therefore the testimony of Scripture is to be evaluated on this basis. What serves the cause of the oppressed is the real kernel of Scripture. Scripture functions only within this more fundamental scheme. In this case one has to ask about the grounds for this belief. A student of human affairs would normally conclude that while oppression and injustice are undoubtedly an important part of the human scene, most people are in an ambivalent position, oppressors in some situations and oppressed in others; that it is not obvious from a survey of world history that God favors the oppressed; and that many other elements in human experience could be candidates for the position of controlling model. Indeed, if the appeal is not to revelation as found in Scripture, but to the knowledge of human affairs which is available to observation and reason, a good case could be made for asserting that the poor are simply those who have failed in the struggle for existence and—in the interests of the race—will be eliminated by those who demonstrate their fitness to survive.

In the second place, namely where the claim for the epistemological privilege of the poor is founded in Scripture, several comments suggest themselves. First, that while the Old Testament undoubtedly contains many passionate expressions of God's concern for justice for the oppressed, it also contains warnings about the chaos which arises when there is no strong government, about the role of a just ruler in God's merciful guiding of human affairs, and about the fact that the victims of today's injustice frequently become tomorrow's oppressors. If we turn to the ministry of Jesus himself, it is of course clear that Jesus shocked the established authorities by being a friend to all—not only to the destitute and hungry, but also to those rich extortioners, the tax-collectors, whom all decent people ostracized; that the shocking thing was not that he sided with the poor against the rich but that he met everyone equally with the same unlimited mercy and the same unconditioned demand for total loyalty. If we look at the end of his earthly ministry, at the cross, it is clear that Jesus was rejected by all—rich and poor, rulers and people—alike. Before the cross of Jesus there are no innocent parties. His cross is not *for* some and *against* others. It is the place where all are guilty and all are forgiven. The cross cannot be converted into the banner for a fight of some against others. And if we look to the beginning of his ministry, to those mysterious days in the desert when he was compelled to face the most searching temptation to take the wrong course, one could sum up the substance of the suggestions of the Evil One in the phrase I have already quoted: "Begin by attending to the aspirations of the people."

I return to the point where I left Roland Allen. I am saying that authentic Christian thought and action begin not by attending to the aspirations of the people, not by answering the questions they are asking in their terms, not by offering solutions to the problems as the world sees them. It must begin and continue by attending to what God has done in the story of Israel and supremely in the story of Jesus Christ. It must continue by indwelling that story so that it is our story, the way we understand the real story. And then, and this is the vital point, to attend with open hearts and minds to the real needs of people in the way that Jesus attended to them, knowing that the real need is that which can only be satisfied by everything that comes from the mouth of God (Matt. 4:4). As we share in the life and worship of the Church, through fellowship, word, and sacrament, we indwell the story and from within that story we seek to be the voice and the hands of Jesus for our time and place. Because we are also driven by our selfish desires and interests we will be aware that we require constant correction and that for this we must look to those who share the life in Christ but inhabit different cultural situations. We must always be ready to recognize that we have misrepresented the intention of Jesus because of our own interests. But that correction comes not from some supposed position of epistemological privilege outside the Christian story; it comes from the story itself when we expose ourselves honestly to the need of all people.

I am thus again stressing the priority of the gospel as the message, embodied in an actual story, of what God has in fact done, is doing, and will do. Christian theology is a form of rational discourse developed within the community which accepts the primacy of this story and seeks actively to live in the world in accordance with the story. It can fail by failing to understand and take seriously the world in which it is set, so that the gospel is not heard but remains incomprehensible because the Church has sought security in its own past instead of risking its life in a deep involvement with the world. It can fail, on the other hand, by allowing the world to dictate the issues and the terms of the meeting. The result then is that the world is not challenged at its depth but rather absorbs and domesticates the gospel and uses it to sacralize its own purposes. We have seen that happen in the history of the old churches of western Christendom. It is the experience of the younger churches of the East and South which has alerted us to this domestication of the gospel in our culture. We shall not be dealing appropriately with our guilt about this if it simply leads us to applaud the same kind of domestication in the cultures of the Third World. Professor Kosuke Koyama has described in unforgettable terms the disasters that follow from a religion which merely applauds and does not radically criticize national aspirations (*Mount Fuji and Mount Sinai*). True contextualization accords to the gospel its rightful primacy, its power to penetrate every culture and to speak within each culture, in its own speech and symbol, the word which is both No and Yes, both judgment and grace. And that happens when the word is not a disembodied word, but comes from a community which embodies the true story, God's story, in a style of life which communicates both the grace and the judgment. In order that it may do this, it must be both truly local and truly ecumenical. Truly local in that it embodies God's particular word of grace and judgment for that people. Truly ecumenical in being open to the witness of churches in all other places, and thus saved from absorption into the culture of that place and enabled to represent to that place the universality, the catholicity of God's purpose of grace and judgment for all humanity.

I began this chapter by saying that the question of contextualization is the question about how the gospel "comes alive" in particular contexts. The history of the Church, and missionary experiences, certainly show that this "coming alive" happens in a myriad of different and unpredictable ways. Nevertheless the gospel is not an empty form into which everyone is free to pour his or her own content. Scripture, it has been wittily said, is not a picnic where the authors bring the words and the readers bring the meaning. The content of the gospel is Jesus Christ in the fullness of his ministry, death, and resurrection. The gospel is this and not anything else. Jesus is who he is, and though our perceptions of him will be shaped by our own situation and the mental formation we have received from our culture, our need is to see him as he truly is. This is why we have to listen to the witness of the whole Church of all places and ages. His word of judgment and grace comes to each person in unique and often mysterious ways. The evangelist may believe that he has so well understood the human situation (for example, as one of oppression) that he knows how to present the gospel (for instance, as liberation). But there are two reasons for questioning this approach. The first is that, however valid may be my understanding of the situation of those to whom I commend the gospel, my knowledge is limited. The situation may look quite different to my hearer. It happens over and over again that the gospel "comes alive" in a way that the evangelist had never dreamed of, and has effects which he never anticipated. The gospel is addressed to the human person as a human person in all the uncountable varieties of predicaments in which human beings find themselves. The gospel has a sovereignty of its own and is never an instrument in the hands of the evangelist. Or, to put it more truly, the Holy Spirit, by whose secret working alone the gospel "comes alive," is not under the evangelist's control. The wind blows freely.

The second reason for questioning the issue-oriented approach to the preaching of the gospel is this. If one begins by defining the situation, for example, as one of oppression, and then offering the Christian message as the answer to the problem, the gospel becomes ancillary to a program. *We* have defined the issues, and *we* are responsible for the program. One is in danger of a new kind of moralism: being a Christian is identified with commitment to a particular "line." But when the gospel truly "comes alive," the one for whom this happens knows that sovereignty now lies elsewhere. A new Lord is in control. That sovereignty will issue in a whole range of actions and in a whole style of life, but these will have about them a spontaneity and a capacity to surprise—probably to surprise even the evangelist.

Of course it is always required of us that we listen sensitively to both the desires and the needs of people, and that we try to understand their situation. But neither these desires and needs, nor any analysis of the situation made on the basis of some principles drawn from other sources than Scripture, can be the starting point for mission. The starting point is God's revelation of himself as it is witnessed to us in Scripture. The dynamic of mission is the presence of God the Holy Spirit with power to convict the world and to bring home the truth of the gospel to each human heart. True contextualization happens when there is a community which lives faithfully by the gospel and in that same costly identification with people in their real situations as we see in the earthly ministry of Jesus. When these conditions are met, the sovereign Spirit of God does his own surprising work.

13. No Other Name

The line of thought which I have been developing in these chapters is one which a very considerable number of contemporary Christians reject altogether. It would be regarded as an expression of a type of exclusive claim for the gospel which was typical of the missionary movement of the past two hundred years. That movement, such critics would say, was obviously intimately related to the imperial expansion of the western European powers. The same triumphalist spirit permeated them both. The famous watchword "The Evangelization of the World in This Generation" was a typical example of this aggressive imperialism. It is inappropriate for today's world. For our grandparents, who were ignorant of the spiritual riches of the great world religions, the idea that these were all to be displaced by a triumphant Christianity was excusable. It is not excusable today. We now know, if we are not wilfully blind and deaf, that we live in a religiously plural world in which the other great world religions show at least as much spiritual vitality as does Christianity, a world moreover in which many Europeans and Americans, disillusioned by the manifest failures of the Christian West, are turning toward the East and the South for fresh ways of understanding and coping with our common human situations. The other world religions, stimulated by the attack of the West, are now themselves active in mission. To maintain, in this new situation, the old missionary attitude is not merely inexcusable but positively dangerous. In a world threatened with nuclear war, a world facing a global ecological crisis, a world more and more closely bound together in its cultural and economic life, the paramount need is for unity, and an aggressive claim on the part of one of the world's religions to have the truth for all can only be regarded as treason against the human race. Even if it is granted that this exclusive claim has been the claim of the Church through nineteen centuries, we must face the fact that it is not now tenable. Just as the Church in the first generation had to face the fact that God's grace was not confined to those who by circumcision were brought into the visible community of Israel but was freely available to uncircumcised gentiles, so now the Church must have the courage to recognize a new fact, recognize that God's grace is at work with undiscriminating generosity among all peoples and in all the great religious traditions, and therefore abandon the claim to be the sole possessor of the truth.

This view is now so widely shared that it has become in effect the contemporary orthodoxy. Pluralism is the reigning assumption, and if one declines to accept it, as I do, one must give reasons. In the following paragraphs I shall refer to three recent expositions of this view. *No Other Name?* by Paul Knitter; *The Myth of Christian Uniqueness*, edited by Paul Knitter and John Hick; and a series of essays and discussions occasioned by the celebration of the fiftieth anniversary of the World Missionary Conference at Tambaram in 1938, published in the volume of the *International Review of Mission* for July 1988.

The basic assumptions from which Paul Knitter and his colleagues write is, on the one hand, the urgent need for human unity, and on the other side the conviction that one particular religious tradition cannot provide the focus for that unity. "Modern Historical Consciousness" (Kaufman in *The Myth,* pp. 5ff.) must necessarily disallow Christian claims to uniqueness. The distinguished Indian theologian Stanley Samartha speaks of our present situation as different from anything else in human history, in that we face the total annihilation of all life either by environmental pollution or by nuclear disaster, and goes on: "Since this is a threat to all humanity, to claim that one religious tradition has the *only* answer to such a global problem seems preposterous" (*International Review of Mission,* July 1988, p. 315). For Samartha and others, the affirmation of the continuing validity of the other great religions is a necessary part of the struggle of their people to emerge from the spiritual and cultural humiliation of colonialism. Dr. Diana Eck, Professor at Harvard and Moderator of the World Council of Churches' program on Dialogue, speaks of the astonishment of a Hindu at the idea that God had had only one incarnation, and continues, "This exclusive understanding of revelation which speaks of it as an event of the past and imprisons it in the first century, is also folly to many Christians" (ibid., p. 384).

It would be tedious to continue with such quotations. For those who have never moved outside the circle of Christian faith and worship, the "folly" of which Dr. Eck complains may not be obvious. But for those who have shared in the multifaith, multiculture, multirace world of today it seems preposterous to maintain that in all the infinite pluralities and relativities of human affairs there should be one absolute against which everything else is to be measured. For the historian there are no absolutes. It is sometimes wrongly said, for instance by Paul Knitter, that science also, since Einstein, has abandoned absolutes and made everything relative. This is, of course, not true. After Einstein there are still absolutes, such as the speed of light and the value of Planck's constant. But, it is urged, if we are to be part of the modern world we must recognize that there is no further place for claims for absolute truth in religion. We must accept pluralism as a reality which God evidently wills.

Writers such as those I have quoted often say that this is a radically new situation which the Church has not faced before, and therefore calls for radically new formulations of the Christian faith. This is clearly not the case. The world into which the first Christians carried the gospel was a religiously plural world and—as the letters of Paul show—in that world of many lords and many gods, Christians had to work out what it means that in fact Jesus alone is Lord. The first three centuries of church history were a time of intense life-and-death struggle against the seductive power of syncretism. But if the issue of religious pluralism is not entirely new, it certainly meets our generation in a new way. We must meet it in the terms of our own time.

One fact that is certainly new is the acute sense that we are part of one global society more and more dependent on each other. The first photographs beamed back to earth from the moon gave us a vivid sense that our planet is not an inexhaustible area in which there will always be fresh frontiers to cross and free space to occupy, but a small and fragile spacecraft in which we are condemned to live together or else perish together. This sense of the paramount need for human unity is one of the genuinely new facts of our time—at least insofar as it now embraces the whole globe. In face of this need, the claim of one group to have the truth for all is seen as potentially disastrous. Thus Professor Christopher Duraisingh, Secretary of the Council for World Mission, writes: "It is not through our *a priori* doctrinal formulations on God or Christ, but rather through our collective human search for meaning and sacredness, that the 'universe of faiths' could be adequately understood."

157

He goes on, therefore, to say that our approach must not be christocentric or even theocentric but rather on the basis of soteriology, of a common search for salvation (ibid., p. 399).

On this two comments are in order:

1. Surely we all seek "salvation" in the sense of total welfare and happiness. The trouble is that we define it differently and seek it at the expense of others. Human beings have different ideas about what "salvation," total welfare, might be, and thus the human search for salvation is a highly competititive affair.

2. All serious seeking involves reliance on some clue. Christians are also seekers, and they believe that the decisive clue, the true and living way, has been given in Jesus. A common search cannot surely mean a search which abandons any specific clue and simply agrees to search.

The Christian points to Jesus as the master-clue in the common search of humanity for salvation and invites others to follow. It is true that this invitation, when it is given by Christians who are in positions of power and privilege, may be radically corrupted into a kind of spiritual imperialism which is oppressive rather than liberating. Missions have been guilty of this distortion and we have to acknowledge it. But it is also worth noting that most of the vigorous evangelism in our contemporary world is being done by the churches of the Third World which have no such power or privilege.

In similar vein Dr. Samartha calls on Christians to "contribute to the pool of human values such as justice and compassion, truth and righteousness in the quest of different people for spiritual and moral values to undergird viable political structures to hold together different religions, cultures, languages and ethnic groups" (ibid., p. 323). He indicates that we must work for secular political structures which will give space for the different religions to make their contributions. It is indeed the duty of Christians in multifaith societies to cooperate with people of other faiths in seeking a just ordering of society, but this is in no sense a substitute for the missionary preaching of the Church. In using the language of values, Dr. Samartha reveals his captivity to the post-Enlightenment worldview which separates facts from values and supposes that what are called values can be permanently sustained apart from some agreement about what are the facts. For centuries Orthodox Hindus believed that the miserable condition of the outcastes or untouchable communities was the result of the sins of their previous birth and that it was therefore part of the cosmic order not to be interfered with. By common consent the preaching of missionaries among these communities was one of the major factors, if not the decisive factor, in bringing about the change of view which has led to legislation (often— alas—ineffective) to give them justice. There is a struggle within Hinduism to relate the demand for justice and compassion to the traditional belief. The "values" of justice and compassion cannot be permanently sustained apart from some belief about the facts which correspond to these values. Christians cannot simply "contribute" these values as if they were contributions to a potluck supper. Questions of ultimate truth are involved.

There is a longing for unity among all human beings, for unity offers the promise of peace. The problem is that we want unity on our terms, and it is our rival programs for unity which tear us apart. As Augustine said, all wars are fought for the sake of peace. The history of the world could be told as the story of successive efforts to bring unity to the world, and of course the name we give to these efforts is "imperialism." The Christian gospel has sometimes been made the tool of an imperialism, and of that we have to repent. But at its heart it is the denial of all imperialisms, for at its center there is the cross where all imperialisms are humbled and we are invited to find the center of human unity in the One who was made nothing so that all might be one. The very heart of the biblical vision for the unity of humankind is that its center is not an imperial power but the slain Lamb.

The truth, of course, is that every program for human unity has implicit in it some vision of the organizing principle which is to make this unity possible. As Andre Dumas has pointed out, if this is not clearly recognized and stated, as it is in the Christian vision of the cross of Jesus as the place where all peoples may find reconciliation, then we shall find that the interests and intentions of the proposer are the hidden center. If there is no explicit statement of the center of unity, then the assumptions and interests of the proposer become the effective center. This becomes very clear in *The Myth of Christian Uniqueness*. Professor Gordon Kaufman of Harvard begins with the need for human unity, assumes without argument that the Christian gospel cannot furnish the center for such unity, and goes on to say that "modern historical consciousness" requires us to abandon the claim to Christ's uniqueness, and to recognize that the biblical view of things, like all other human views, is culturally conditioned (*The Myth*, pp. 5ff.). This same "modern

159

historical consciousness" will enable us to enter into the mental worlds of the other religions without supposing that we can impose our Christian norms on them. But to a person living in another culture it is not obvious that the modern historical consciousness of twentieth-century Western intellectuals provides us with a vantage point which can displace the one provided by the Christian story, or that it can furnish a basis for human unity. It is true that modern historical studies enable us to see that people in other times and places were looking at the world through culturally conditioned lenses and that their claim to "see things as they really are" is relativized by our studies in the history of cultures. But to suppose that modern historical consciousness gives us a privileged standpoint where we really do see things as they are, is of course unsupported dogma. Modern historical consciousness is also the product of a particular culture and can claim no epistemological privilege. Kaufman's theology of religions is thus similar to that of the Christian in that it finally rests on an ultimate faith-commitment which does not and cannot seek validation from some more ultimate ground. In this case the ultimate faith-commitment is to the validity of the "modern historical consciousness."

The same is true for the often made claim that all religions are variants of one central human experience, namely that which has been explored most fully by the great mystics. It is indeed true that mystical experience has played a very important role in all the world's great religions, including Christianity. But in no religious tradition is it the only reality. There is much else in all religious traditions, much about the conduct of human life, about justice, freedom, obedience, and mutual charity. To select the mystical element in religion as the core reality is a decision which can be questioned in the name of other elements in the religious life. And the claim that the mystical experience is that which provides the primary clue to what is real, and therefore the one road to salvation for all humanity, is—once again—to choose a particular faith-commitment among others which are possible. It does not enable one to evade the question: Why this, rather than that?

Wilfred Cantwell Smith in the same volume restates his familiar view that all the religions have as their core some experience of the Transcendent; that whether we speak of images made of wood and stone or images made in the mind, or even of such an image as the man Jesus, all are equally the means used by the Transcendent to make himself, herself, or itself present to us humans. To claim uniqueness for one particular form or vehicle of this contact with the Transcendent is preposterous and even blasphemous. Much rather accept the truth so beautifully stated in the *Bhagavadgita* and in the theology of Ramanuja, that God is so gracious that he (or she or it) accepts everyone who worships whatever be the form through which that worship is offered (*The Myth*, p. 65).

It is clear that in Smith's view "The Transcendent" is a purely formal category. He, she, or it may be conceived in any way that the worshipper may choose. There can therefore be no such thing as false or misdirected worship, since the reality to which it is directed is unknowable. Smith quotes as "one of the theologically most discerning remarks that I know" the words of the *Yogavasistha*: "Thou art formless. Thy only form is our knowledge of Thee" (*The Myth*, p. 55). Any claim for uniqueness made for one concept of the Transcendent, for instance the Christian claim that the Transcendent is present in fullness in Jesus (Col. 1:19), is to be regarded as wholly unacceptable. There are no criteria by which different concepts of the Transcendent may be tested. We are shut up to a total subjectivity: the Transcendent is unknowable.

This belief (or, rather, this declining of the possibility of belief) is taken to its logical conclusion in the frank polytheism with which the *Myth* volume concludes. In his final essay Tom Drive writes:

> God has different "natures". In pluralist perspective, it is not simply that God has one nature variously and inadequately expressed by different religious traditions. It is that there are real and genuine differences within the Godhead itself, owing to the manifold involvement that God has undertaken with the great variety of human communities. (*Myth*, p. 212)

Readers of the preceding chapters of the present book will of course recognize this as a typical (though extreme) illustration of the cultural collapse which has abandoned the struggle to find truth in the welter of human experiences. But, as I have tried to show in the earlier chapters, this collapse is a feature of only one side of our culture. In the world of science the effort to grasp the coherent rationality of things has not been abandoned. There is an unresting passion to find those patterns of thought which will enable us to grasp the coherence of things. Thus the physicists, faced with the problem of reconciling relativity with quantum theory, do not fall back on the supposition that reality has different natures, acts in different ways, is fundamentally incoherent. They continue with unwearied energy to seek a unified theory which will hold the whole of physics together. The religious pluralism represented in *The Myth* is evidence of cultural collapse. And, very obviously, if even

God is not one but many; if ultimate reality is such that he, she, or it behaves in mutually incoherent ways, what possible hope is there for human unity? The corollary of this intellectual collapse is the abandonment of hope for human unity.

In another essay in the same volume, Langdon Gilkey shows himself much more aware than the other essayists of the problems which this kind of total relativism raises. In this total relativism, he writes, we have no ground for speaking of salvation at all. Pluralism has its shadow side—the demonic movements which operate under the names of religion or quasi-religions such as nationalism. We must resist these, but in order to do so we must have somewhere to stand. And that means we must be committed to some belief not merely about what we personally desire (our "values") but about what is really the case. Against Hitler, only the absolute commitment of the signatories to the Barmen Confession could mount a real resistance. There has to be an absolute commitment if we are to act effectively against demonic powers. So, writes Gilkey, "paradoxically, plurality, precisely by its own ambiguity, implies both relativity and absoluteness, a juxtaposition or synthesis of the relative and the absolute that is frustrating intellectually and yet necessary practically" (*The Myth*, pp. 43-44). How does Gilkey resolve this dilemma? By relying on what he calls the venerable American tradition of pragmatism. He falls back on John Dewey and William James. We have to act or else conform. For this purpose we *need* an absolute, but we must recognize that our standpoint is only relative, otherwise our absolute will become another source of domination and repression.

On this point it seems to me that two comments are in order even after one has gone through the difficult process of understanding how an absolute can be relative. The first comment is this: an absolute is surely, by definition, something which cannot be acquired because we need it for the fulfillment of some purpose which we have embraced on other grounds. If it really is absolute truth, then it is not at our disposal. What Gilkey's program points to is something all too familiar, namely the employment of absolutist language to support claims which are in fact only the desires, or—if you like—values of some people. We are back again with Nietzsche: the only reality is the will. We *want* a certain kind of society, and in order to get it we need to be able to appeal to an absolute. The absolute in this scene is no absolute at all but merely a mask for a certain kind of desire. It is not surprising that this kind of liberalism was powerless in the face of Hitler and is powerless in the face of people like Ayatollah Khomeini.

The second comment is this: Gilkey suggests that a claim to absolute truth must be oppressive. It is certainly true that any community which claims to *possess* absolute truth must inevitably, if it gains power, become oppressive. But the Christian claim is not such, although in the course of history it has been wrongly understood as such. The claim of the Christian community is that in Jesus the absolute truth has been made present amid the relativities of human cultures, and that the form which this truth took was not that of dominance and imperial power but that of one who was without power, or—rather—whose power was manifest in weakness and suffering. The Church in its journey through history and in its embodiment in many different cultures seeks to express its allegiance to this truth in forms of theological statement and practical living. These forms are always temporary and always flawed by human sin and error. But insofar as they are constantly held under the critical control of the original witness as embodied in Scripture they are always capable of reformation. The Church thus does not claim to *possess* absolute truth: it claims to know where to point for guidance (both in thought and in action) for the common search for truth.

But is it possible to believe that the absolute has become part of history, history which is all a matter of relativities? Many of the writers I am discussing see it as axiomatic that there can be no absolutes in history. How absurd, says Cantwell Smith, to believe that it is only in Jesus that God was personally present. He is present everywhere, in the music of Bach as in the eucharist. How preposterous, says Dr. Eck, that there should be only one incarnation and only one gospel. In fact it is wrong to speak of God's revelation as if it were an event in past history. "The locus of revelation," says Dr. Eck, quoting Cantwell Smith, "is always the present, always the person. The channel of revelation in the Christian case, Christ, is a figure in history, but history moves forward and is the process by which He comes to us" (*International Review of Mission*, p. 385). Since revelation is always in the present and always to the person, I cannot speak of an absolute revelation since it is obvious that I at this moment have not grasped the whole of what God wills to reveal.

I think four comments are in order:

1. In the first place, the statement that there are no absolutes in history is obviously a pure assertion for which no proof is offered or can be offered. It is simply one of the axioms of our contemporary Western culture. It is pure unsupported dogma. There is nothing in the nature of things and nothing in the necessities of human thought which

163

requires us to deny the possibility that history might have a center just as the solar system has a center. In fact, of course, the denial of the Christian belief that the center of all history is the incarnation of the *Logos* in Jesus is always the other side of another belief about the real meaning and end of history. The very heart of the Christian message, as it is set forth for instance in the Fourth Gospel, is that the particular life-story which it tells is the decisive manifestation within history of the one who is the source and goal of all history. One may dismiss this belief as preposterous, as the writers of these essays do, but that merely demonstrates their captivity within the plausibility structures of our contemporary Western society.

2. The second comment is with reference to the statement that revelation is always in the present and always to the person. Behind this seemingly innocent statement there is the very ancient seduction of a purely individualistic spirituality, the understanding of the human person as a being existing apart from the history of which every human life is a part. Granted that there are profound and deeply personal spiritual experiences of many kinds which have many elements in common even though occurring in many different cultural and religious contexts, it is a distortion of the human reality to suppose that these can be taken in isolation from the continuing shared life of the human race as the clue to the ultimate meaning of life. Human life is both personal and corporate. No human life can be rightly understood apart from the whole story of which each life-story is a part. The trinitarian faith brings together these two aspects of human existence, assuring us that the one who is the source and sustainer and goal of all reality, and the one who is made known in the deepest experiences of the human spirit, is one with the man, this particular man, who went his humble way from Bethlehem to Calvary. There is thus no dichotomy between the inward experiences of the heart and the outward history of which each of us is a part. God's self-revelation in Jesus is not simply an event which recedes farther and farther into the past; through the work of the Spirit we are led into an ever fuller understanding of it as the Spirit takes of the things of Jesus and shows them to us through the experiences of our place and time. And, by the same token, our spiritual experience is not an affair of our own individual subjectivity; it is sustained, nourished, and tested by continual reference to the original witnesses of the revelation and by reference to the continuing experience of those who share with us the allegiance to Jesus.

Dr. Samartha strongly attacks the traditional understanding of the

Christian mission on the grounds that "conversion, instead of being a vertical movement towards God, a genuine renewal of life, has become a horizontal movement of groups of people from one community to another" (*International Review of Mission,* p. 321). Here again we meet the same fundamentally false view of what it is to be a human person. Samartha sees the human person as an isolated monad "vertically" related to God through an inward spiritual experience which is unrelated to the "horizontal" relations of human beings with each other. A true relation to God cannot be independent of our relation with other people, and allegiance to Christ must necessarily be expressed in relationship with those who share that allegiance.

3. This leads to a third comment. When Cantwell Smith writes: "God is not revealed fully in Jesus Christ to me, nor indeed to anyone else that I have met" (*International Review of Mission,* p. 423), he is no doubt correct in the sense that neither he nor anyone else has fully grasped the revelation. But from this statement one can move in two different directions. One would be to say, I find in Jesus the most compelling clue to God's being and purpose, therefore I shall try to grasp the revelation in Jesus more fully." But that is not the move that Smith advocates. Rather, it is to claim that God reveals himself everywhere to every human being however varied may be the forms in which they express that revelation. But certainly Smith does not in practice accept all these forms as equally valid. Hitler was certain that he had a divine mission. On what grounds do we reject his claim? Dr. Eck, in her criticism of Kraemer, says that he was wrong to presume to answer the question, Does God reveal himself to Muslims? since it is only the Muslims themselves who can answer that question, and it was presumptuous of Kraemer to presume to answer it for them (*International Review of Mission,* pp. 380-81). But certainly none of these writers would be ready to accept every claim to divine revelation. Some, such as that of Hitler, will certainly be rejected. On what ground? No explicit answer is given to that question, but from the writers concerned it is clear that the criterion is the general consensus of liberal-minded Western Christians. And when these same Christians ask, "What grounds have you for taking Jesus as your criterion of revelation? Why this one and not any of the others offered by people of other faiths?" one must put the counter-question: What grounds are there for thinking that this contemporary opinion is the valid measuring rod for assessing claims to divine revelation?

4. Fourth, if the answer is given that the criteria are to be found

in such permanently enduring values as justice, compassion, love, and mercy, one must ask, Why should these abstract nouns have a more ultimate status than a concrete life lived out on the actual plane of history? The gospel is not the assertion that in Jesus certain qualities such as love and justice were present in an exemplary manner. If this were so, we could of course dispense with the example once we had learned the lesson which the example teaches. The gospel is not just the illustration (even the best illustration) of an idea. It is the story of actions by which the human situation is irreversibly changed. The concreteness, the specificity, the "happenedness" of this can in no way be replaced by a series of abstract nouns. The difficulty of words like justice and love is that their content has to be given them in particular situations where action has to be taken. Both "justice" and "love" can be used and are frequently used as masks for special interests. One has always to ask, "Whose justice? What kind of love?" Where there is no Judge, each of us is judge in our own cause. On the other hand, when we point to Jesus, and to the story which has its center in the cross, we are invoking a criterion by which all our claims to justice are humbled and relativized. To affirm the unique decisiveness of God's action in Jesus Christ is not arrogance; it is the enduring bulwark against the arrogance of every culture to be itself the criterion by which others are judged. The charge of arrogance which is leveled against those who speak of Jesus as unique Lord and Savior must be thrown back at those who assume that "modern historical consciousness" has disposed of that faith.

Some of those who advocate the abandonment of a claim to Christian uniqueness seek to show that the Bible itself authorizes this move. Appeal is made to the early chapters of Genesis and especially to the Noachic covenant with its unconditional promise of blessing on Noah and all his descendants. The blessing is manifest in the procreation of the seventy nations as it is recounted in the following chapter. The gentiles are thus introduced at the beginning of our Bible as existing because of the blessing of God and as under his unbreakable promise of blessing. That is true and profoundly important. All the nations live by the blessing of God. The New Testament reaffirms that faith. But one cannot stop the reading of the Bible at the tenth chapter of Genesis. That chapter is followed at once by the story of the tower of Babel, the first great imperial project for human unity, which ends, as do all imperialisms, in confusion and alienation. And so there follows the beginning of the story of election, the choosing of one among the seventy nations to be the bearer of the blessing for all. It is a very misguided exegesis which sets these two elements in the biblical story against each other. God's love for all his creation, his purpose of blessing for all human beings is fundamental from beginning to end. But—for the reasons that I have already suggested—that purpose is fulfilled by way of election, of the choosing of one for the blessing of all. Both dimensions of the divine purpose, the universal and the particular, show themselves in different ways throughout the Bible. To set one against the other is to misunderstand both.

Thus, for example, appeal is made to the words of Amos 9: "'Are you not like the Ethiopians to me, O people of Israel?'" says the Lord. "'Did I not bring up Israel from the land of Egypt, and the Philistines from Caphtor and the Syrians from Kir? Behold, the eyes of the Lord are upon the sinful kingdom, and I will destroy it from the surface of the earth.'" Do these words negate the teaching of the rest of the Old Testament about the special election of Israel? Not at all; they confirm it. They are in line with the earlier words of Amos, which immediately follow the terrible catalogue of crimes in which Israel is as bad as or worse than all the gentiles: "You only have I known of all the families of earth; therefore I will punish you for all your iniquities" (Amos 3:2). God's guiding and providing hand is over all his works and over all the nations. His purpose is blessing for them all. For that purpose he has chosen Israel. Israel has rejected the call and behaved just like any of the nations which do not know God. Therefore his wrath descends on Israel. To take this text as ground for denying the biblical doctrine of the special calling of Israel is to reverse its whole intention. So also in the wonderfully ironic story of Jonah, where God's unlimited kindness to the wicked city of Nineveh and all its inhabitants, even the cattle, is contrasted with the surly, spiteful, and disobedient messenger of the Lord, Jonah *alias* Israel. The contrast is as sharp as it could be. The pagan sailors on the ship and the pagan rulers and people of the wicked city are both so tenderhearted that they repent and turn to the Lord at the first invitation, while Jonah is stubborn and unbelieving. And yet it is Jonah and no other who is chosen, called, and sent to bring God's message. God deals with Nineveh through this unlikely missionary. Jonah must go.

In the New Testament the text most often appealed to is the story of the conversion of Cornelius, which was also the conversion of Peter and of the Church. According to Wesley Ariarajah, the story shows that "there is no need to channel God to people; God has direct access" (*The*

Bible and People of Other Faiths, p. 17). Now it is certainly true that this story shows how God's mission is not simply an enterprise of the Church. It is a work of the Spirit who goes ahead of the Church, touches the Roman soldier and his household, prepares them for the message, and teaches the Church a new lesson about the scope of God's grace. But it is a complete misreading of the story to conclude from it that the going of the missionary is unnecessary. On the contrary, if Peter had not gone to Cornelius's house there would have been no conversion and no story. God prepared the heart of Cornelius before Peter came. But God also sent Peter, and Peter had to go and tell the story of Jesus. It was the telling of the story that provided the occasion for the radically new experience which made Cornelius a Christian, and which radically changed the Church's own understanding of its gospel. To use this story to suggest that the missionary journey is unnecessary or even improper is to distort it beyond recognition. It is indeed true, gloriously true, that God goes ahead of his Church. But it is also true that he calls the Church to follow. The Holy Spirit is not domesticated within the Church, but it is through the Church, the company of those (often unworthy like Jonah) who confess Jesus as Lord, that the Spirit brings others to that confession.

I venture to offer two concluding comments on the pluralist position as it is set out in *The Myth of Christian Uniqueness.* One is from the perspective of the sociology of knowledge. The culture in which this type of thinking has developed is one in which the most typical feature is the supermarket. In a society which has exalted the autonomous individual as the supreme reality, we are accustomed to the rich variety offered on the supermarket shelves and to the freedom we have to choose our favorite brands. It is very natural that this mentality should pervade our view of religion. One may stick to one's favorite brand and acclaim its merits in songs of praise; but to insist that everyone else should choose the same brand is unacceptable.

And that leads to a second point, which is more fundamental. The *Myth* volume celebrated a decisive move beyond exclusivism, and beyond the inclusivism which acknowledges the saving work of Christ beyond Christianity, to a pluralism which denies any uniqueness to Jesus Christ. This move, the "crossing of the Rubicon," is the further development of what was described by John Hick as a Copernican revolution—the move from a christocentric view of reality to a theocentric one (Hick, *God and the Universe of Faiths*). The further move is described as "soteriocentric"—it has its center in the common quest for salvation.

Even the word "God" excludes some concepts of the Transcendent Reality and is therefore exclusivist. But what is "salvation"? It is, according to Hick, "the transformation of human experience from self-centredness to God—or Reality—centredness" (*Myth*, p. 23). The Christian tradition affirms that this salvation has been made possible because God, the creator and sustainer of all that is, has acted in the historical person of the man Jesus to meet us, take our burden of sin and death, invite us to trust and love him, and so to come to a life centered in God and not in the self. The authors of the *Myth* deny this. "Reality" is not to be identified with any specific name or form or image or story. Reality "has no form except our knowledge of it." Reality is unknowable, and each of us has to form his or her own image of it. There is no objective reality which can confront the self and offer another center—as the concrete person of Jesus does. There is only the self and its need for salvation, a need which must be satisfied with whatever form of the unknown Transcendent the self may cherish. The movement, in other words, is exactly the reverse of the Copernican one. It is a move away from a center outside the self, to the self as the only center. It is a further development of the move which converted Christian theology from a concern with the reality of God's saving acts, to a concern with "religious experience," the move which converts theology into anthropology, the move about which perhaps the final word was spoken by Feuerbach who saw that the "God" so conceived was simply the blown-up image of the self thrown up against the sky. It is the final triumph of the self over reality. A "soteriocentric" view makes "reality" the servant of the self and its desires. It excludes the possibility that "reality" as personal might address the self with a call which requires an answer. It is the authentic product of a consumer society.

It is not easy to resist the contemporary tide of thinking and feeling which seems to sweep us irresistibly in the direction of an acceptance of religious pluralism, and away from any confident affirmation of the absolute sovereignty of Jesus Christ. It is not easy to challenge the reigning plausibility structure. It is much easier to conform. The overwhelming dominance of relativism in contemporary culture makes any firm confession of belief suspect. To the affirmation which Christians make about Jesus, the reply is, "Yes, but others make similar affirmations about the symbols of their faith; why Jesus and not someone or something else?" Thus a reluctance to believe in something leads to a state of mind in which the *Zeitgeist* becomes the only ruling force. The true statement that none of us can grasp the whole truth is made an excuse for disqualifying any claim to have a valid clue for at least the beginnings of understanding. There is an appearance of humility in the protestation that the truth is much greater than any one of us can grasp, but if this is used to invalidate all claims to discern the truth it is in fact an arrogant claim to a kind of knowledge which is superior to the knowledge which is available to fallible human beings. We have to ask, "How do you know that the truth about God is greater than what is revealed to us in Jesus?" When Samartha and others ask us, "What grounds can you show for regarding the Bible as uniquely authoritative when other religions also have their sacred books?" we have to ask in turn, "What is the vantage ground from which you claim to be able to relativize all the absolute claims which these different scriptures make? What higher truth do you have which enables you to reconcile the diametrically opposite statements of the Bible and the Qur'an about Jesus? Or are you in effect advising that it is better not to believe in anything?" When the answer is, "We want the unity of humankind so that we may be saved from disaster," the answer must be, "We also want that unity, and therefore seek the truth by which alone humankind can become one." That truth is not a doctrine or a worldview or even a religious experience; it is certainly not to be found by repeating abstract nouns like justice and love; it is the man Jesus Christ in whom God was reconciling the world. The truth is personal, concrete, historical.

To make that confession does not mean, as critics seem to assume, that we believe that God's saving mercy is limited to Christians and that the rest of the world is lost. In the next chapter, taking for granted the faith that Christ is indeed unique Lord and Savior, we must ask what this means for our understanding of and relations with the other great world faiths.

14. The Gospel and the Religions

1. If, as I have affirmed, we are to reject religious pluralism and acknowledge Jesus Christ as the unique and decisive revelation of God for the salvation of the world, what is the proper attitude which believers in that revelation ought to take toward the adherents of the great world religions? Perhaps one should begin by making the elementary point that the word "religion" covers an extremely wide and varied range of entities, and the way in which we relate to them as Christians will vary accordingly. One might divide the religions, as Nicol Macnicol does in his fine book *Is Christianity Unique?*, into those which understand God's self-revelation in historical terms—Judaism, Christianity, Islam—and those for whom the essential religious experience is a-historical—Hinduism, Jainism, Sikhism, Buddhism. Within the first group one would again have to distinguish between Judaism, which looks for a Messiah still to come, Christianity, which confesses Jesus as the Messiah who has come and is to come, and Islam, which affirms not a Messiah but a succession of messengers culminating in the Prophet. One should perhaps also include in this list Marxism, which functions in some respects as a religion in which the proletariat is the messianic people whose victory will inaugurate the final removal of human alienation from the sources of being. Clearly the gospel is related to each of these in differing ways.

One could also classify the religions in a different way which takes account of the very important group of religions which are known as primal religions. Dr. Harold Turner, well known as a student and interpreter of new religious movements in primal societies, says that there are only three possible ways of understanding the world: the atomic,

171

the oceanic, and the relational—symbolized respectively by billiard balls, the ocean, and the net. This is a classification of worldviews rather than of religions, but all religions embody some kind of worldview. The atomic, which is characteristic of contemporary Western society and has deep roots in Greek philosophy, sees reality in terms of its individual units. The atom, conceived as a minute piece of matter, is the ultimate constituent of the visible world. The human individual, conceived as an autonomous center of knowing and willing, is the ultimate constituent of society. The oceanic view, on the other hand, sees all things ultimately merged into one entity which is both the soul and all that exists. Atma is Brahma. The third view sees everything as constituted by relationships, whether it is the material world or human society. This view, characteristic of what we are accustomed to call primitive societies and primal religions, is also the view of the Bible. That is probably why the gospel is more readily accepted by so-called primitive peoples than by those who inhabit atomic or oceanic worldviews. It also calls into question the conventional use of the term "higher religions" to denote the other world faiths.

2. These preliminary remarks about classifications of religions and worldviews should serve to remind us that in using the word "religion" we are already making assumptions which need to be examined. In most human cultures religion is not a separate activity set apart from the rest of life. Neither in practice nor in thought is religion separate from the rest of life. In practice all the life of society is permeated by beliefs which western Europeans would call religious, and in thought what we call religion is a whole worldview, a way of understanding the whole of human experience. The sharp line which modern Western culture has drawn between religious affairs and secular affairs is itself one of the most significant peculiarities of our culture and would be incomprehensible to the vast majority of people who have not been brought into contact with this culture. It follows that in thinking about the implications of the claim that Jesus is God's unique self-revelation for our relation to the world religions, we must take into view more than what we call religion. The contemporary debate about Christianity and the world's religions is generally conducted with the unspoken assumption that "religion" is the primary medium of human contact with the divine. But this assumption has to be questioned. When the New Testament affirms that God has nowhere left himself without witness, there is no suggestion that this witness is necessarily to be found in the sphere of what we call religion. The parables of Jesus are notable for the fact that they speak of

secular experiences. When the Fourth Gospel affirms that the light of the Logos who came into the world in Jesus shines on every human being, there is no suggestion that this light is identified with human religion. The text goes on to say that this light shines in the darkness, and the ensuing story constantly suggests that it is religion which is the primary area of darkness, while the common people, unlearned in religious matters, are the ones who respond to the light. And it is significant that Justin Martyr, one of the earliest apologists to use this Johannine teaching in making contact with the unbelieving world, affirms that the true light did indeed shine on the great philosophers like Socrates, but that the contemporary religion was the work of devils. Our thought must therefore be directed not just to the religions so called; we must ask about the relation of the gospel to all who live by other commitments, whether they are called religious or secular.

3. We must look first at the strictly exclusivist view which holds that all who do not accept Jesus as Lord and Savior are eternally lost. We shall look later at the question whether this is in fact what fidelity to Scripture requires us to hold. There are several reasons which make it difficult for me to believe this. If it were true, then it would be not only permissible but obligatory to use any means available, all the modern techniques of brainwashing included, to rescue others from this appalling fate. And since it is God alone who knows the heart of every person, how are we to judge whether or not another person truly has that faith which is acceptable to him? If we hold this view, it is absolutely necessary to know who is saved and who is not, and we are then led into making the kind of judgments against which Scripture warns us. We are in the business of erecting barriers: Has she been baptized? Has he been confirmed by a bishop in the historic succession? Or has she had a recognizable conversion and can she name the day and the hour when it happened? We are bound to become judges of that which God alone knows. Moreover, every missionary knows that it is impossible to communicate the gospel without acknowledging in practice that there is some continuity between the gospel and the experience of the hearer outside the Christian Church. One cannot preach the gospel without using the word "God." If one is talking to a person of a non-Christian religion, one is bound to use one of the words in her language which is used to denote God. But the content of that word has necessarily been formed by his experience outside the Church. By using the word, the preacher is taking the non-Christian experience of the hearer as the starting point. Without this there is no way of communicating.

This fact by itself does not refute the position we are considering, but it makes it impossible to affirm a total discontinuity between Christian faith and the religions. And anyone who has had intimate friendship with a devout Hindu or Muslim would find it impossible to believe that the experience of God of which his friend speaks is simply illusion or fraud.

4. An important group of writers who reject both this exclusivism on the one hand and a total pluralism on the other, take an inclusivist position which acknowledges Christ as the only Savior but affirm that his saving work extends beyond the bounds of the visible church. Probably the most influential exponent of this view has been Karl Rahner with his conception of anonymous Christianity. It is important to note here that Rahner is not merely affirming that individual non-Christians can be saved—certainly no new doctrine—but that the non-Christian religions as such have a salvific role. Rahner (*Theological Investigations,* vol. 5) set out his position in four theses:

a. Christianity is the absolute religion, being founded on the unique event of the incarnation of the Son of God. But, since this event occurred at a certain point in history, we have to ask about God's relation to those who lived before it occurred or before it was brought to their knowledge. This question will not be just about individuals but about the religions to which they adhered. To quote Rahner, "Man who is required to have a religion is also commanded to seek and accept a social form of religion" (p. 120).

b. It follows that non-Christian religions, even if they contain error (as they do), are lawful and salvific up to the time at which the gospel is brought to the attention of their adherents. The gospel requires us to assume that God's grace is offered to all, and that "in a great many cases at least" it is accepted (p. 124). But after the time when the gospel has been preached and heard, the non-Christian religion is no longer lawful.

c. The faithful adherent of a non-Christian religion must therefore be regarded as an "anonymous Christian." He can be saved through his faithful practice of his religion. But the one who accepts Christ "has a greater chance of salvation than the anonymous Christian" (p. 132).

d. The other religions will not be displaced by Christianity. Religious pluralism will continue and conflict will become sharper.

5. While Rahner's idea of "anonymous Christianity" has not proved widely acceptable, the idea that the non-Christian religions as such are to be understood as vehicles of salvation is widely accepted. It has indeed

become a sort of orthodoxy and those who are not willing to accept it are dismissed as simply out-of-date (as by Wesley Ariarajah—see *International Review of Mission,* July 1988, pp. 419-20). He attacks the position of those who are not willing to make this judgment but wish to leave it in God's hands as "theological neutrality," and says that we cannot now afford this neutrality because we urgently need to have a basis for praying together with people of other faiths for world peace. An alleged practical need overrides the question of truth. What are we to say, on the basis of a scriptural faith, about the status and role of the great world religions?

6. I believe that we must begin with the great reality made known to us in Jesus Christ, that God—the creator and sustainer of all that exists—is in his own triune being an ocean of infinite love overflowing to all his works in all creation and to all human beings. I believe that when we see Jesus eagerly welcoming the signs of faith among men and women outside the house of Israel; when we see him lovingly welcoming those whom others cast out; when we see him on the cross with arms outstretched to embrace the whole world and when we hear his whispered words, "Father, forgive them; they know not what they do"; we are seeing the most fundamental of all realities, namely a grace and mercy and loving-kindness which reaches out to every creature. I believe that no person, of whatever kind or creed, is without some witness of God's grace in heart and conscience and reason, and none in whom that grace does not evoke some response—however feeble, fitful, and flawed.

7. The same revelation in Jesus Christ, with its burning center in the agony and death of Calvary, compels me to acknowledge that this world which God made and loves is in a state of alienation, rejection, and rebellion against him. Calvary is the central unveiling of the infinite love of God and at the same time the unmasking of the dark horror of sin. Here not the dregs of humanity, not the scoundrels whom all good people condemn, but the revered leaders in church, state, and culture, combine in one murderous intent to destroy the holy one by whose mercy they exist and were created.

8. All true thinking about this, as about every matter, must be held within the magnetic field set up between these two poles: the amazing grace of God and the appalling sin of the world. To live in this magnetic field is to live in an atmosphere which is charged with power, tingling, as it were, with electricity. One is always in the (humanly speaking) impossible position of knowing that one is—along with all others—

at the same time the enemy of God and the beloved child of God. To live in this charged field of force is always at the same time supremely demanding and supremely affirming. But we are always tempted to slacken the tension by drawing away from one or other of the two poles. Nowhere is this more clear than in the attitude we take to people outside the household of faith. We can opt for a solution which relies wholly on the universality and omnipotence of grace and move toward some form of universalism. Here the sharpness of the issue which God's action in Christ raises for every human soul is blunted. There is no life-or-death decision to be made. We can relax and be assured that everything will be all right for everybody in the end. Over much theological writing about the gospel and the world's religions one is tempted to write the famous words of Anselm: "Nondum considerasti quanti ponderis sit peccatum"—"You have not yet taken full account of sin." Or, on the other hand, the Christian may be so conscious of the abyss of sin from which only the grace of God in Jesus Christ could rescue him that he is unwilling to believe that the same grace can operate in ways beyond his own experience and understanding. His relation to the man or woman outside the Church, or outside the particular embodiment of Christianity to which he adheres, can only be that of the saved to the lost. In both cases genuine dialogue is impossible. In the first case there is no real dialogue because nothing vital is at stake; it is merely a sharing of varied experiences of the same reality. In the second case dialogue is simply inappropriate. The person in the lifeboat and the person drowning in the sea do not have a dialogue. The one rescues the other; the time to share their experiences will come only afterward.

9. If we are to avoid these two dangers, if we are to live faithfully in this spiritual magnetic field between the amazing grace of God and the appalling sin of the world, how are we to regard the other commitments, faiths, worldviews to which the people around us and with whom we live and move adhere? I believe that the debate about this question has been fatally flawed by the fact that it has been conducted around the question, "Who can be saved?" It has been taken for granted that the only question was, "Can the good non-Christian be saved?" and by that question what was meant was not, "Can the non-Christian live a good and useful life and play a good and useful role in the life of society?" The question was, "Where will she go when she dies?" I am putting this crudely because I want to make the issue as clear as possible. The quest for truth always requires that we ask the right questions. If we ask the wrong questions we shall get only silence or confusion. In

the debate about Christianity and the world's religions it is fair to say that there has been an almost unquestioned assumption that the only question is, "What happens to the non-Christian after death?" I want to affirm that this is the wrong question and that as long as it remains the central question we shall never come to the truth. And this for three reasons:

a. First, and simply, it is the wrong question because it is a question to which God alone has the right to give the answer. I confess that I am astounded at the arrogance of theologians who seem to think that we are authorized, in our capacity as Christians, to inform the rest of the world about who is to be vindicated and who is to be condemned at the last judgment. There has been an odd reversal of roles here. There was a time when Protestants accused Catholics of lacking assurance of salvation, and Catholics accused Protestants of being too sure. Today Roman Catholic theologians accuse Protestants of a failure in responsibility when they say that God alone knows the ultimate fate of unbelievers. Hans Küng (*On Being a Christian*, p. 99) is scathing in his contempt for Protestant theologians who say that we must leave the question of the ultimate fate of non-Christians in the hands of God. Rahner is equally sure that it is the duty of Christian theologians to tell the faithful adherent of a non-Christian religion that he can be saved but that he will have a better chance of salvation if he becomes a Christian and no chance at all if he refuses this invitation. And Wesley Ariarajah rebukes Visser 't Hooft for what he calls a "theology of neutrality" because the latter said, "I don't know whether a Hindu is saved: I only know that salvation comes in Jesus Christ" (*International Review of Mission*, pp. 419-20). I find this way of thinking among Christians astonishing in view of the emphatic warnings of Jesus against these kinds of judgments which claim to preempt the final judgment of God. Nothing could be more remote from the whole thrust of Jesus' teaching than the idea that we are in a position to know in advance the final judgment of God. It would be tedious to repeat again the innumerable warnings of Jesus in this matter, his repeated statements that the last day will be a day of surprises, of reversals, of astonishment. In his most developed parable of the last judgment, the parable of the sheep and the goats, both the saved and the lost are astonished. Surely theologians at least should know that the judge on the last day is God and no one else. Perhaps the "feel" of Jesus' teaching is best captured in the brief story of the rich young ruler who had kept all God's commandments but turned away from the call to surrender his wealth, prompting Jesus' famous statement that for a

177

rich man to enter the kingdom of God was harder than for a camel to go through the eye of a needle. When Peter protests, "Then who can be saved?" Jesus answers, "With men it is impossible, but with God all things are possible." I repeat that I find it astonishing that a theologian of the stature of Küng can so contemptuously reject the position of writers like Barth and Kraemer who refuse to pronounce on the final salvation of the non-Christian. If a theologian is really serious he must learn to understand the impossible possibility of salvation.

In St. Paul we find this same tension of confidence and awareness of the abyss that lies beneath. Paul, who is certain that nothing can separate him from the love of God in Christ Jesus, also tells his friends that he has to exercise severe self-discipline "lest having preached to others I myself should be disqualified" (1 Cor. 9:27). The Christian life, lived in the magnetic field between the two poles of the amazing grace of God and the appalling sin in which I share, has a corresponding synthesis of a godly confidence and a godly fear. The fear is lest I should put my trust in anything other than God's grace in Jesus Christ; the confidence is in the infinite abundance of his grace to me and to every one of his creatures.

b. The second reason for rejecting this way of putting the question is that it is based on an abstraction. By concentrating on the fate of the individual soul after death, it abstracts the soul from the full reality of the human person as an actor and sufferer in the ongoing history of the world. Once again we have to insist that the human person is not, essentially, a soul which can be understood in abstraction from the whole story of the person's life. This reductionist move is as misleading as the corresponding move of the materialists and behaviorists who want to explain the human person simply as a bundle of physical activities. If we refuse both these forms of reductionism, then the question we have to ask is not, "What will happen to this person's soul after death?" but "What is the end which gives meaning to this person's story as part of God's whole story?" It has often been pointed out that the verb "to save" is used in the New Testament in three tenses — past, present, and future. We were saved, we are being saved, and we look for salvation. By common consent it is agreed that to understand the word we must begin from its eschatological sense, from the end to which it all looks. Salvation in this sense is the completion of God's whole work in creation and redemption, the summing up of all things with Christ as head (Eph. 1:10), the reconciling of all things in heaven and earth through the blood of the cross (Col. 1:20), the subjecting of all hostile powers under the feet of Christ (1 Cor. 15:24-28). The other uses of the verb (we have been saved, we are being saved) must be understood in the light of the end to which they look. The question of salvation is wrongly posed if it is posed in respect of the human soul abstracted from God's history of salvation, abstracted therefore from the question, "How do we understand the human story?" Being saved has to do with the part we are playing now in God's story and therefore with the question whether we have understood the story rightly. It follows that our dialogue with people of other faiths must be about what is happening in the world now and about how we understand it and take our part in it. It cannot be only, or even mainly, about our destiny as individual souls after death. Insofar as the debate has concentrated on this latter question, it has been flawed.

c. The third reason for rejecting this way of putting the question is the most fundamental: it is that the question starts with the individual and his or her need to be assured of ultimate happiness, and not with God and his glory. All human beings have a longing for ultimate happiness, and the many worldviews, religious or otherwise, have as part of their power some promise of satisfying that longing. We must believe that this longing is something implanted in us by God. He has so made us that we have infinite desires beyond the satisfaction of our biological necessities, desires which only God himself can satisfy. Our hearts are restless till they find rest in him. On our journey he gives us good things which whet our appetite but do not finally satisfy, for they are always corrupted by the selfishness that desires to have them as our own possession. The gospel, the story of the astonishing act of God himself in coming down to be part of our alienated world, to endure the full horror of our rebellion against love, to take the whole burden of our guilt and shame, and to lift us up into communion and fellowship with himself, breaks into this self-centered search for our own happiness, shifts the center from the self and its desires to God and his glory. It is true, God forgive us, that Christians have turned even this into something that they thought they could possess for themselves; that they have privatized this mighty work of grace and talked as if the whole cosmic drama of salvation culminated in the words "For me; for me"; as if the one question is "How can I be saved?" leading inevitably to the question, "How can anyone be saved?" But this is a perversion of the gospel. For anyone who has understood what God did for us all in Jesus Christ, the one question is: "How shall God be glorified? How shall his amazing grace be known and celebrated and adored? How

179

shall he see of the travail of his soul and be satisfied?" The whole discussion of the role of the world religions and secular ideologies from the point of view of the Christian faith is skewed if it begins with the question, Who is going to be saved at the end? That is a question which God alone will answer, and it is arrogant presumption on the part of theologians to suppose that it is their business to answer it. We have to begin with the mighty work of grace in Jesus Christ and ask, How is he to be honored and glorified? The goal of missions is the glory of God.

What are the practical consequences of taking this as the starting point in our relation to people of other faiths? I suggest four immediate implications.

1. The first is this: we shall expect, look for, and welcome all the signs of the grace of God at work in the lives of those who do not know Jesus as Lord. In this, of course, we shall be following the example of Jesus, who was so eager to welcome the evidences of faith in those outside the household of Israel. This kind of expectancy and welcome is an implication of the greatness of God's grace as it has been shown to us in Jesus. For Jesus is the personal presence of that creative word by which all that exists was made and is sustained in being. He comes to the world as no stranger but as the source of the world's life. He is the true light of the world, and that light shines into every corner of the world in spite of all that seeks to shut it out. In our contact with people who do not acknowledge Jesus as Lord, our first business, our first privilege, is to seek out and to welcome all the reflections of that one true light in the lives of those we meet. There is something deeply repulsive in the attitude, sometimes found among Christians, which makes only grudging acknowledgment of the faith, the godliness, and the nobility to be found in the lives of non-Christians. Even more repulsive is the idea that in order to communicate the gospel to them one must, as it were, ferret out their hidden sins, show that their goodness is not so good after all, as a precondition for presenting the offer of grace in Christ. It is indeed true that in the presence of the cross we come to know that, whoever we are, we are sinners before the grace of God. But that knowledge is the result, not the precondition of grace. It is in the light of the amazing grace of God in Jesus Christ that I am compelled to say, "God, be merciful to me a sinner." Indeed, as the Fourth Gospel teaches us, it is only the presence of the living Holy Spirit that can convict the world in respect of sin and righteousness and judgment. The

preacher of the gospel may well be mistaken in regard to these matters; he may see sin where no sin is, and may be blind to the sins of which he himself is a party. As a fellow human being and a fellow sinner, his relation to the man or woman of another faith must be modeled on that of Jesus to all who came to him.

2. The second consequence of the approach I suggest is that the Christian will be eager to cooperate with people of all faiths and ideologies in all projects which are in line with the Christian's understanding of God's purpose in history. I have repeatedly made the point that the heart of the faith of a Christian is the belief that the true meaning of the story of which our lives are a part is that which is made known in the biblical narrative. The human story is one which we share with all other human beings—past, present, and to come. We cannot opt out of the story. We cannot take control of the story. It is under the control of the infinitely patient God and Father of our Lord Jesus Christ. Every day of our lives we have to make decisions about the part we will play in the story, decisions which we cannot take without regard to the others who share the story. They may be Christians, Muslims, Hindus, secular humanists, Marxists, or of some other persuasion. They will have different understandings of the meaning and end of the story, but along the way there will be many issues in which we can agree about what should be done. There are struggles for justice and for freedom in which we can and should join hands with those of other faiths and ideologies to achieve specific goals, even though we know that the ultimate goal is Christ and his coming in glory and not what our collaborators imagine.

3. Third, it is precisely in this kind of shared commitment to the business of the world that the context for true dialogue is provided. As we work together with people of other commitments, we shall discover the places where our ways must separate. Here is where real dialogue may begin. It is a real dialogue about real issues. It is not just a sharing of religious experience, though it may include this. At heart it will be a dialogue about the meaning and goal of the human story. If we are doing what we ought to be doing as Christians, the dialogue will be initiated by our partners, not by ourselves. They will be aware of the fact that, while we share with them in commitment to some immediate project, our action is set in a different context from theirs. It has a different motivation. It looks to a different goal. Specifically—and here I am thinking of the dialogue with secular ideologies—our partners will discover that we do not invest our ultimate confidence in the intrahistorical goal

of our labors, but that for us the horizon is one that is both nearer and farther away than theirs. They will discover that we are guided by something both more ultimate and more immediate than the success of the project in hand. And they will discover that we have resources for coping with failure, defeat, and humiliation, because we understand human history from this side of the resurrection of the crucified Lord. It is—or it ought to be—the presence of these realities which prompts the questions and begins the dialogue. And, once again, the dialogue will not be about who is going to be saved. It will be about the question, "What is the meaning and goal of this common human story in which we are all, Christians and others together, participants?"

4. Therefore, the essential contribution of the Christian to the dialogue will simply be the telling of the story, the story of Jesus, the story of the Bible. The story is itself, as Paul says, the power of God for salvation. The Christian must tell it, not because she lacks respect for the many excellencies of her companions—many of whom may be better, more godly, more worthy of respect than she is. She tells it simply as one who has been chosen and called by God to be part of the company which is entrusted with the story. It is not her business to convert the others. She will indeed—out of love for them—long that they may come to share the joy that she knows and pray that they may indeed do so. But it is only the Holy Spirit of God who can so touch the hearts and consciences of the others that they are brought to accept the story as true and to put their trust in Jesus. This will always be a mysterious work of the Spirit, often in ways which no third party will ever understand. The Christian will pray that it may be so, and she will seek faithfully both to tell the story and—as part of a Christian congregation—so conduct her life as to embody the truth of the story. But she will not imagine that it is her responsibility to insure that the other is persuaded. That is in God's hands.

It has become customary to classify views on the relation of Christianity to the world religions as either pluralist, exclusivist, or inclusivist, the three positions being typically represented by John Hick, Hendrik Kraemer, and Karl Rahner. The position which I have outlined is exclusivist in the sense that it affirms the unique truth of the revelation in Jesus Christ, but it is not exclusivist in the sense of denying the possibility of the salvation of the non-Christian. It is inclusivist in the sense that it refuses to limit the saving grace of God to the members of the Christian Church, but it rejects the inclusivism which regards the non-Christian religions as vehicles of salvation. It is pluralist in the sense of acknowledging the gracious work of God in the lives of all human beings, but it rejects a pluralism which denies the uniqueness and decisiveness of what God has done in Jesus Christ. Arguments for pluralism and inclusivism usually begin from the paramount need for human unity, a need hugely increased by the threats of nuclear and ecological disaster. We must surely recognize that need. But the recognition of the need provides no clue as to how it is to be met, and certainly does not justify the assertion that religion is the means by which human unity is to be achieved. The question of truth must be faced. C. S. Song is one of those who wishes to play down the role of truth because, as he says, truth judges, polarizes, divides. Truth, he says, cannot unite the ununitable; only love can. So the Christian mission must be an affair of love, not an affair of truth (*Tell Us Our Names*, Orbis Books, 1984, p. 114). But it is not love which encourages people to believe a lie. As a human race we are on a journey and we need to know the road. It is not true that all roads lead to the top of the same mountain. There are roads which lead over the precipice. In Christ we have been shown the road. We cannot treat that knowledge as a private matter for ourselves. It concerns the whole human family. We do not presume to limit the might and the mercy of God for the ultimate salvation of all people, but the same costly act of revelation and reconciliation which gives us that assurance also requires us to share with our fellow pilgrims the vision that God has given us the route we must follow and the goal to which we must press forward.

15. The Gospel and the Cultures

In the two previous chapters I have been exploring the issue of religious pluralism. I have given reasons for rejecting a total relativism among religious options and have tried to suggest what is implied for our understanding of the religions by our confession that Jesus is the way, the truth, and the life. I want to turn now to another aspect of pluralism, the plurality of human cultures. These two different issues are easily confused because, from the point of view of a sociologist, religion is part of culture, and no religious belief is without implications for culture. On the other hand, religions may be multicultural, and that is certainly true of Christianity. There are enormous cultural variations between the ways in which Christians in Nigeria, India, Samoa, and the USA express their faith. The question of the relation between the gospel and the different human cultures is a very live one in contemporary missiology. At one extreme Dr. McGavran and the "Church Growth" school of missiologists affirm—in McGavran's words—that "God accepts culture" (Lausanne Congress for World Evangelisation, 1974); they therefore tend to absolutize culture and to minimize the cultural changes which conversion ought to imply. People who accept the gospel, they affirm, ought to retain their traditional culture. Surely, however, the Church Growth missiologists are thinking here of such aspects of culture as music, art, dress, habits of eating and drinking, and—of course—language. They would not, certainly, agree that the gospel leaves unchallenged such elements of culture as cannibalism, the death penalty for petty offenses, or the ancient Indian custom of *sati*—the burning of a man's widow with his body on the funeral pyre. So if we do not accept a total relativism in respect of the varieties of human culture, what degree of relativism can there be?

The most fundamental element in culture is language. When people are forbidden to use their traditional language, as for instance the highlanders of Scotland in the eighteenth century, or the Taiwanese in our own time, then they feel that the very foundations of their common life have been destroyed. Do the nations of the world, with their many thousands of different languages, have to lose their language in order to become part of the universal Christian church? Perhaps the early church was spared the sharpness of that question by the fact that Greek was available as a common language throughout such a large part of the known world. A similar situation today, when English is so widely used throughout the world, helps us to evade the sharpness of the problem. For many centuries the Roman Catholic Church insisted that the only language in which the gospel could be properly expressed was Latin. And everyone who has wrestled with the task of communicating the gospel in a language which has been formed in total isolation from Christendom knows that every translation involves a fresh interpretation. Islam insists to this day that God's word as given to the Prophet can only be heard in Arabic. According to strict Islamic teaching the Qur'an cannot be translated, only interpreted. Yet at the birth of the Christian Church we have the story of what happened on the day of Pentecost, when people of a score of different nations heard the mighty works of God communicated to them in their own languages. In the Eastern tradition this is spoken of as the baptism of the languages, and it is on the basis of this understanding that the pioneers of Greek missionary outreach, such as Cyril and Methodius in their work for the conversion of the Slavic peoples, began by translating the Bible and the liturgy into the Slavic languages. Russians did not have to learn Greek in order to be Christians. Pentecost is our biblical warrant for saying that God accepts languages.

But does that mean that God accepts all the elements of human culture? Human culture is simply the way in which human societies order their corporate life, and as such it is corrupted by sin. I have mentioned such very ancient elements of certain human cultures as cannibalism and *sati*, which are now almost universally condemned. It is worth remembering that even these have had their defenders. Missionaries in Papua New Guinea have told us how shocked tribal peoples were at the idea of burying the bodies of their loved ones in the ground to be eaten by worms, and how much more appropriate it seemed to them that they should be eaten by members of the family; and *sati* had, and still has, defenders who see it as the ultimate symbol of wifely devotion. Slavery is another extremely ancient element in many human cultures, and in the culture in which the Church first developed. While St. Paul affirms that there is a new creation in Christ which makes slaves and their masters brothers in one family, and which therefore radically subverts the whole institution of slavery, yet he seems to imply that it remains a permanent part of the social order within which Christians must live their lives. It took seventeen centuries for the Church to become persuaded that the institution of slavery was incompatible with the gospel.

It seems clear that no one is willing, in the last resort, to accept a total relativism about culture. All of us judge some elements of culture to be good and some bad. The question is whether these judgments arise from the gospel itself or from the cultural presuppositions of the person who makes the judgment. And, if one replies that they ought to be made only on the basis of the gospel itself, the reply must be that there is no such thing as a gospel which is not already culturally shaped. Missionary history is replete with examples of judgments made on another culture by missionaries who were unaware of the extent to which their judgments were shaped by their own cultures rather than by the gospel. The difficulty of these issues is well illustrated in the long-running and still continuing debate about the relation of the gospel to one of the most fundamental elements in Indian culture—caste. Missionaries from Europe in the eighteenth century, both Catholic and Protestant, regarded caste as a social arrangement with which missionaries had no business to interfere. It was seen as analogous to the hierarchical social structure which was then normal in Europe. Indian Christians were not asked to drop their caste identity, any more than English Christians abandoned their place in the social order, or European Christians abandoned their national identities. There was no embarrassment about adding the caste name to the personal name. But the new generation of missionaries who came to India in the nineteenth century, filled with the egalitarian ideas of the French Revolution, regarded this situation with horror. They saw it as a betrayal of the gospel. They accused their missionary predecessors, and the Indian Christians of their time, of having fatally compromised the gospel. Modern secular opinion in India, very largely shaped by 150 years in which all higher education has been in the English language and in which generations of national leadership have been deeply influenced by modern European culture, endorses the condemnation of caste—whether or not one judges the condemnation to have been effective. Looking back on this controversy from our perspective at the end of the twentieth century, one is bound to ask whether the outright condemnation of caste by the nineteenth-century missionaries was primarily the fruit of their biblical study or primarily the fruit of the new movement of Enlightenment in Europe. Perhaps one might judge that this was an occasion when the Enlightenment brought to light neglected elements of biblical teaching. One is bound to ask, however, whether these "enlightened" missionaries did not, perhaps, communicate an atomic individualism which was farther from the biblical picture than the strongly cohesive, albeit narrowly exclusive texture of the traditional society. Surely every Christian today must condemn the inhuman treatment of the so-called "untouchables" under the traditional caste system, and must applaud the courage with which the nineteenth-century missionaries attacked it and upheld the cause of those excluded from Hindu society; but it is arguable, too, that missionary impact was flawed by a kind of individualism which failed to do justice to elements of value in the tradition, namely the sense of mutual responsibility in the extended family.

A similar issue is raised by missionary experience in Africa. Polygamy is part of the traditional culture in many parts of Africa. Protestant missionaries took it for granted that anyone wishing to be a Christian must acknowledge that monogamy is God's will and must therefore put away all but the first wife. Very large numbers of men, desirous of giving their lives to Christ, have nevertheless refused to do what the missionaries told them and therefore remain noncommunicant adherents of the Church. Many of us would conclude that these refusals were justified, since it would surely be a very great wrong to send away a woman married in good faith, with the knowledge that she can have no future except perhaps as a prostitute (as would be the case in India) or in another polygamous marriage. To contemporary African Christians, looking at Western society with its serial polygamy, it seems obvious that the traditional African pattern is more true to the gospel, since it at least acknowledges binding covenant obligations while the Western model dissolves them. When one looks back at the whole argument, it seems obvious that the difference between the two estimates of polygamy was not based only on biblical teaching (in regard to which Africans could and did appeal to Old Testament models of polygamy among revered patriarchs) but also, and perhaps much more, on different estimates of the role of the individual in society. For African society the human person is seen as a partner in a whole network of relationships binding him or her horizontally across a widely extended family and vertically to the ancestors who have died and to the children yet to be born. To be human is to be part of this closely woven fabric of relationships. By contrast, the Western post-Enlightenment understanding of the human person centers on the autonomy of the individual who is free to make or to break relationships at will. It can indeed, and I think must be said that the biblical teaching as a whole leads to the conclusion that the proper, God-ordained pattern is truly embodied only in a lifelong partnership of one man with one woman. When measured by this standard, both European and African cultures must be judged wanting. But it is by no means clear that the former is nearer to the biblical model than the latter.

The discussion of this particular African case leads to a more basic question. The question of the relation of gospel to culture is one of the most vigorously debated subjects in contemporary missiology. But one has to ask whether the way in which the question is posed does not imply already an unacknowledged and disastrous dualism. Culture is simply the social aspect of human living. It is defined in my dictionary as "the sum total of ways of living built up by a group of human beings and transmitted from one generation to another." Culture is human behavior in its corporate aspect. The gospel comes to any human community in words of a particular language which is the primary vehicle of a culture, and in a community (the Church) which itself embodies and illustrates a culture. The question of gospel and culture is sometimes discussed as though it were a matter of the meeting of two quite separate things: a disembodied message and a historically conditioned pattern of social life. And the reason why this dualism is present is, one must suggest, that in fact the gospel has been reduced to a matter of individual belief and conduct as though this could be separated from the shared life of society. The point is very vividly illustrated in a contrast between two missionary experiences in Africa. Ronald Wynne was sent as a missionary to a remote and isolated African community which had had no contact whatever with Christianity, the Hambukushu of Etsha in Botswana. Wynne lived with them for eight years, learning their language, entering deeply into their culture, sharing with them stories from the Old Testament which resonated deeply with their own experience of exile and persecution, and becoming part of their life, before he took the momentous step of naming the name of Jesus and inviting them— as a community—to accept him as Lord (*The Pool That Never Dries Up*, London). In other words, the gospel was seen from the very beginning as something which would affect the entire life of the community and all their customs and traditions. A decision for Christ would be a decision that put the whole of their shared life, their culture, into a new setting. The result was a profound change in the whole corporate life of the community. Wynne contrasts this with what happened in many parts of Africa where a religion of individual salvation had been taught, along with a wholesale rejection and condemnation of traditional culture. The result has been, as he says, a superficial Christianity with no deep roots, and then—later—a reaction to an uncritical and sentimental attachment to everything in the discarded culture.

This raises, it seems to me, sharp questions for us in the old Western Christendom. The very way in which we raise the question, with its dichotomizing of gospel and culture, reveals the dualism in our thinking: a purely individualistic Christianity which reflects the individualism of our culture with its enthronement of the autonomous human reason as the judge of all things has to face—as though it were a separate question from conversion—the matter of relating gospel to culture. I was recently in a meeting where a missionary home from Africa remarked that it had struck him that when his African Christian friends were faced with a difficult decision, he often found that, although they were devout and committed Christians, it was often the traditional African way of thinking which determined the decision. He seemed to be quite unconscious of the fact that the same was obviously true of an English or American Christian. The individual has accepted the gospel, but the culture has not been converted. Or, to put it more accurately, one part of the person has been converted, but not the whole person.

We must recognize the falsity of this dualism and acknowledge the fact that there is not and cannot be a gospel which is not culturally embodied. This is simply another way of affirming, as I have tried to do in the earlier chapters, the historical nature of the gospel. The gospel is about events which happened at a particular time and place in history. The events were in Palestine and not in Japan or Africa. The language in which they were told was Hebrew and Greek, not Sanskrit or Chinese. Wherever the gospel is preached it is preached in a human language, which means the language of one particular culture; wherever a community tries to live out the gospel, it is also part of one particular human culture. Wherever and whenever missionaries have gone preaching the gospel, they have brought not an ethereal something disinfected of all human cultural ingredients; they have brought a gospel expressed in the language and the life-style of a particular culture. It seems to be almost inevitable that, when the gospel is first received, it is accepted in

189

the form in which it was brought, with all the cultural particularities of the missionaries. The first converts reproduce faithfully the forms of Christian life and worship which the missionaries brought. This is not always or only because of pressure by the missionaries; the new thing is often welcomed just because it is new, for there are always in any society both conservatives who cherish the old traditions and radicals who question them. Later, when there has been time for deep study of the Bible in their own language, the new Christians—or more probably their children and grandchildren—will begin to look critically at the forms of Christianity which they have received and begin to make distinctions which the missionaries could not make between what is proper to the gospel according to the Scriptures and what is simply part of the traditional culture of the missionaries. And if, as Wynne says, the conversion has been superficial, there will then be a sentimental reaction which applauds the ancient culture as indiscriminately as it had previously rejected it.

The history of cross-cultural missions in the nineteenth and twentieth centuries is extremely complex, full of unexpected twists and also full of ironies. Chinese intellectuals rejected the invasion of missionaries in the nineteenth century partly at least on the ground that they brought with them a foreign culture. Today missionaries like Timothy Richard are honored by the leadership precisely because they brought China into touch with Western society and so prepared the way for what is now called modernization. The work of missionaries in India is praised by non-Christians because they brought Western science, medicine, and technology. European Christians criticize the Indian Church for being too Western and express their enthusiasm for Indian cultural styles—not recognizing that the reason why they appreciate things Indian is the same as the reason why many Indians appreciate things Western—namely that they are a welcome change from the tradition. Modern critics of nineteenth-century missions have often criticized the early missionaries in the South Pacific for making the women put on more clothes, although there seems to be evidence that the women regarded this as a way of asserting their new-found dignity in the Christian society. Today Christians in the South Pacific are scandalized by the clothing—or absence of clothing—of the tourists from Europe.

Reference to these twists and turns in the story of cross-cultural missions reminds us of the fact that our judgments are very much governed by the emotions generated by the profound cultural changes in the Western world in the past seventy-five years. The world missionary conference of Edinburgh 1910, with its vision of the evangelization of the world in that generation, is criticized for its alleged confusion of confidence in the gospel with confidence in the expansive power of Western civilization. The charge is not entirely true, for there were strong voices bringing a Christian critique to bear on elements of the so-called Christian civilization. But it is certainly true that there was then still a great confidence in the onward spread of civilization—the kind of civilization which Europe and North America had produced, and that this confidence was also—inevitably—a factor in the confidence of missions. For many at that time, Christianity and modern civilization went together. After the experiences of the past seventy-five years that is no longer so. There is a profound collapse of belief in the future of our civilization. The missionary movement is widely perceived as simply one element of what the Indian historian Panikkar calls the Vasco de Gama era—an era now definitely over. Many sensitive people, including Christians, sensing that our culture is bankrupt, look elsewhere for salvation. Salvation, if it is to be found anywhere, will surely not (in this view) be found in Europe or America: we must now learn to listen humbly to the voice of other cultures. In this climate all judgments about culture and about the relation of the gospel to culture are colored by this profound pessimism about our own. If our own culture has proved bankrupt, and if all expressions of the gospel are culturally embodied, it is understandable that a collapse of confidence in our culture goes along with a faltering of confidence in the gospel. And that is certainly what has happened in the old heartlands of the great missionary movements of the past two centuries.

If this is the true diagnosis of our situation, what is the next move? If the gospel is always and everywhere culturally embodied—in a particular language and a particular life-style, how can it be possible for the gospel to have a critical relation to culture? To be specific, can we who are both Christian believers and also products of this collapsing Western post-Enlightenment culture, can we find a stance from which we can criticize our own culture? A recent writer in *Theology*, reviewing my book *Foolishness to the Greeks*, says bluntly that it is impossible. Trying to criticize one's own culture is, he says, like pretending to move a bus when you are sitting in it. We are what our culture has made us and we have to accept that fact. To appeal to the Bible is futile. After two centuries of scientific historical-critical analysis of the contents of the Bible, we know that it also is simply part of human culture. We can examine its texts more and more minutely and place them more and more precisely within the continuum of human culture, but there is no sense in which the Bible can speak a critical word *to* our culture. In fact we have no way of understanding the Bible except through the reason and imagination, the concepts and categories which our culture supplies. What answer can be given to this?

It is obviously true that we have no way of understanding the Bible except through the concepts and categories of thought with which our culture has equipped us through our whole intellectual formation from earliest childhood. But the Bible speaks of things which are not simply products of human culture but are words and deeds of God, creator and sustainer of all that is. How can we know that these biblical stories are more than an objectified representation of the religious experiences of a particular people, the peoples of Israel and of the Eastern Mediterranean, with their own particular cultural conditioning? It is also true that we have no way of understanding the natural world around us except through the experience of our five senses. How do we know that these experiences convey valid information about what is really "out there"? How can we know that we are not misled by our sense experiences? Only by making our perceptions public, sharing them with others, comparing our different perceptions and checking their reliability against those of others. On the one hand we have to take responsibility for what we claim to know by seeing and hearing and touching; on the other hand these claims, because they are claims to be in contact with a reality beyond ourselves, must be made "with universal intent." We must seek to show others that they are valid.

The way in which any Christian perceives God's revelation in Christ and in the whole biblical story will be shaped by the culture through which that individual was formed. It is simply a fact of history that Jesus has been and is portrayed in an amazing variety of portraits from the Byzantine Pantocrator through the medieval crucifix and the Jesus of the sacred heart, to the blue-eyed blond of American protestantism and the Che Guevara freedom fighter of liberation theology. For some writers it seems obvious that Jesus can be portrayed in any guise that is (as they would say) "meaningful" for them and their contemporaries. But "Jesus" is not a name to which we can attach any character we like to imagine. Jesus is the name of a man of whom we have information in the books of New Testament interpreted (as they must be) in the light of the books which were Jesus' own scriptures. The Jesus of whom the New Testament writers bear witness is not an inaccessible figure. Our varying perceptions of him—and of course they will vary because we are culturally different people—have to be checked in the same way that all our claims to perceive reality have to be checked. We have to share them with others who perceive Jesus with the different lenses furnished by their different cultures. And this is a matter on which we can speak with solid experience. It is a matter of fact, for example, that in an Assembly of the World Council of Churches, where Christians from an enormously wide variety of cultures, with correspondingly varied perceptions of Jesus, long periods of Bible study shared by people with these clashing perceptions lead to a fresh assurance of the reality of Jesus' authority and a more fully shared perception of his nature and purpose. Not that all differences are removed, but that there is a fresh assurance that—from different perspectives—they are speaking of the same person.

And in this experience we are being faithful to the nature of the biblical witness. It is, for example, a matter of scandal to Muslims that Christians have four Gospels and not one. Muslims speak of the Gospel ("Injil"), but it is axiomatic for them that there is one gospel, and if Christians have four then that is proof that the four are not authentic. This is of course in line with the Muslim conviction that the Qur'an cannot be translated. God has only one speech, and that is Arabic. The same kind of logic underlay the attempts from early times to eliminate the discrepancies in the Gospels by producing a harmonized version. But the church's canon includes four Gospels, each of which gives a somewhat different portrait of Jesus. Modern scholars have devoted great energy and skill to drawing out the differences, and that is of value. But for millions of Christians in past centuries and today, the devout study of these four Gospels has led to a growing assurance that there is indeed one Lord Jesus whom they are learning to know and to follow.

It will of course be pointed out that my reasoning is defective, since the sharing of our experiences of sight and sound and touch is potentially a sharing with the whole human race, whereas the sharing of experience of Jesus is limited to the community of believers. This is of course true. And it is to be understood, as I have been pointing out earlier, in terms of the biblical doctrine of election. It is our faith that God has called this community to be the bearer of his gospel for all communities. Once again, of course, this faith cannot be shown to be valid by reference to some more ultimate belief. Like every other human belief, it is part of the tradition of belief developed and handed down in one particular human community. But this community is one which is more and more fully represented in all the vast variety of human cultures. Those who belong to it are people formed both by the human cultures in which they have been nourished and also by the traditions which they share with all Christian believers. They belong to two cultures. In Pauline language, while living as the people of Philippi or Corinth or Rome, they have a citizenship in heaven (Phil. 3:20). What, then, is the relation between these two citizenships, these two affiliations?

There have been and are situations in which Christians feel a deep attachment only to their heavenly citizenship, in which they reject and are rejected by the earthly city. Such was—in large measure—the situation for many in the earliest decades of the Church. It is a situation reflected on many pages of the New Testament. It is a situation which has its paradigmatic form in the crucifixion of Jesus. The cross, where Jesus was rejected and cast out by the representatives of human cultures in religion, politics, law, and morals, would (if it were the last word) imply that the normal situation for Christians is that they reject and are rejected by the world. That is the implication of the words of Jesus, "Whoever would be my disciple, let him take up his cross and follow me." Nothing could suggest more forcibly a total rejection of the believer by the world and of the world by the believer.

But the cross is not God's last word. In raising his beloved Son from the dead, God has given the pledge and the foretaste of his unconquerable grace in kindness and patience toward the world which rejects him. In the resurrection of Jesus, the original covenant with creation and with all human life, the covenant with Noah and his descendants, is reaffirmed. The world of human culture rejects God and is under God's judgments. But God in his patient and long-suffering love sustains the created world, and the world of human culture in being, in order that there may still be time and space for repentance and for the coming into being of the new creation within the womb of the old. God stills cherishes and sustains the world of creation and of culture, in spite of its subjection to illusion and vanity. The covenant with Noah and its rainbow sign refer explicitly to one of the most basic elements in human culture, namely the work of the farmer who cultivates the wilderness in order that it may bring forth food for human beings (Gen. 8:22). Here the interdependence of human beings and nature, and the dependence of both on the grace of God, are at their most manifest. God's promise that while earth remains seedtime and harvest shall not cease stands over the entire story of human culture. It is an assurance and an invitation to cherish and care for the earth and all that is in it, because God their creator cherishes and cares for them. And one of the counterthemes of the Old Testament is the perpetual tendency of Israel to forget the awesome and holy God who was the true author of prosperity, and to turn to the gods whose only function was to provide plenty of grain and oil and wine. Israel had to be reminded again and again by devastating disasters that the work of the farmer is only rightly undertaken when it is done as graceful acknowledgment of a gracious God. This double theme is also illustrated from another area of culture, that of politics. The same double theme runs through the Old Testament account of the political life of Israel: the king as one anointed by God to bring peace, justice, and good order, the true son of David; and—on the other hand—the king who uses his God-given power to serve his own ends and so brings disaster on the people (cf. 1 Samuel 8 and 9).

If this biblical interpretation of the human story, with its center in the double event of Jesus' death and resurrection, is our clue, then it will follow that we are called neither to a simple affirmation of human culture nor to a simple rejection of it. We are to cherish human culture as an area in which we live under God's grace and are given daily new tokens of that grace. But we are called also to remember that we are part of that whole seamless texture of human culture which was shown on the day we call Good Friday to be in murderous rebellion against the grace of God. We have to say both "God accepts human culture" and also "God judges human culture." There will have to be room in the Christian life for the two attitudes which Von Hügel used to call the homely and the heroic. Christian discipleship can never be all homeliness nor all heroism. It has to have elements of both and it has to learn from day to day when to accept the homely duties of life as it is, and when to take the heroic road of questioning and challenging the accepted ways. It was necessary for the early church, at crucial moments, to take the heroic path and to accept martyrdom rather than submit to what the vast majority of people took for granted. But it was also right that, when the time came with the conversion of Constantine, the Church should accept the role of sustainer and cherisher of the political order. It is right for churches to be dissenting communities challenging accepted norms and structures. It is right also in other circumstances for the Church to be the church for the nation or the parish, the cherisher and sustainer of the ordinary work of the farmer, the judge, and the soldier. What is wrong is the absolutizing of one position against the other and the corresponding ex-communication of those who take the other role. What is needed is the discernment to know, from day to day and from issue to issue, when the one stance is appropriate and when the other.

But how shall we find that discernment? Once again we face the problem posed by the critic who said that we cannot pretend to move a bus while sitting in it. We *are* what our culture has made us: our Christianity is part of our culture. We read the Bible in our own language and it is full of resonances which arise from past cultural experience. Where do I find the stance from which I can look at myself from the point of view of the Bible when my reading of the Bible is itself so much shaped by the person that I am, formed by my culture? I think that we can be helped toward an answer by looking at the experience of the churches in the present century. During the 1914-1918 war the churches on both sides made an almost total identification of the cause of Christ with the cause of their own nation. Christianity had become almost absorbed into national identity. It was the scandal of that situation which shocked many—including notably a young pastor in Safenwil called Karl Barth—and caused them to realize that European Christianity was guilty of a fatal syncretism, and to send them back to a fresh and more humble listening to the Bible. Out of that grew the ecumenical developments of the 1930s and '40s. In the Second World War the blasphemies of the First were not repeated, at least not on anything like the same scale. Spiritual bonds remained through the years of conflict, and almost as soon as the war was over the church leaders on the two sides were meeting together to work and pray for a new form of Christian presence in Europe. They knew that it was no longer tolerable that the churches should be content to be domestic chaplains to their nations: there had to be a supranational entity which could in some measure embody and express the supranational and supracultural character of the gospel. That recognition was given concrete form when, at Amsterdam in 1948, churches whose nations had been so recently at war pledged themselves to be faithful to one another in a mutual commitment to receive correction from one another. That reference to mutual correction is the crucial one. All our reading of the Bible and all our Christian discipleship are necessarily shaped by the cultures which have formed us. In Europe over the past four hundred years these cultures have been embodied in nations which have taken the place of God as the supreme reality, calling for absolute and total devotion. The fruit of that idolatry was reaped in two terrible wars. In that situation, the only way in which the gospel can challenge our culturally conditioned interpretations of it is through the witness of those who read the Bible with minds shaped by other cultures. We have to listen to others. This mutual correction is sometimes unwelcome, but it is necessary and it is fruitful.

As so often, the answer to the complex questions about the relation of the gospel to human culture has to be a practical one and not merely a theoretical one. It is only by being faithful participants in a supranational, multicultural family of churches that we can find the resources to be at the same time faithful sustainers and cherishers of our respective cultures and also faithful critics of them. The gospel endorses an immensely wide diversity among human cultures, but it does not endorse a total relativism. There is good and bad in every culture and there are developments continually going on in every culture which may be either creative or destructive, either in line with the purpose of God as revealed in Christ for all human beings, or else out of that line. The criteria for making judgments between the one and the other cannot arise from one culture. That is the familiar error of cultural imperialism. There can only be criteria if God has in fact shown us what his will is. He has done so in Christ. If that is denied in the name of religious pluralism, then there is no valid criterion by which the positive and negative developments in human culture can be assessed. On the other hand, the content of the revelation in Christ, defined crucially by the twin events of cross and resurrection, provides a basis on which the great diversity of cultures can be welcomed and cherished and the claim of any one culture to dominance can be resisted.

16. Principalities, Powers, and People

My previous chapter was about the gospel and culture. This is a very familiar theme in contemporary theological and especially missiological discussion. The World Council of Churches has recently taken it as a major theme. But why should this become a theme for discussion? Why is there not an equally widespread discussion about the gospel and personal behavior? After all, "culture" is simply the word we use for the way in which a whole community of men and women behaves. The very formulation of the theme "Gospel and Culture" indicates (as I suggested in the last chapter) that a dualism has appeared in our thinking. It is a dualism which arises from our tendency to regard individual behavior as something which can be understood, explained, and perhaps changed, apart from the behavior of the society to which the individual belongs. In other words, the dualism arises from the individualism in our culture, and from the resultant privatization of our ethical thinking. It would not occur to people in a traditional African society to develop a theory of personal behavior apart from the way in which this is related to the life of the whole community. And, in accordance with this way of seeing things, the gospel would be seen as something which affects the way in which the whole society behaves and not just the way in which individuals behave. By contrast, one often hears in our Western society such statements as "The gospel is about changing people; it is addressed to the individual conscience, not to societies and institutions. Societies and institutions will only be changed when people are changed. It is therefore the business of the Church to address the individual conscience and to seek conversion there. The reformation of society will follow."

That way of thinking would seem strange to many human societies today. And surely even in our own highly individualistic society we
know that the relation between individual behavior and the behavior of
societies is not one-way; it is reciprocal. Professor Donnison has given
a vivid illustration of this from personal experience in the Navy. He
speaks of days spent in a transit camp where men were coming and
going all the time and no enduring bonds were formed between them.
In that camp, he says, one had to nail everything down or it would be
stolen. Then he speaks of life on board ship on active service. The same
men are his companions. But now he knows that any of his fellow crew
members would without hesitation risk his own life for one of his mates.
The same men were involved in both situations: in one they were bound
together by a common purpose; in the other they were not. In the two
different social contexts, their personal behavior was totally different
(*Just Sharing*, Ed Duncan Forrester and Danus Skene, 1988, pp. 3-4). The
society shapes the person as much as the person shapes the society.
What exactly we are talking about when we speak of "the society" as
distinct from the people who form the society is a matter we must come
back to. It is the fundamental matter of this chapter.

Alasdair MacIntyre in his seminal book *After Virtue* contrasts the
contemporary way of discussing ethical issues as though they were simply a matter of how each individual decides, in sovereign autonomy,
how to act, with the Greek way of seeing behavior as sharing in the life
of a *polis,* an ordered community. So the question "How shall I behave?"
is only to be answered by asking the more basic question, "What kind
of a community do I want to share in?" As a vivid illustration of the difference MacIntyre quotes the often repeated saying of E. M. Forster that
if he had to choose between betraying his country and betraying his
friends, he hoped he would betray his country. On this MacIntyre comments that a man who can write those words has never had a country.
In the Greek sense, he has never been citizen of a city. The only human
community he has known is that of his personally, individually chosen
friends.

The idea that the gospel is addressed only to the individual and
that it is only indirectly addressed to societies, nations, and cultures is
simply an illusion of our individualistic post-Enlightenment Western
culture. Very plainly when we turn to the Old Testament we find no
such separation of the individual from the society which nurtures and
forms him and of which he is a part. The Torah, God's gracious instruction of his people, is addressed as much to the life of the nation as to

that of the individual. It is as much about law and order, hygiene, economics, social welfare, and politics as it is about personal morals. It is Israel as a whole which is addressed in the Torah. That is obvious; but many would say that this is one of the matters on which the teaching of the New Testament is radically different from that of the Old. In the New Testament, they would say, God's word is addressed to the individual, not to a nation, and the new Israel is not a nation but a community of individuals living in many cities and states but bound together by their individual commitment to Jesus Christ. The New Testament, it is said, does not envisage a social or political reformation of Greek and Roman society; it simply accepts that society as the milieu within which individuals have to work out their own salvation. Is this true? I do not believe that it is, and in order to correct what I believe to be a flawed reading of the New Testament, I want to direct attention to an element in its teaching which has been neglected in the modern period of the historical-critical approach to the Scriptures but is—once you open your eyes to it—extremely prominent.

I refer to the whole mass of teaching in St. Paul's letters about what are variously called principalities, powers, dominions, thrones, authorities, rulers, angels, and other names. With these we must also look at what the Gospels have to say about hostile spiritual powers, about Satan, and about what the Fourth Gospel calls "the ruler of this world." If I am not mistaken, most scholarly readers of the New Testament in the past 150 years have regarded all this language as something which we can for practical purposes ignore because it belongs to a thought-world which we have grown out of. We imagine a host of angelic or demonic beings flying around in the air somewhere above our heads, suppose that Paul and his contemporaries believed in these, just as people once believed in fairies and elves, and conclude that we can ignore this part of his writing. The domination of a reductionist materialism, which supposed that when we had discovered the atomic and molecular and biological facts about any phenomemon we had explained it, has prevented us from discerning the realities that Paul and other New Testament writers are talking about, and they *are* realities.

When we read right through the whole New Testament looking for words which speak of power, authority, rule, dominion, or lordship, we find such words on almost every page. The central phrase of the gospel, the kingdom of God, is obviously about power, authority, rule. In a vast number of cases, of course, the words refer to what we would recognize as human rulers and authorities—magistrates, priests, elders, a governor like Pilate, or a petty rajah like Herod. When Paul writes about "the powers that be" in Romans 13, it is clear that they are human beings, for they wear swords and collect taxes. But what are we to make of the principalities and peers in the heavenly places against which we are to wrestle (Eph. 6:12)? And how on earth is the church to set about making known the manifold wisdom of God to the principalities and powers in the heavenly places (Eph. 3:10)? Are these powers the same as or quite different from the powers that collect taxes on earth? When Paul says that none of the rulers of this world understood the wisdom of God, for if they had they would not have crucified the Lord of glory (1 Cor. 2:8), is he just talking about Herod and Pilate, or about something else? A couple of verses earlier Paul has said that these rulers are doomed to pass away. But Herod and Pilate had disappeared from the scene before Paul wrote these words. Does he mean that these two men are doomed to pass away? If so, it seems hardly worth saying: they are already dead. So does he mean that their roles, their offices, their authority is doomed to pass away? Are we talking about an individual called Herod or Pilate or Smith or Jones, or are we talking about something which is temporarily embodied in these officeholders, about the role rather than the individual who plays it? And when (according to the Fourth Gospel) Jesus speaks of his coming death and says, "Now is the judgment of this world; now shall the ruler of this world be cast out" (John 12:31), he cannot be speaking just of Herod or Pilate; neither of them could be called "ruler of this world." Clearly this language does not simply refer to certain human beings who hold these offices of power and authority for a few years and are then dead and gone. They refer to something behind these individuals, to the offices, the powers, the authority which is represented from time to time by this or that individual. It is these powers, authorities, rulers, dominions which have been confronted in Christ's death with the supreme power and authority of God. That is why it is the business of the Church to make manifest to them the wisdom of God. That is why we are told in the brief, hymn-like words of 1 Timothy 3:16 that God was "manifested in the flesh, vindicated in the Spirit, seen by angels, preached among the nations, believed on in the world." What was done in the incarnation, death, and resurrection of Jesus confronts the powers before it is preached among the nations. That is why we are told that the risen Christ has been seated at God's right hand with all the principalities and powers under his feet (Eph. 1:21). That is why we are also told that Christ in his cross disarmed the principalities and powers and made a public example of them, triumphing over them in his cross (Col. 2:14). But what exactly are these principalities and powers?

It seems clear from the examples already quoted that these powers do not exist apart from the human agencies in which they are embodied—Pilate, Herod, Caiaphas. Yet they are not identical with these particular individuals. They refer, I suggested, to that which is behind them, to the power which they represent and exercise but which is not identical with them. We are talking about power and authority which is real, which is embodied in and exercised by individual human beings, but is not identical with them. The king dies, but the kingship goes on. Another king steps into the place. But what is this thing that we call "kingship"? I used a spatial metaphor when I spoke of the authority which is "behind" the particular person who holds office and exercises authority for the moment. A spatial metaphor is obviously very inadequate. You do not find a thing called kingship by looking behind the king's back. We say that kingship is a reality which is more than, which transcends the particular exercise of kingship by this man or this woman. But we do not escape the spatial metaphor, for "transcendence" means being above something else. When in contemporary English we speak of the relation of a spiritual reality to its visible embodiment, we tend to think of inwardness—another spatial metaphor. We cannot avoid spatial metaphors but we can be saved from being misled by acknowledging that a variety of metaphors is possible. Shall we speak of the spiritual power within, behind, or above its visible embodiment? We all know very well that long-enduring institutions have something, an inwardness which can be recognized in those who form the institution at any one time, but outlasts and transcends them. This "something" may be benevolent or malevolent. A good school has a spirit, an ethos, which molds the characters of the pupils. It was there before they came, and it will be there after all the present pupils have left. A nation similarly has something which is not just the sum of the attitudes of its individual citizens. And a mob can become an embodiment of evil, an evil which its individual members would never have wished for on their own. Clearly this "something" has reality. But we cannot locate it spatially within, behind, or above its visible embodiment. It is not something which hovers in the air above the heads of living human beings. We have tended to read the New Testament as though this was how its writers conceived of this spiritual reality. We have assumed that "the heavenly places," where the principalities and powers dwell, are above our heads. But Paul is not a victim of his own inevitably spatial language. According to Paul, those who are in Christ are already seated in the heavenly places where Christ is (Eph. 1:20). This "something" which is invisible, and which cannot be located spatially either within or behind or above its earthly manifestations, is nevertheless real—terribly real. When Christians have to fight their battles, they are not just fighting with this or that person, this magistrate or that temple priest, or that angry mob in the theater; they are not fighting against flesh and blood. Their conflict is not against human beings. It is against the spiritual power that is—how shall we say it?—behind, within, and above human beings. It is this that we have to address. So when John the Seer addresses the churches in Asia, he does not address their members as individuals whom he could name; he addresses the angels of the churches, the spiritual reality, the power—good, bad, or mixed—which is embodied in the congregation, which is more than the personal conduct of each individual. And so throughout the Book of Revelation, there is always a correspondence between the war in heaven and the wars and disasters on earth. The happenings on earth are only understood in terms of the spiritual battle between the victorious Christ who is seated on the throne in the heavenly places, and the spiritual powers that challenge his rule.

Paul's use of words in relation to these unseen realities is extremely flexible. Such words as principalities, powers, dominions, thrones, angels, authorities, and others are used without any apparent attempt to distinguish between their meanings if indeed there is any difference. Just as no one spatial metaphor can describe the relation between these invisible entities and their visible embodiments, so no one word is adequate to denote them. There is, however, one other word which Paul uses in this connection and which helps us to get to the heart of his meaning. It occurs in the passage of Colossians where we are told that Christ in his cross has disarmed the powers (Col. 2:15). This is the word *stoicheion*, used always in the plural, *stoicheia*. It is variously translated in our versions: "rudiments," "elements," "elementary spirits," "ruling spirits of the universe." Its basic meaning is simply expressed in the word "elements." It is very frequently used in contemporary Greek writing for the four elements—air, earth, fire, and water. It is used for the letters of the alphabet. It is used in the Letter to the Hebrews (5:12) for the first principles, the elementary matters of the gospel. It may seem strange that Paul brings this word into close relation with his language about principalities and powers, as he does in two places. In Galatians Paul seems to identify it with the law. He tells his readers that before

Christ came they were like children under the law which was their cus-
todian, but that now in Christ we have been set free from this control
so as to live in the freedom of the Spirit. And to those who want to
creep back again under the protection of the law, by receiving circumcision, he says, "Formerly you were in bondage to beings that by nature are no gods; but now that you have come to know God, or rather
to be known by God, how can you turn back again to the weak and
beggarly *stoicheia,* whose slaves you want to be once more?" (Gal. 4:8-
9). In the Letter to the Colossians his readers are warned against becoming a prey to "philosophy and empty deceit, according to human
traditions, according to the *stoicheia* of the universe and not according
to Christ," and later on they are told that having died to the *stoicheia,*
they should not live as if they belonged to this world, submitting to all
sorts of rules and regulations (Col. 2:8, 20). In both passages it is the
work of Christ which has delivered Christians from the power of the
stoicheia and in the Colossians passage it is stated that this is because
Christ has disarmed the principalities and powers.

What is clear in these as in other passages is that the powers have
been disarmed but not destroyed. They are put under the supreme dominion of Christ by what he has done on the cross, but they still exist.
We have to wrestle with them. And the Church has to make manifest
to them the wisdom of God as revealed in Jesus (Eph. 3:10). Moreover,
in the letter to the Colossians it is explicitly stated that the powers were
created through Christ and for Christ and in him alone they have their
coherence (Col. 1:15-17). So these things, whatever they are, have a
good purpose. They are intended to serve the purpose of God as
manifest in Christ. And yet it is these things, these principalities and
powers, which crucified the Lord of glory. There has been a rebellion
of these powers against their proper sovereign Lord. The rebellion has
been put down. The rebellious powers are not destroyed; they are disarmed. They still have a function to perform in God's ordering of the
universe, but they must now subserve their Lord. They are under his
feet, and in the end they will disappear when (according to 1 Cor. 15:24)
Christ destroys them and hands over the kingdom to his Father.

How do we interpret this language? Simply to ignore it as some
sort of outdated mythology would be a disastrous mistake. It is obviously
an extremely important element in Paul's teaching. Nor are we without
clues to its meaning.

Let us begin with the matter which is at issue in Galatians, namely
the law. Paul has repeatedly affirmed that the law is a good gift of God.

Yet it has become a power that enslaves, from which Christ had to deliver us by his death. It was the representatives of the law who put Jesus on the cross. But Caiaphas and his colleagues were not just a few wicked men. They were acting as the temporary agents and embodiments of something more fundamental and more enduring than their own individual opinions. The Colossians passage speaks of "human traditions" about eating and drinking and the observance of seasons and festivals. The passage in Romans 13 refers to the state authorities. The passages in 1 Corinthians 2 refer simply to "the rulers of this age," which no doubt includes all those elements which had a hand in the decision to destroy Jesus—legal, political, ecclesiastical, and other. If one can summarize all these as referring to the structural elements in human life, one brings them into relation with the language about the *stoicheia*. All human life is lived and has to be lived within limits which are set by certain structural features, both of the natural world and of the world of human society. In the former category belong the fundamental elements of the physical universe (the original meaning of *stoicheia*), the invariances which are the subject of natural science and which make it possible for us to behave rationally in the world. If we could not rely on these invariances, on the fundamental stability of the natural world, we could not live a human life. So also our life in society is structured by law, custom, and tradition. Without these we could not develop into responsible beings. No one lives and no one could live a rational life if there were no given norms (which may be different in different places and times) which govern behavior. Most of the time even the most eccentric human being does from moment to moment what the normal customs and traditions of his or her society indicate. Nor can we function without the help of accepted roles. A person appointed to a public office, or ordained to the Christian ministry, may in course of time develop very fresh and original ways of interpreting his role. But she has to begin by accepting the guidance of the tradition. One cannot begin by a sort of *creatio ex nihilo*, developing a totally original model of behavior unrelated to the expectations of the society which has appointed her to this role. A person who tried to do this simply could not function in her role. So also with our life in larger political units. There has to be some kind of ordered structure of power. Without it, human life would dissolve into anarchy. These structural elements are necessary to guide and protect human life. They serve God's purpose. But, as we well know, they can also become demonic. The God-given authority of the state can be used for tyranny. Roles can become dehumanizing so that even our best efforts at goodness can become—as Jesus said—play-acting, hypocrisy.

I have been speaking of entities which are not just individual human beings, flesh and blood in Pauline language, but which yet exist and have power. I have been speaking of norms, roles, and structures. We have to acknowledge the reality and the power of these things, and we have to ask what the gospel has to do with them. And we have seen that a great deal of New Testament writing is addressed exactly to that question. These things, says Paul, are good creations of God. They have a part to play in his purpose. But they can come to usurp the place to which they have no right, the place which belongs to Christ and to him alone. They can be, as we say, absolutized, and then they become demonic. The power ordained by God of Romans 13 becomes the Beast of Revelation. The Torah, that loving instruction which God gives his people and the beauty of which is celebrated in Psalm 119, becomes a tyrant from which Christ has to deliver us. Tradition, the handing on of good practice from parent to child as it is so beautifully described in Deuteronomy, becomes an evil power which comes between human beings and the living God.

These are examples from the New Testament itself of the ways in which the powers, created in Christ and for Christ, become agents of tyranny. One could give many more examples from outside the New Testament. Number is one of the *stoicheia* which has fascinated thinkers of various schools. Numbering enables us to measure and quantify. It is an element of order in the universe. But it can become a tyrant when, as in modern reductionist thinking, it is absolutized and nothing is valued except what can be measured and quantified.

Chance seems to be a fundamental element in this contingent universe which God has created. In past times it was made into a goddess and named Fortuna. And, though not given a personal name, the same power rules wide swathes of contemporary thought. Chance mutations in the transmission of genes becomes the sovereign power governing the emergence of life. The chance workings of the free market become the "Invisible Hand" of Adam Smith which mysteriously converts private selfishness into public good. This particular example of an invisible power ruling over human affairs is particularly relevant at present, since it is one of the key arguments of the religious Right against the religious Left that one cannot speak of justice or injustice when describing the huge differences between rich and poor in our society. These, on this view, cannot be called unjust because they are not the work of conscious human agency but the result of chance. Thus in our economic life we are no longer responsible to Christ; we are not responsible at all, for economic life has been handed over to the goddess Fortuna. It is not difficult to recognize that as one of the principalities and powers of which Paul speaks.

Race is another element in the structuring of human life. Family, kinship, tribal community—these are all parts of the structure of human life which play a vital part in the nurturing the developing of authentic humanity. It was therefore with good intention that missionaries in South Africa insisted that African Christians should be able to organize their churches and conduct their worship in their own traditional ways and using their own languages. But when this good provision was given an absolute status as part of the order of creation, not subject to Christ, it became the demonic power of *apartheid*. No one who lives in South Africa can doubt its reality and power, and the task of Christians in that country is not to wrestle against flesh and blood, not to attack the God-fearing Afrikaners, but to wrestle against the demonic power which is as real as it is invisible.

Money is perhaps another example of the principalities and powers of our time. As is well known, Marx used the word "fetishism" to speak of the attitude to money which he found in capitalist society. Money, which is a useful means for facilitating exchange, has become a power in itself, so that we do not measure human wealth in terms of real goodness and happiness but in terms of cash. Money has truly become a fetish, a power which demands and receives absolute devotion. In the vision of Marx the proletariat was to be a sort of corporate Messiah which would overthrow the power of this false god and create a society of free and responsible human relationships. Alas, the proletariat is not Christ. The Marxist ideology has itself become a power in the Pauline sense, which controls human behavior and forces those under its power to crush the free expression of the human spirit. The wrestling of men and women like Solzhenitsyn is not against flesh and blood, not against particular human beings, but against the invisible but terribly powerful spiritual force that controls their actions.

The principalities and powers are real. They are invisible and we cannot locate them in space. They do not exist as disembodied entities floating above this world, or lurking within it. They meet us as embodied in visible and tangible realities—people, nations, and institutions. And they are powerful. What is Christ's relation to them? To recapitulate briefly: they are created in Christ and for Christ; their true end is to

207

serve him; some do—for the New Testament speaks of good angels who perform his service; but they become powers for evil when they attempt to usurp the place which belongs to Christ alone. In his death Christ has disarmed them; he has put them under his feet; they must now serve him; and the Church is the agency through which his victory over them is made manifest and is effected as the Church puts on the whole armor of God to meet and master them. The language is pictorial, mythological if you like, because we have no other language. But the things described are real and are contemporary. They are at the heart of our business as Christians. Let me try to spell this out in terms of contemporary Christian duty.

In the cross Christ has disarmed the powers. He has unmasked them. He has not destroyed them, but—in Johannine language—has cast the ruler of this world out of his usurped throne. What I have called the structural elements in the world as we know it, from the basic structure of the physical world to the social and political structures of the nations, to the customs and traditions by which human beings are normally guided, to what the sociologists call the "plausibility structures" by which all human thinking is guided: all of these are part of God's good ordering of his creation. Yet it was these things which at the decisive *denouement,* the moment when they were confronted by the living God in person, by him in whom the fullness of Godhead was present bodily, were found ranged in unanimous and murderous hostility against him. The death of Christ was the unmasking of the powers. Caiaphas and Herod and Pilate were not uniquely wicked men; they were acting out their roles as guardians of the political and moral and religious order. They acted as representatives of what the New Testament calls the world, this present age. When God raised the crucified Jesus, this present age and its structures was exposed, illuminated, unmasked—but not destroyed. Cross and resurrection seen together mean both judgment and grace, both wrath and endless patience. God still upholds the structures; without them the world would collapse and human life would be unthinkable. But the structures lose their pretended absoluteness. Nothing now is absolute except God as he is known in Jesus Christ; everything else is relativized. That is the bottom line for Christian thinking and the starting point for Christian action in the affairs of the world. What does it imply in practice?

Let me begin with some negatives. It does *not* mean anarchy. It does not mean an attack on structures as such. Many people are tempted this way. There are those for whom Christian freedom means a rejection of institutions, traditions, laws, and structures. And they can always show good reasons, for all human traditions, institutions, and structures are prone to evil—including religion and including Christianity and the Church. They are all part of this present age. They are all prone to make absolutist claims. They are all ambiguous. There are always good reasons for attacking them. But human life is impossible without them, and God in his mercy preserves them in order to give time for the Church to fulfill its calling to make manifest to them the wisdom of God. Our relation to the structures has to contain both the judgment that is inevitable in the searing light of the cross, and also the patience which is required of us as witnesses to the resurrection. We are not conservatives who regard the structures as part of the unalterable order of creation, as part of the world of what we call "hard facts" beyond the range of the gospel, and who therefore suppose that the gospel is only relevant to the issues of personal and private life. Nor are we anarchists who seek to destroy the structures. We are rather patient revolutionaries who know that the whole creation, with all its given structures, is groaning in the travail of a new birth, and that we share this groaning and travail, this struggling and wrestling, but do so in hope because we have already received, in the Spirit, the firstfruit of the new world (Rom. 8:19-25).

But, second, as Paul tells us, our wrestling is not against flesh and blood but against the principalities and powers in the invisible world (Eph. 6:12). What are we talking about when we speak of confronting the institutions of state and market economy and culture with the gospel? We are not fighting against the individuals who perform their roles within these institutions. We know well that when we get a chance to talk intimately with them, they feel themselves powerless. To the outsider they appear to wield great power, but they know that they are under the control of forces greater than their own and that their freedom to change things is very narrowly limited. Those who call for a Christian assault on the worlds of politics and economics often make it clear that the attack belongs to the same order of being as the enemy to be attacked. The aim of the attack is to seize the levers of power and take control. We have seen many such successful revolutions, and we know that in most cases what has happened is simply that the oppressor and the oppressed have exchanged roles. The structure is unchanged. The throne is unshaken, only there is a different person occupying it. How is the throne itself to be shaken? How is the power to be disarmed and placed at the service of Christ? Only by the power of the gospel itself, announced in word and embodied in deed. As Walter Wink reminds us, the victory of the Church over the demonic power which was embodied in the Roman imperial system was not won by seizing the levers of power: it was won when the victims knelt down in the Colosseum and prayed in the name of Jesus for the Emperor. The soldiers in Christ's victorious army were not armed with the weapons of this age; they were the martyrs whose robes were washed in blood. It was not that a particular Emperor was discredited and displaced; it was that the entire mystique of the Empire, its spiritual power, was unmasked, disarmed, and rendered powerless. A conversion of individuals which failed to identify, unmask, and reject that spiritual, ideological power would have been as futile as an attempt by Christians to wrest that power from its holders. Evangelism which is politically and ideologically naive, and social action which does not recognize the need for conversion from false gods to the living God, both fall short of what is required.

The principalities and powers are realities. We may not be able to visualize them, to locate them, or to say exactly what they are. But we are foolish if we pretend that they do not exist. Certainly one cannot read the Gospels without recognizing that the ministry of Jesus from beginning to end was a mighty spiritual battle with powers which are not simply human frailties, errors, diseases, or sins. And one cannot read St. Paul, or the other books of the New Testament, without recognizing that this drama of Christ's disarming of the powers is central to their meaning. If we dismiss this as merely outworn mythology, we shall be incapable of grasping the central message of the New Testament. If we try to systematize the diffuse and flexible language of the writers and develop a sort of systematic demonology, we shall also go astray. But if we live in the real world and take the Bible as our clue for understanding and coping with it, we shall certainly know what it means that our wrestling is not against flesh and blood but against the invisible principalities and powers, and we shall learn what it means to put on the whole armor of God for the conflict.

17. The Myth of the Secular Society

The word "myth" has become rather useful to theologians because of its ambiguity. In frequent popular use it is just another word for a falsehood. When it is used in the title of books such as *The Myth of Christ Incarnate,* or *The Myth of Christian Uniqueness,* the authors have a convenient shield to protect them from the charge that they are simply denying the truth of these hallowed beliefs and will claim that they are using the word in a technical sense. In respect of these two works, I have to confess that I find it hard to discover what this technical sense might be, and what (in these works) is the difference between "myth" and "mistake." One of the definitions of myth used in its more technical sense is: "An unproved collective belief that is accepted uncritically to justify a social institution" (*Random House Dictionary,* s.v.). I am proposing to use the word "myth" both in this technical and its popular sense: I am suggesting both that the belief in a secular society is an unproven belief accepted uncritically to justify a social institution, and also that the belief is mistaken.

Put very briefly, the belief is that modern society is on a steady and irreversible course toward increasing secularization, and that this is to be welcomed since it enables us to put the wars of religion behind us and to create a society in which the conflicting truth-claims of the religions do not tear society to pieces. The articulation of this belief is frequently attributed in the first place to Max Weber, who taught that the threefold process of rationalization, industrialization, and bureaucratization was creating a society in which there would necessarily be less and less room for the supernatural, the magical, the transcendent. The modern world, as he saw it, was undergoing a process of disenchantment. There would be no more room for gods or fairies, for providence or for miracles. Rational planning, forecasting, and organizing would create a world in which there was no place for God. While religious people of a conservative temper might regret this, it could nevertheless be welcomed by those who had the wider interests of humanity at heart. Especially in a country like India, long riven by interreligious tensions and struggling to create a single, strong nation, the vision of a genuinely secular society was and is compelling. Such a society, it was believed, would provide free space for the exercise of religion. It would not be in any sense antireligious. It would safeguard the freedom of each person to follow the religion of his or her choice. But it would not allow any particular religious belief to govern national policy or to have a privileged place in education. This has been and is the hope of many devoutly religious people. But beyond this and especially in the so-called developed world, there has been and is a further expectation—namely that the process of secularization would inevitably lead to the gradual disappearance of religious belief, that secularization is an irreversible process, and that the farther any society moves along the road of rationalization, industrialization, and urbanization, the more certain it is that religion will have a receding role in that society.

The first thing to be said about this belief is that it appears to be a myth in the popular sense of that word. It appears to be—quite simply—untrue. In the face of the statistical evidence of the survival and vigor of religion in the most highly secularized societies, sociologists no longer accept the theory which has had so much currency since the time of Weber's writing. Sociologists have accumulated a great mass of statistical material which demonstrates the continuing and often greatly increased vigor of religious belief in that society which has proceeded farthest along the road of rationalization, industrialization, and urbanization—namely the United States. The main facts are well known. The strongly conservative and evangelical elements in the Protestant Churches have undergone a remarkable renaissance, while the churches which have tried to adjust their beliefs and practices to the temper of modernity are in decline. Religious belief has become a serious factor in public politics—something which sociologists even up to twenty years ago regarded as a feature of the past which would not reappear. And, as is well known, new religious movements have appeared in a bewildering number and variety not only in the United States but all over the "developed" world. Moreover, these movements are not mainly among the marginalized and disadvantaged sections of society. It has been well known by sociologists of religion for a long time that peoples on the margins of society who feel that they have no hope in the present world are prone to welcome religious beliefs, often of an apocalyptic kind, which offer hope for a new order and another world. But the new religious movements which are such a prominent feature of the "developed" world are attracting not these disadvantaged people but—on the contrary—the young people of the most affluent sections of society. In a recent collection of essays by leading sociologists, mainly from the United States, there is an almost unanimous confession that the belief which was accepted uncritically up to ten or twenty years ago, namely that the process of modernization would necessarily lead to the decline of religion, was totally mistaken. To quote only one of these writers, Professor Rodney Stark, Professor of Sociology at Washington University, the evidence "leads to the conclusion that secularization will not usher in a post-religious era. Instead, it will repeatedly lead to a resupply of vigorous otherworldly religious organizations by prompting revival" (*The Sacred in a Secular Age,* Berkeley 1985, p. 146).

It would seem to be proved beyond doubt that human beings cannot live in the rarified atmosphere of pure rationality as the post-Enlightenment world has understood rationality. There are needs of the human spirit which simply must be met. It seems that those religious bodies which have tried to accommodate as much as possible of the rationalism of the Enlightenment are those which are in decline, and that those which have maintained a strong emphasis on the supernatural dimension of religion have flourished. Here I am not equating religion with Christianity. There is much in the flourishing of new religions and the revival of old ones which is more pagan than Christian. But this flourishing does seem to prove that what is loosely called "modernity" does not provide enough nourishment for the human spirit. Moreover, quite apart from religion properly so-called, one has to look at the enormous growth of belief in astrology, precisely among the most "developed" societies. This is surely evidence of the fact that the human spirit cannot live permanently with a form of rationality which has no answer to the question "Why?" Even if the whole infinitely complex pattern of events could be completely mapped and all the links uncovered so that one could explain the antecedent cause of everything that happened, one would still be left with the question "Why did this happen to me?" and if there is no belief in a divine providence it seems almost inevitable that one will either deify chance under the name of Fortune, or else fall back on something like astrology.

A large amount of statistical material has been gathered and analyzed by sociologists of religion in the effort to discover what correlation exists, if any, between religious belief and achievement in the natural and human sciences. Two conclusions from these studies are of interest in my present discussion. The first is this. To quote Professor Robert Wuthnow, professor of sociology at Princeton, "virtually all surveys and polls, whether of the general public, college students, church members or clergy, show inverse relations between exposure to higher education and adherence to core religious tenets" (*The Sacred in a Secular Age*, p. 189). In other words, the better educated you are in our modern society, the less time you have for religion. But, and this is the significant point, the surveys show that, to quote Wuthnow again, "it is the irreligious who are selected into academic careers in the first place, not that the process of being socialized into the academic life causes them to become less and less religious" (p. 191). The second finding is this. The correlation between academic life and irreligion is much higher in the social sciences and the humanities than it is among the natural sciences—physics, chemistry, and biology. Atomic physicists are much more likely to believe in God than sociologists. These two facts taken together lead Professor Wuthnow to make an interesting suggestion, based on the work of the sociology of science. Science, like every human activity, is a socially embodied exercise and therefore scientists are under the necessity of demarcating the boundaries of their exercise. The editor of a scientific magazine has to be able to recognize what is science and what is not. This boundary definition is much easier in the case of the natural sciences like physics and chemistry. These sciences have a high degree to clarity and internal consistency. It is more difficult in the case of sciences like sociology, economics, psychology, and even more in the humanities, to say where exactly the boundary is to be drawn. Yet the drawing of the boundary is essential to the corporate sense of identity without which the scientific community cannot flourish. Wuthnow suggests that the two facts which I have referred to can best be explained on the hypothesis that the irreligion of academics is essentially a matter of boundary demarcation. It is clear that it is not the contents of these academic disciplines themselves which cause alienation from religion. The irreligion, insofar as it has been documented, is a factor at the point of entry into the study, not a product of it. And further confirmation of this thesis is obtained, says Wuthnow, from the fact that the enormous expansion of scientific work in the United States since the Second World War has not been accompanied by any decline in religion. In the period of twenty-five years from 1955 expenditure on scientific research in the USA increased by over 1,000 percent, which must mean that a vastly greater number of people were giving their full-time commitment to science; yet in the same period commitment to religion as measured by church membership remained steady. There seem to be good grounds for taking seriously Professor Wuthnow's conclusion. "While the evidence clearly documents the irreligiosity of scientists themselves, it shows that this irreligiosity is far more pronounced among the least scientific disciplines—the social sciences and humanities—than it is among the natural scientists. And closer inspection of the scientific role itself suggests that scientists in these fields may adopt an irreligious stance chiefly as one of the boundary-posturing mechanisms they use to distance themselves from the general public and thereby maintain the precarious reality of the work they do. . . . The proverbial conflict between science and religion may be more a function of the precariousness of science than of the precariousness of religion" (*The Sacred*, p. 199).

If, then, we may see good ground for thinking that the idea of secularization is an irreversible process which must lead to the inevitable marginalization of religion as a myth in the popular sense, namely something which is untrue, we may turn now to the more technical use of the word "myth." There are good grounds for saying that the secularization theory has been accepted uncritically by Christians to justify a social institution. The idea of a secular society has been attractive to Christians because it seemed to hold out the hope of peaceful coexistence between the religions and worldviews. It promised a society in which public affairs were governed by beliefs which are shared by all "enlightened" people, and in which there would be freedom for individuals and voluntary associations of individuals to profess and practice their particular religious or nonreligious beliefs. It promised deliverance from the tyranny of dogma, and peaceful coexistence in an accepted framework of shared rationality. Just because the idea of a secular society has been such a powerful symbol, offering the hope of peace among the warring religions and ideologies, it is necessary to scrutinize it in order to see whether the failure of the secularization theory is due to accidental circumstances or to weakness inherent in the idea itself.

One of the most influential statements of the idea of a secular society was set forth in a book with that title written by the Oxford economist, Denis Munby. He wrote at the beginning of the 1960s, that decade which saw the secular as something to be welcomed and not

shunned by Christians. It was the decade which saw the wide circula-
tion of such books as Harvey Cox's *The Secular City* and Paul van Buren's
The Secular Meaning of the Gospel. It was the decade which celebrated a
misunderstood Bonhoeffer and "Man's Coming of Age." Munby's book
appeared at the beginning of the decade. Its title was a deliberate rebut-
tal of the book of T. S. Eliot written twenty-three years earlier, *The Idea
of a Christian Society*. The background for Eliot's book was the miserable
period of the 1930s when the nations of Europe were drifting helplessly
toward a second world war, when millions were rotting in unemploy-
ment, and when the bright hopes kindled after the first war had been
extinguished. Democratic governments in most of the European countries appeared to be rudderless and helpless, mere victims of economic
forces which were not understood and could not be controlled. Eliot
had seen movements, mostly of young people, taking control of these
drifting hulks, rejecting the ideology of liberal capitalism, and proclaiming a new ideology which would insure that the life of their nations
would not be left to the blind forces of the market but would be directed
to deliberately chosen ends. Eliot was one of a number of Christian
thinkers in several countries who asked: If small determined minorities
can do this in the power of a pagan ideology, is it not possible that a
Christian minority could impart to a whole nation a sense of purpose
directed by the Christian faith?

Munby, on the other hand, was writing at the beginning of the
1960s, that decade which was supremely confident of the power of technology to solve every human problem, the decade which acclaimed the
secular as the truly human. Munby was in tune with his times when he
advised Christians to reject Eliot's vision, to shake off the lingering nos-
talgia for a Christian past and to embrace wholeheartedly the ideal of a
secular society. It was Munby and those who thought like him who captured the ear of many Christians in the decade which followed the publication of his book. Reading it now, one is chiefly aware of its failure
to grasp the real human problem.

The secular society for which Christians should work will, according to Munby, have the following six essential marks:

1. It is uncommitted to any particular view of the universe and
man's place in it.

2. It is therefore a pluralist society, not merely plural in fact but
pluralist in principle.

3. It will therefore be a tolerant society, its tolerance limited only

by the need to resist activities which are directed against the accepted policies of the society.

4. It must, however, have some common aims for which citizens can work together. But it will deflate the pretensions of judges and magistrates to represent anything more august than these agreed aims of society. A secular society will therefore eliminate the relics of the sacred which still hang around the role of the judge.

5. The secular society will solve its problems by eliminating emotion and irrational impulses; it will work by ascertaining the facts of the situation so that society may be organized to enable the citizens to achieve their actual aims. It does not pretend to pass judgment on these aims.

6. Finally, therefore, a secular society will be without official images, ideal types, or models held up for imitation. It will aim, rather, to provide a framework within which people of different allegiances can work together.

Thus, in his own words, Munby outlined the idea of a secular society and advised the Christians of his day to accept it and to reject Eliot's idea of a Christian society. His advice has been widely followed. And yet its illusions and self-contradictions are obvious. Consider each of the six elements in Munby's secular society.

1. It is obvious from Munby's own outline that his secular society *is* committed to a very particular view of society. It is a view which excludes the belief, shared by Islam, Judaism, and Christianity, that all human society, like all creation, is under the sovereign rule of God, and that the word "God" is not a meaningless cipher but refers to one whose purpose for human society has been made known. The secular society is effectively committed to a worldview which excludes this belief. But here at the outset we meet the power of the myth in the technical sense of that word—the power of an uncritically accepted belief to justify a social institution. It is widely believed in our society that to introduce the name of God into the discussion of a public issue, or into an academic study, is to intrude a private opinion into a sphere which is governed by other criteria. These other criteria are not normally brought into the open for scrutiny. The "modern worldview" is simply "how things actually are." Munby himself is plainly a victim of this very familiar illusion. His whole book, *The Idea of a Secular Society*, is itself a comprehensive refutation of his opening statement that the secular

society is not committed to any particular view of the world or man's place in it.

2. The second mark of Munby's secular society is that it is pluralist in principle. It is not necessary to repeat here what I have said earlier about the limits of this pluralism. Clearly Munby, like other advocates of the pluralist society, understands pluralism to apply to the *aims* of people (what are more often now called their "values") but not to the facts. In regard to what are called "facts" the secular society is not pluralist. Its distinctive feature, as I have argued earlier, is its sharp dichotomy between "facts" and "values," its implied belief that "values" or "aims" are purely a matter for personal choice and are not under the control of the world of "facts." This is made clear in Munby's third mark of a secular society, namely that it will draw a strict boundary between public and private morality.

3. This boundary, one of the distinctive features of a secular society, is drawn in order to insure tolerance for a wide variety of private lifestyles. In Munby's secular society tolerance will not be extended to activities which are directed against the accepted policies of society. Thus the secular society, while it does not have an accepted public view of the world and man's place in it, does have accepted policies. Presumably these are the policies approved by the majority, or by whoever is able to gain power. But it would draw a clear boundary separating public and private behavior. Here, plainly, we have one of the key elements in the picture—a concept of the human person which separates morals from public life. This separation is surely impossible in the long term. The way societies behave, and the policies they accept, will be a function of the commitments the members of the society have, the values they cherish, and—ultimately—the beliefs they hold about the world and their place in it.

4. In his fourth point Munby proposes to deflate the pretensions of judges to represent anything more than the agreed aims of society. This is, of course, what Marxists have always insisted on. The courts are "people's courts" where the will of the people is carried out. In this situation language about justice becomes meaningless. If courts exist to carry out the will of society, then it would be quite absurd to complain that a particular judgment was unjust. The claim that a judgment is unjust is—whether or not the claimant is aware of it—an implicit appeal to a tribunal higher than the courts of the state. What Munby wishes to remove, as the last vestiges of sacredness still clinging to the role of judges in our society, are those elements which are the reminder to

judges, if not to plaintiffs, that there *is* such a higher tribunal and that judges will in the end have to plead before it.

5. Munby's fifth point calls for the elimination of "emotion and irrational impulse" so that society may ascertain the facts and act on them. Here we have again the familiar dichotomy of fact and value which has been discussed in previous chapters. The concept of facts as simply raw data presented to us apart from any conceptual framework within which they are understood, is—as we have seen—one of the characteristic illusions of a secular culture. All facts are interpreted facts and the interpretation depends upon a whole range of social and personal factors rooted in the tradition of the society in question. The decision as to what are the significant facts in relation to a given problem is one which, plainly, cannot be decided on the basis of "facts" which are prior to any decision about importance. And the decision about importance will be related to the world of beliefs, aims, purposes, values—all that world which Munby would dismiss as emotion and irrationality. But the secular society, as acclaimed by Munby, will simply establish the facts so that individual citizens may achieve their aims; it will not pass judgment on these aims. But can a human society thus divest itself of all responsibility to distinguish between good and bad, right and wrong? If society—and here presumably we must be talking about the institutional structures of society such as the state, business, universities, and professional associations—if society is not to pass judgment on the aim of citizens, this must also mean that citizens have no right to pass judgment on the performance of these institutions of society. We are driven inevitably to the tyranny of institutions: the state is no longer a moral subject which can be held responsible for doing right or wrong. There is a final divorce between politics and ethics.

6. One could say that everything in Munby's picture of the secular society comes to a point in the statement that a secular society is without official images or models held up for emulation. If that is so, then there has never been a secular society and there never can be. For, as Calvin said, the mind of man is an image-factory. No society exists without models held up for emulation. In contemporary Western society it is very easy to identify these models. They are presented hour after hour on the television screens in almost every home in the land. They are the images of the good life as our society conceives it, and the presentation is fueled by the most powerful commercial interests in society.

In twenty-five years since Munby wrote his book, we have learned something about the secular society. We have learned, I think, that what has come into being is not a secular society but a pagan society, not a society devoid of public images but a society which worships gods which are not God. But the myth of the secular society remains powerful. Let me remind you again of the definition of myth which I quoted at the outset: "an unproved collective belief that is accepted uncritically to justify a social institution." The idea of the secular society has been accepted by many Christians uncritically because it seemed to offer the Church the possibility of a peaceful coexistence with false gods, a comfortable concordat between Yahweh and the Baalim. But the promise is illusory. It is not surprising that there are violent countermovements which threaten to destroy the good with the bad, to throw away the gains of the Enlightenment along with its illusions. It is not surprising that the age which called itself secular has produced an unprecedented crop of new religions. The secular society is a myth, and it has the power of a myth to blind people to realities. A powerful myth, such as this, has in it the power about which I was speaking in the chapter on "principalities and powers." Christian affirmation in this context requires the unmasking of the powers. It calls for a new kind of enlightenment, namely the opening up of the underlying assumptions of a secular society, the asking of the unasked questions, the probing of unrecognized presuppositions.

Christian affirmation in this context cannot mean simply the affirmation of a way of personal salvation for the individual. It must mean this, and no less than this. To call men and women into discipleship of Jesus Christ is and must always be central in the life of the Church. But we must be clear about what discipleship will mean. It cannot mean that one accepts the lordship of Christ as governing personal and domestic life, and the life of the Church, while another sovereignty is acknowledged for the public life of society. It cannot mean that the Church is seen as a voluntary society of individuals who have decided to follow Jesus in their personal lives, a society which does not challenge the assumptions which govern the worlds of politics, economics, education, and culture. The model for all Christian discipleship is given once and for all in the ministry of Jesus. His ministry entailed the calling of individual men and women to personal and costly discipleship, but at the same time it challenged the principalities and powers, the ruler of this world, and the cross was the price paid for that challenge. Christian discipleship today cannot mean less than that. I do not think that any of us yet knows what this will involve. We have accepted for too long the position of a voluntary society among other such societies, conceived as alternative options within a religiously and ideologically neutral society. It was the rise of the totalitarian ideologies of the 1930s which prompted T. S. Eliot and others to ask about the possibility of a society which would not be neutral but would be a Christian society. That question has not been seriously followed up. We have settled for what seemed the easier option—a secular society within which Christianity would be a permitted option. We have tended to suppose that the kind of open democratic societies which have grown out of the European experience in the past five hundred years can be reproduced and can continue without the rooting in the Christian worldview within which they developed. Contemporary political events do not encourage that optimism.

The Church is an entity which has outlasted many states, nations, and empires, and it will outlast those that exist today. The Church is nothing other than that movement launched into the public life of the world by its sovereign Lord to continue that which he came to do until it is finished in his return in glory. It has his promise that the gates of hell shall not prevail against it. In spite of the crimes, blunders, compromises, and errors by which its story has been stained and is stained to this day, the Church is the great reality in comparison with which nations and empires and civilizations are passing phenomena. The Church can never settle down to being a voluntary society concerned merely with private and domestic affairs. It is bound to challenge in the name of the one Lord all the powers, ideologies, myths, assumptions, and worldviews which do not acknowledge him as Lord. If that involves conflict, trouble, and rejection, then we have the example of Jesus before us and his reminder that a servant is not greater than his master.

18. The Congregation as Hermeneutic of the Gospel

If the preceding chapters have succeeded in their purpose, the reader will be ready to acknowledge that the gospel cannot be accommodated as one element in a society which has pluralism as its reigning ideology. The Church cannot accept as its role simply the winning of individuals to a kind of Christian discipleship which concerns only the private and domestic aspects of life. To be faithful to a message which concerns the kingdom of God, his rule over all things and all peoples, the Church has to claim the high ground of public truth. Every human society is governed by assumptions, normally taken for granted without question, about what is real, what is important, what is worth aiming for. There is no such thing as an ideological vacuum. Public truth, as it is taught in schools and universities, as it is assumed in the public debate about political and economic goals, is either in comformity with the truth as it is given in Jesus Christ, or it is not. Where it is not, the Church is bound to challenge it. When we speak of a time when public truth as it was understood and accepted in Europe was shaped by Christianity, we do not—of course—mean that every person's behavior was in accordance with Christ's teaching. In that sense there has never been and there can never be a Christian society. But Europe was a Christian society in the sense that its public truth was shaped by the biblical story with its center in the incarnation of the Word in Jesus.

What can it mean in practice to "claim the high ground" for Christianity? Certainly it cannot mean going back to the past. The claim that I am making has often been and is now confused and corrupted by being represented as a conservative move, a move to restore the past. That is impossible and undesirable. We are—as always—in a new situation. The Church of the first three centuries was essentially a martyr church, bearing witness against the public doctrine of the time. It could have accepted, but did not accept, the protection offered by Roman law to the private exercise of religion as a way of personal salvation. Though a small minority, it challenged the public doctrine of the time as false— and paid the price. When the old classical worldview lost its confidence and disintegrated, it was perhaps inevitable that the ruling power should turn to the Church as the integrating power for a new social order. That had enormous consequences for good over the succeeding millennium. It created the Christian civilization of Europe. But it also led the Church into the fatal temptation to use the secular power to enforce conformity to Christian teaching. It is easy to condemn this with hindsight, but one has to ask: How can any society hold together against the forces of disruption without some commonly accepted beliefs about the truth, and— therefore—without some sanctions against deviations which threaten to destroy society? These are agonizingly difficult questions and there are no simple answers valid for all circumstances. What is clear, however, is that the cohesion of European Christendom was shattered by internal dispute erupting into bloody warfare, and that in the seventeenth and eighteenth centuries Europe turned to another vision of public truth, a vision inspired by the achievements of the new science and eventually embodied in the idea of a secular state. No one, surely, can fail to acknowledge with gratitude the achievements of this period of human history. But no one can be blind to the evidence that the liberal, secular democratic state is in grave trouble. The attacks on it from powerful new religious fanaticisms are possible only because its own internal weaknesses have become so clear: the disintegration of family life, the growth of mindless violence, the vandalism which finds satisfaction in destroying whatever is comely and useful, the growing destruction of the environment by limitless consumption fueled by ceaseless propaganda, the threat of nuclear war, and—as the deepest root of it all—the loss of any sense of a meaningful future. Weakened from within, secular democratic societies are at a loss to respond to religious fanaticism without denying their own principles. What could it mean for the Church to make once again the claim which it made in its earliest centuries, the claim to provide the public truth by which society can be given coherence and direction?

Certainly it cannot mean a return to the use of coercion to impose belief. That is, in any case, impossible. Assent to the claim of Christ has to be given in freedom. But it is never given in a vacuum. The one to whom the call of Jesus comes already lives in a world full of assumptions about what is true. How is this world of assumptions formed? Obviously through all the means of education and communication existing in society. Who controls these means? The question of power is inescapable. Whatever their pretensions, schools teach children to believe something and not something else. There is no "secular" neutrality. Christians cannot evade the responsibility which a democratic society gives to every citizen to seek access to the levers of power. But the issue has never confronted the Church in this way before; we are in a radically new situation and cannot dream either of a Constantinian authority or of a pre-Constantinian innocence.

What is to be done? How is it possible that the one who was nailed helpless to a cross should be seen by society as the ultimate source of power? Here is the piercing paradox at the heart of any attempt to talk about "claiming the high ground." No text of the Old Testament is more frequently quoted in the New than the terrible words of Yahweh to Isaiah: "Go and say to this people: 'Hear and hear but do not understand; see and see but do not perceive.' Make the heart of this people fat and their ears heavy and shut their eyes, lest they see with their eyes and hear with their ears and understand with their hearts, and turn and be healed" (Isa. 6:9-10). It is quoted in all the Gospels, in Acts, by St. Paul. Yet Paul is tireless in his effort to bring the gospel to the Gentiles, and is confident that God's purpose cannot fail. He is sure that in the end the fullness of the Gentiles will come in and all Israel will be saved (Rom. 11:25-26). How do we reconcile these elements in the New Testament teaching? It is only when we hold them both together that we begin to grasp the "impossible possibility" of salvation. This ought to deliver us from being impressed by the various proposals which are frequently made to the effect that if we will adopt the proper techniques for evangelism, we can be assured of success. It ought to inoculate us against the Pelagianism which tends to infect missionary thinking, the Pelagianism which supposes that the conversion of the world will be our achievement. It ought to direct our minds away from our programs to the awesome reality of God whose sovereignty is manifest in what the world calls failure, and whose "folly" is wiser than the wisdom of the world (1 Cor. 1:25). It ought to help us to understand why, at the end of his long discussion of these matters, St. Paul can only exclaim: "O the depth of the riches and wisdom and knowledge of God. How unsearchable are his judgments and how inscrutable his ways!" (Rom. 11:33). The conversion of the nations is, and can only be, the supernatural work of God. What, then, is our role?

In a necessary reaction against the idea of a Church which acts as God's viceroy on earth, a triumphalist Church, we have in recent years emphasized the servant role of the Church. We are here rightly seeking to follow the example of Jesus, who defined his role as that of servant (for example, Mark 10:45). But this servant role can be misunderstood. Jesus did not allow himself to be simply at the disposal of others. The temptations at the outset of his ministry were temptations to do what people wanted the Messiah to do. While he responded instantly to the touch of human need, he yet retained the sovereignty in his own hands. He chose the times, place, and manner of his acts. Even at the end he was in control. "No one," he said, "takes my life from me; I lay it down of my own accord" (John 10:18). The most sustained discussion of this issue is given in the Johannine account of the feeding of the multitude and its sequel (John 6).

The story begins with an act of pure compassion. A great crowd has gathered around Jesus, not because they believe his teaching but because they have seen his healing (vv. 1-2). They are hungry. Jesus sees that they are hungry and—without any request from the crowd—he provides enough and more than enough to satisfy them (vv. 3-13). The result is a surge of popular enthusiasm to make Jesus their leader. A real "people's movement" is about to be born (v. 14)! The response of Jesus is to distance himself completely from this movement. He will have nothing to do with it (v. 15). The disciples, perplexed, set off for home. The crowds are determined to find him, and eventually succeed (vv. 16-25). Jesus tells them the real reason for their pursuit. They have been fed, but now they are hungry again. They should seek the food that gives not temporary but enduring life. When they (naturally) ask what work they must do to get this eminently desirable food, they are told that what is required is not a work, but faith. They are to believe the one whom God has sent (vv. 26-29). After further perplexed questioning the crowd is finally told that the food in question is Jesus himself (vv. 30-40). In response to the "murmuring" (which forms the background to the story of the giving of manna in the desert) Jesus quietly replies that no one can come to him unless the Father draws him (vv. 41-44). In the ensuing debate the lines harden and the hearers refuse to hear more. Even many of Jesus' disciples leave him. Jesus is left

225

with "the twelve" and warns them that even in this group of his closest friends there is treachery (vv. 45-71).

If we take this as a picture of what is involved in the offering of the gospel to the world, we have something very different from the picture of a successful exercise in public relations. Jesus is both totally compassionate and yet totally uncompromising about what is involved in coming to the fullness of life. There can be no compromise with false ideas about what it is that makes for fullness of life. To give bread to the hungry is an action of divine compassion and as such a sign of that which alone can satisfy the infinite desires and needs of the human spirit. If the sign is confused with that which it signifies, the gift of life is forfeited. In serving human need, Jesus remains master. The servant who washes the feet of his disciples is their master and lord, and it is in serving that he exercises his lordship (John 13:13-14).

What does this say about the way in which the Church is authorized to represent the kingdom of God in the life of society? It excludes, certainly, the idea that it will be by exercising the kind of power which "the rulers of the Gentiles" exercise (Luke 22:25-26). But it excludes also the idea that the Church simply "responds to the aspirations of the people." And it excludes ideas which have been too prevalent in "evangelical" circles, ideas which portray the Church in the style of a commercial firm using modern techniques of promotion to attract members. How is it possible for the Church truly to represent the reign of God in the world in the way Jesus did? How can there be this combination of tender compassion and awesome sovereignty? How can any human society be both the servant of all people in all their needs, and yet at the same time responsible only to God in his awesome and holy sovereignty? How can the Church be fully open to the needs of the world and yet have its eyes fixed always on God? I think there is only one way.

One of the very few missionary leaders of this century who recognized at an early date that the greatest contemporary challenge to the missionary movement is presented by "modern" Western society was J. H. Oldham. No one did more to shape the ecumenical movement in its early days and to direct the attention of the churches to the need to challenge the assumptions of contemporary society. It was said of him by close colleagues that, when he spoke of "the Church," "it was never quite clear whether he was talking about the ordinary, parson-led congregation, or about something more exciting but less visible" (letter to the author from J. Eric Fenn, January 1937). Oldham did not expect very much from the "ordinary, parson-led congregation," and one can scarcely blame him. Much of the vitality which was imparted to the early organs of ecumenical action was due to the fact that professional ecclesiastics were balanced by a goodly sprinkling of highly competent laypersons from business, government, and the professions. And yet I confess that I have come to feel that the primary reality of which we have to take account in seeking for a Christian impact on public life is the Christian congregation. How is it possible that the gospel should be credible, that people should come to believe that the power which has the last word in human affairs is represented by a man hanging on a cross? I am suggesting that the only answer, the only hermeneutic of the gospel, is a congregation of men and women who believe it and live by it. I am, of course, not denying the importance of the many activities by which we seek to challenge public life with the gospel—evangelistic campaigns, distribution of Bibles and Christian literature, conferences, and even books such as this one. But I am saying that these are all secondary, and that they have power to accomplish their purpose only as they are rooted in and lead back to a believing community.

Jesus, as I said earlier, did not write a book but formed a community. This community has at its heart the remembering and rehearsing of his words and deeds, and the sacraments given by him through which it is enabled both to engraft new members into its life and to renew this life again and again through sharing in his risen life through the body broken and the lifeblood poured out. It exists in him and for him. He is the center of its life. Its character is given to it, when it is true to its nature, not by the characters of its members but by his character. Insofar as it is true to its calling, it becomes the place where men and women and children find that the gospel gives them the framework of understanding, the "lenses" through which they are able to understand and cope with the world. Insofar as it is true to its calling, this community will have, I think, the following six characteristics:

1. It will be a community of praise. That is, perhaps, its most distinctive character. Praise is an activity which is almost totally absent from "modern" society. Here two distinct points can be made.

a. The dominant notes in the development of the specifically "modern" view of things has been (as we have noted earlier) the note of scepticism, of doubt. The "hermeneutic of suspicion" is only the most recent manifestation of the belief that one could be saved from error by the systematic exercise of doubt. It has followed that when any person, institution, or tradition has been held up as an object worthy of reverence, it has immediately attracted the attention of those who undertook to demonstrate that there was another side to the picture, that the golden image has feet of clay. I suppose that this is one manifestation of that "disenchantment" which Weber regarded as a key element in the development of "modern" society. Reverence, the attitude which looks up in admiration and love to one who is greater and better than oneself, is generally regarded as something unworthy of those who have "come of age" and who claim that equality is essential to human dignity. With such presuppositions, of course, the very idea of God is ruled out. The Christian congregation, by contrast, is a place where people find their true freedom, their true dignity, and their true equality in reverence to One who is worthy of all the praise that we can offer.

b. Then, too, the Church's praise includes thanksgiving. The Christian congregation meets as a community that acknowledges that it lives by the amazing grace of a boundless kindness. Contemporary society speaks much about "human rights." It is uncomfortable with "charity" as something which falls short of "justice," and connects the giving of thanks with an unacceptable subservience. In Christian worship the language of rights is out of place except when it serves to remind us of the rights of others. For ourselves we confess that we cannot speak of rights, for we have been given everything and forgiven everything and promised everything, so that (as Luther said) we lack nothing except faith to believe it. In Christian worship we acknowledge that if we had received justice instead of charity we would be on our way to perdition. A Christian congregation is thus a body of people with gratitude to spare, a gratitude that can spill over into care for the neighbor. And it is of the essence of the matter that this concern for the neighbor is the overflow of a great gift of grace and not, primarily, the expression of commitment to a moral crusade. There is a big difference between these two.

2. Second, it will be a community of truth. This may seem an obvious point, but it needs to be stressed. As I have tried to show in these chapters, it is essential to recognize that all human thinking takes place within a "plausibility structure" which determines what beliefs are reasonable and what are not. The reigning plausibility structure can only be effectively challenged by people who are fully integrated inhabitants of another. Every person living in a "modern" society is subject to an almost continuous bombardment of ideas, images, slogans, and stories which presuppose a plausibility structure radically different from that which is controlled by the Christian understanding of human nature

and destiny. The power of contemporary media to shape thought and imagination is very great. Even the most alert critical powers are easily overwhelmed. A Christian congregation is a community in which, through the constant remembering and rehearsing of the true story of human nature and destiny, an attitude of healthy scepticism can be sustained, a scepticism which enables one to take part in the life of society without being bemused and deluded by its own beliefs about itself. And, if the congregation is to function effectively as a community of truth, its manner of speaking the truth must not be aligned to the techniques of modern propaganda, but must have the modesty, the sobriety, and the realism which are proper to a disciple of Jesus.

3. Third, it will be a community that does not live for itself but is deeply involved in the concerns of its neighborhood. It will be the church for the specific place where it lives, not the church for those who wish to be members of it—or, rather, it will be for them insofar as they are willing to be *for* the wider community. It is, I think, very significant that in the consistent usage of the New Testament, the word *ekklēsia* is qualified in only two ways; it is "the Church of God," or "of Christ," and it is the church of a place. A Christian congregation is defined by this twofold relation: it is God's embassy in a specific place. Either of these vital relationships may be neglected. The congregation may be so identified with the place that it ceases to be the vehicle of God's judgment and mercy for that place and becomes simply the focus of the self-image of the people of that place. Or it may be so concerned about the relation of its members to God that it turns its back on the neighborhood and is perceived as irrelevant to its concerns. With the development of powerful denominational structures, nationwide agencies for evangelism or social action, it can happen that these things are no longer seen as the direct responsibility of the local congregation except insofar as they are called upon to support them financially. But if the local congregation is not perceived in its own neighborhood as the place from which good news overflows in good action, the programs for social and political action launched by the national agencies are apt to lose their integral relation to the good news and come to be seen as part of a moral crusade rather than part of the gospel. The local congregation is the place where the proper relation is most easily and naturally kept.

4. Fourth, it will be a community where men and women are prepared for and sustained in the exercise of the priesthood in the world. The Church is described in the New Testament as a royal priesthood, called to "offer spiritual sacrifices acceptable to God" and to "declare

229

the wonderful deeds of him who called you out of darkness into his marvellous light" (1 Pet. 2:5, 9). The office of a priest is to stand before God on behalf of people and to stand before people on behalf of God. Jesus is himself the one High Priest who alone can fulfill and has fulfilled this office. The Church is sent into the world to continue that which he came to do, in the power of the same Spirit, reconciling people to God (John 20:19-23). This priesthood has to be exercised in the life of the world. It is in the ordinary secular business of the world that the sacrifices of love and obedience are to be offered to God. It is in the context of secular affairs that the mighty power released into the world through the work of Christ is to be manifested. The Church gathers every Sunday, the day of resurrection and of Pentecost, to renew its participation in Christ's priesthood. But the exercise of this priesthood is not within the walls of the Church but in the daily business of the world. It is only in this way that the public life of the world, its accepted habits and assumptions, can be challenged by the gospel and brought under the searching light of the truth as it has been revealed in Jesus. It may indeed be the duty of the Church through its appointed representatives—bishops and synods and assemblies—to speak a word from time to time to the nation and the world. But such pronouncements carry weight only when they are validated by the way in which Christians are actually behaving and using their influence in public life. It is, of course, also true that individual Christians will be weakened in their efforts to live out the gospel in secular engagements if what they are doing does not have the support of the Church as a whole. There is a reciprocal relationship between official pronouncements and individual commitment. It has to be said, I think, that in recent years there has been a widely perceived disjunction between official pronouncements and individual commitment, and it is important to stress the fact that the former without the latter are ineffective.

Two implications of this need to be stated:

a. The congregation has to be a place where its members are trained, supported, and nourished in the exercise of their parts of the priestly ministry in the world. The preaching and teaching of the local church has to be such that it enables members to think out the problems that face them in their secular work in the light of their Christian faith. This is very difficult. It is divisive. One pastor, trained in the kind of theology which is traditional, is not equipped to fulfill this function. There is need for "frontier-groups," groups of Christians working in the same sectors of public life, meeting to thrash out the controversial issues of their business or profession in the light of their faith. But there is also need to consider how far the present traditions of ministerial training really prepare ministers for this task. The report of the Archbishop's Committee on Urban Priority Areas contained devastating comments on the inappropriateness of current ministerial training as perceived by those working in these areas (*Faith in the City* 6:56, p. 119). I realize how extremely difficult it is to find the way forward in this matter, but it seems clear that ministerial training as currently conceived is still far too much training for the pastoral care of the existing congregation, and far too little oriented toward the missionary calling to claim the whole of public life for Christ and his kingdom.

b. A second implication is this: a Christian congregation must recognize that God gives different gifts to different members of the body, and calls them to different kinds of service. St. Paul's letters contain many eloquent expositions of this fact. Yet there is a persistent tendency to deny this and to look for a uniform style of Christian discipleship. People look for a church which is all geared to explicit evangelism, or to radical social action; a church where all speak in tongues and dance in the aisles, or a church where all is decorous and staid. This is, of course, exactly the danger against which Paul warns in the long description of the body in 1 Corinthians 12. The ear should not demand that the whole body be ears, nor the eye that all should be eyes. A bagful of eyes is not a body. Only when a congregation can accept and rejoice in the diversity of gifts, and when members can rejoice in gifts which others have been given, can the whole body function as Christ's royal priesthood in the world.

5. Fifth, it will be a community of mutual responsibility. If the Church is to be effective in advocating and achieving a new social order in the nation, it must itself be a new social order. The deepest root of the contemporary malaise of Western culture is an individualism which denies the fundamental reality of our human nature as given by God — namely that we grow into true humanity only in relationships of faithfulness and responsibility toward one another. The local congregation is called to be, and by the grace of God often is, such a community of mutual responsibility. When it is such, it stands in the wider community of the neighborhood and the nation not primarily as the promoter of programs for social change (although it will be that) but primarily as itself the foretaste of a different social order. Its members will be advocates for human liberation by being themselves liberated. Its actions for justice and peace will be, and will be seen to be, the overflow of a life

231

in Christ, where God's justice and God's peace are already an experienced treasure.

6. And finally it will be a community of hope. As I have already said, I think that one of the most striking features of contemporary Western culture is the virtual disappearance of hope. The nineteenth-century belief in progress no longer sustains us. There is widespread pessimism about the future of "Western" civilization. Many Christian writers speak of our culture in accents of embarrassment, guilt, and shame. In his study of contemporary Western society, the Chinese Christian writer Carver T. Yu finds as its two key elements "technological optimism and literary pessimism" (*Being and Relation: A Theological Critique of Western Dualism and Individualism*, p. 1). Technology continues to forge ahead with more and more brilliant achievements; but the novels, the drama, and the general literature of the West are full of nihilism and despair. It is not surprising that many Western people are drawn toward Eastern types of spirituality in which the struggle to achieve the purpose of a personal creator is replaced by the timeless peace of pantheistic mysticism. As I have tried to suggest in an earlier chapter, the gospel offers an understanding of the human situation which makes it possible to be filled with a hope which is both eager and patient even in the most hopeless situations. I must repeat again that it is only as we are truly "indwelling" the gospel story, only as we are so deeply involved in the life of the community which is shaped by this story that it becomes our real "plausibility structure," that we are able steadily and confidently to live in this attitude of eager hope. Almost everything in the "plausibility structure" which is the habitation of our society seems to contradict this Christian hope. Everything suggests that it is absurd to believe that the true authority over all things is represented in a crucified man. No amount of brilliant argument can make it sound reasonable to the inhabitants of the reigning plausibility structure. That is why I am suggesting that the only possible hermeneutic of the gospel is a congregation which believes it.

If the gospel is to challenge the public life of our society, if Christians are to occupy the "high ground" which they vacated in the noontime of "modernity," it will not be by forming a Christian political party, or by aggressive propaganda campaigns. Once again it has to be said that there can be no going back to the "Constantinian" era. It will only be by movements that begin with the local congregation in which the reality of the new creation is present, known, and experienced, and from which men and women will go into every sector of public life to claim it for Christ, to unmask the illusions which have remained hidden and to expose all areas of public life to the illumination of the gospel. But that will only happen as and when local congregations renounce an introverted concern for their own life, and recognize that they exist for the sake of those who are not members, as sign, instrument, and foretaste of God's redeeming grace for the whole life of society.

19. *Ministerial Leadership for a Missionary Congregation*

If I am right in believing, as I do, that the only effective hermeneutic of the gospel is the life of the congregation which believes it, one has to ask about how such congregations may be helped to become what they are called to be. I referred in the last chapter to the contrast, which I suppose everyone has made at some time or another, between the "ordinary parson-led congregation" and "something more exciting but less visible." The idea of an invisible Church is, of course, always attractive for the simple reason that one chooses in the privacy of one's own mind who are the members and who are not. By contrast, the Church in the New Testament is represented by visible communities of men and women located in places which can be visited and to which letters can be written. This is not to deny the very important point, which was the subject of Chapter 16, that there is a spiritual reality "in the heavenly places" which is not visible to the eye of flesh but which is the reality which has visible embodiment in these congregations; that there are "angels" of the churches, spiritual realities which are more than simply the sum of the individual members; and that the "angels" can be accused of behavior which is not in accordance with the will of God (for example, Rev. 3:15ff.). But the "angels" do not have any impact on events except as they are represented by visible congregations which have a specific location—whether in the primary geographical sense, or in the sense of location within one of the sectors of public life in a complex and multisectional modern society. I have already said that I believe that the major impact of such congregations on the life of society as a whole is through the daily work of the members in their secular vocations and not through the official pronouncements of ecclesiastical bodies. But the developing, nourishing, and sustaining of Christian faith and practice is impossible apart from the life of a believing congregation. It is therefore important for my thesis to consider, however briefly, the question of the leadership of such congregations.

In some Christian circles it is unfashionable to talk much about the ordained ministry, because of the fear of being guilty of elitism, one of contemporary society's catalogue of unforgivable sins. Without going into an elaborate discussion of this fear, I will make two simple points. First, I hope I have made clear my belief that it is the whole Church which is called to be—in Christ—a royal priesthood, that every member of the body is called to the exercise of this priesthood, and that this priesthood is to be exercised in the daily life and work of Christians in the secular business of the world. But this will not happen unless there is a ministerial priesthood which serves, nourishes, sustains, and guides this priestly work. The priestly people needs a ministering priesthood to sustain and nourish it. Men and women are not ordained to this ministerial priesthood in order to take priesthood away from the people but in order to nourish and sustain the priesthood of the people. Just as we observe one day of the week as "the Lord's Day," not in order that the other six days may be left to the devil but in order that they may all belong to the Lord; so we set apart a man or woman to a ministerial priesthood not in order to take away the priesthood of the whole body but to enable it. To be chosen ("elite") for this ministry becomes an occasion for sin only if this fundamental fact is forgotten. And, second, one can put the same point from the other side. The full participation of the members of a body in its activity does not happen without leadership. The business of leadership is precisely to enable, encourage, and sustain the activity of all the members. To set "participation" and "leadership" against each other is absurd. Clericalism and anticlericalism are simply two sides of one mistake.

What kind of ministerial leadership will nourish the Church in its faithfulness to the gospel in a pluralist society? It is frequently said that the Church in Britain is now in a missionary situation. It is not clear that the full meaning of this has been understood. We have lived for so many centuries in the "Christendom" situation that ministerial training is almost entirely conceived in terms of the pastoral care of existing congregations. In a situation of declining numbers, the policy has been to abandon areas (such as the inner cities) where active Christians are few and to concentrate ministerial resources by merging congregations and deploying ministers in the places where there are enough Christians to support them. Needless to say, this simply accelerates the decline. It is the opposite of a missionary strategy, which would proceed in the opposite direction—deploying ministers in the areas where the Christian presence is weakest. The large-scale abandonment of the inner cities by the "mainline" churches is the most obvious evidence of the policy that has been pursued.

If the gospel is the good news of the reign of God over the whole of life, public no less than private; if the Church is therefore called to address the whole public life of the community as well as the personal lives of men and women in the private and domestic affairs, what kind of ministerial leadership is needed? I suppose that the problem is (in some respects) simpler in a small village community than in a city. In the traditional way of life in a small English village it was the case, and sometimes still is the case, that the "Parson" was seen as a leadership figure for the whole community—for regular churchgoers and for those who hardly ever look inside the church door. In a modern city the situation is different. Society is fragmented. People are "plugged into" a variety of networks. Moreover, the presence of television has the effect of atomizing society; people spend most of their leisure hours glued to the TV screen as separate individuals gripped (if only for a time) by the message that is being beamed into the living room. The local community of neighbors becomes a much less powerful element in people's lives. It is much more difficult for the church and the minister to relate to the whole community. The minister is tempted to "look after" those individuals and families who attend church, and they—in turn—expect him to spend his time doing so. The vision of the church as a body which exists for the neighborhood and not just for its members, as the sign of God's rule over all, is much harder to sustain. Some years ago a survey was conducted in the South Indian city of Bangalore to find out something of the attitudes of clergy and people to the role of the Church and the clergy. Among the results of the survey was the discovery that while a majority of the lay members thought the clergy were far too much involved in business outside their congregations, a majority of the clergy thought they were not enough involved. This failure of communication and consequent divergence between the clerical and the lay view of the role of the minister is certainly not unique to Bangalore. Is it the primary business of the ordained minister to look after the spiritual needs of the church members? Is it to represent God's kingdom to the whole community? Or—and this is surely the true answer—is it to lead the whole congregation as God's embassage to the whole community?

The Bible shows us two images of the city. There is the theme of the wicked city, the point of concentration for all that opposes God's purpose, from Babylon through all the great imperialisms to Rome as the seat of the great harlot. And there is the other image of the city as the place of God's dwelling, Zion the place where he has made his sanctuary and the type of the holy city which will come down from heaven as a bride adorned for her husband. In regard to the wicked city, there are at least two different strands of teaching as well. By far the most powerful in Christian history has been that strand which emphasizes the need to flee from the wicked city in order to escape the destruction which will come upon it. The picture of Lot and his wife fleeing from Sodom has been an immensely powerful one in shaping Christian imagination. In the English-speaking world it has been reinforced by the vivid imagery of Bunyan's *Pilgrim's Progress*. "Come out from among them and be separate from them, says the Lord" (2 Cor. 6:16) has been an immensely powerful text in Christian history. It suggests a model of ministry in the city which has as its central thrust the effort to draw individuals out of the wicked city and bring them one by one into the ark of salvation.

But there is another image in the Bible, one that has had less impact on the Christian imagination. Its classic representation in the Old Testament is the story of Jonah, that improbable missionary who tries to run away from the wicked city but is stopped in his tracks by the Lord and ordered to go into the city to call it to repentance. The call meets with a fantastic response, but Jonah is left at the end in a thoroughly ambivalent position, not quite inside the city and not quite far from it, but sitting on its edge waiting to see what will happen, caring more about himself than about the fate of the city. Is this where the Church can stay—half in and half out, more concerned about itself than about the city? The end of the book of Jonah leaves us in no doubt. Jonah may not care, but God cares deeply—even for the dumb animals in their stalls.

Neither Lot fleeing from Sodom nor Jonah sitting under his gourd in the outer suburbs of Nineveh can provide us with the definitive image of the Church's relation to the city. That is given to us in the picture of Jesus riding into Jerusalem at the feast of the Passover. Jesus loved Jerusalem. He had wept over it. But Jerusalem had rejected him. He could have turned his back on it and led his disciples away into the desert and there—like the Essenes of his time—devoted their corporate life to praying and waiting for God to bring in his kingdom. Or he could have put himself at the head of the Zealots, taken up the sword, and made himself master of the city. What he did was neither of these things. He chose for his moment the festival of Passover, the moment of maximum national feeling, the moment when thoughts of a mighty deliverance for Israel were in all hearts. He chose for his mount not a warhorse or a chariot, but a mount that would call to mind the ancient prophecy of a king who would come in lowliness to claim his kingdom. By what he did he challenged the public life of the city and the nation. He claimed rightful kingship. He challenged all the powers that usurped God's rule over public life. He came as a king claiming the throne that was his by right. And he accepted, with open eyes, the cost of the claim. The throne would be a cross. But it was, and is, the throne. The death of Jesus was the place where "the ruler of this world" was cast out of his usurped throne (John 12:31). It was the place where the principalities and powers were disarmed (Col. 2:15).

This, surely, is the image that must control our thinking about the relation of the Church to the city, of the Church to the world. And it will therefore control the way ministry is conceived. The task of ministry is to lead the congregation as a whole in a mission to the community as a whole, to claim its whole public life, as well as the personal lives of all its people, for God's rule. It means equipping all the members of the congregation to understand and fulfill their several roles in this mission through their faithfulness in their daily work. It means training and equipping them to be active followers of Jesus in his assault on the principalities and powers which he has disarmed on his cross. And it means sustaining them in bearing the cost of that warfare.

It seems to me that, if this is our model, it will preclude our being captive to either of the two models which are often presented as the only alternatives. One model lays all the stress on personal conversion, the other on a diffused influence through the community. Those who accept one of these models are often deeply suspicious of those who accept the other. I have noticed this particularly in the context of mission to industry. There is, on the one side, a tendency to regard with contempt the "holy huddle" of those who claim to have been converted, who therefore keep themselves separate from the unconverted, who pray and study their Bibles but do not seem to take the risks involved in taking costly public positions on specific issues such as working conditions in the factory or bargaining rights for workers. On the other hand, there are those who do not like to talk about "the call to conversion" but speak much about applying Christian principles to the working of industry, and who therefore appear to be purveyors of good advice rather than of good news. A similar split in the Christian view of the relation of Church to world occurs in other contexts. Defenders of the "parish church" approach are criticized by those who call for gathered communities of those who have a definite experience of conversion. Those in the former camp can be plausibly portrayed as people who have made a comfortable concordat with the world and fail seriously to challenge it; those on the other side can with equal plausibility be portrayed as selfish people who are concerned only with their own salvation and fail to love the world as God loves it.

I cannot doubt that the call to conversion is essential to any authentic understanding of the gospel. The ministry of Jesus began with such a call: "Repent, for the kingdom of God is at hand." The crucial question concerns the content of conversion. The widespread misunderstanding of the word is illustrated in the mistranslation of this word of Jesus in the *Good News Bible*. There *metanoeite* is translated as "turn away from your sins." If this were the true translation, Jesus would be merely a preacher of revival. In fact he was calling for something much more radical, a conversion of the mind which leads to a totally new view of life. As the story unfolds, it becomes clear that the "sinners" are the ones who understand and the "righteous" are the ones who do not. The call to conversion is much more than a call to turn away from those things which society (even apart from the events of Jesus' ministry) can recognize as sins. It involves, in fact, proving that the world's idea of what is sin and what is righteousness is wrong (John 16:8). The conversion for which Jesus calls, and which the Spirit now effects in those who turn to him, is a radically new way of understanding: it involves at the same time a demand for total self-surrender and the gift of utter security. It involves both calling and promise, demand and gift, at the same time. And it concerns the whole of life—the public life of the world, the nation, the factory, the society, and the personal life of each believer. There can be no muffling of the call to conversion, but equally there can be no limiting of its range, no offer of a "cheap grace" which promises security without commitment to that mission for which Jesus went to the cross. The bearer of this call has to be a community which is both committed to that mission and also enjoying and celebrating that security.

What, then, will be the relation of the minister to this community? I have used such words as "enabling," "sustaining," and "nourishing" to describe his role in mobilizing the congregation for its mission. But how shall this be done? Once again, I think, we have to look at alternative images. The typical picture of the minister, at least in the Protestant tradition, has been that of a teacher. He faces the congregation as a teacher faces the class. They all, preacher and people alike, have their backs turned to the outside world. They face one another, and the minister encourages, exhorts, and teaches. Many biblical pictures portray Jesus in this relation to his disciples. The Italian director Pasolini (himself a Marxist) in the film *The Gospel according to St. Matthew* gives a picture of Jesus' teaching which is quite different and, once seen, unforgettable. It shows Jesus going ahead of his disciples, like a commander leading troops into battle. The words he speaks are thrown back over his shoulder to the fearful and faltering followers. He is not like a general who sits at headquarters and sends his troops into battle. He goes at their head and takes the brunt of the enemy attack. He enables and encourages them by leading them, not just by telling them. In this picture, the words of Jesus have a quite different force. They all find their meaning in the central keyword, "Follow me."

If one has once seen this picture, one cannot think of ministry in the way I have just described. Ministerial leadership for a missionary congregation will require that the minister is directly engaged in the warfare of the kingdom against the powers which usurp the kingship. Of course the minister cannot be directly involved in each of the specific areas of secular life in which the members of the congregation have to fight their battles. But there will be situations where the minister must represent the whole Church in challenging abuse of power, corruption, and selfishness in public life and take the blows that follow. As he or she does this, the way will be open for standing in solidarity with members of the congregation who have to face similar conflict. There is a sense in which the Christian warfare against the world, the flesh, and the devil is all one warfare. Those who display courage in one sector of the line encourage everyone. The minister will encourage the whole company by the courage with which he or she engages the enemy. And of course, as Paul reminds us, "the weapons of our warfare are not worldly but have divine power to destroy strongholds" (2 Cor. 10:4). The minister's leadership of the congregation in its mission to the world will be first and foremost in the area of his or her own discipleship, in that life of prayer and daily consecration which remains hidden from the world but which is the place where the essential battles are either won or lost.

I find warrant for this way of seeing ministry in the final chapter of St. John's Gospel, where—in the person of Peter—we have given to us a picture of apostolic leadership in the Church. Peter is first presented to us as an evangelist. He is a fisherman who, however, catches nothing until he submits to the Master's instruction. When he does so, there is a mighty catch which he brings, with the net intact and as the fruit of his work, one undivided harvest, to the feet of Jesus. Then the image changes and Peter is a pastor to whom Jesus entrusts his flock. He can so entrust it because Peter loves him more than all. But then, finally, the image changes again. Peter is a disciple who must go the way the Master went, the way of the cross. He is not to look around to see who else is following. He is to look one way only—to the Master who goes before him. Ministerial leadership is, first and finally, discipleship.

20. Confidence in the Gospel

I have given these chapters the title *The Gospel in a Pluralist Society*. The gospel is news of what has happened. The problem of communicating it in a pluralist society is that it simply disappears into the undifferentiated ocean of information. It represents one opinion among millions of others. It cannot be "the truth," since in a pluralist society truth is not one but many. It may be "true for you," but it cannot be true for everyone. To claim that it is true for everyone is simply arrogance. It is permitted as one opinion among many.

Churches, at least in Britain, have been eager to avoid the charge of arrogance. They have been eloquent in their efforts to distance themselves from what is now judged to have been the arrogance of missionaries who talked of the evangelization of the world in their generation. They are eager to repent of the arrogance of their predecessors. In reaction to this arrogance, two moods are widely discernible. One is timidity. This is, I think, the most obvious feature of much contemporary English theology. Most theology in this country is carried on within the universities whose curricula are governed by the assumptions of "modernity." It is difficult for theologians to step outside these boundaries. Literary, historical, and phenomenological studies in religious history and practice can be carried on without transgressing these boundaries. "Religious studies" can flourish, since they are—in general—descriptive rather than normative. They do not pass judgment on the truth or otherwise of the religious beliefs studied, much less on what is taught as truth in other faculties. But Christian dogmatics, the teaching as truth of beliefs which run counter to the accepted assumptions of our culture, is much more difficult. Academic theology tends to live within the frontiers which the reigning "plausibility structure" dictates. The resulting tension between academic theology and the beliefs of ordinary church-goers is a familiar matter of comment.

The other mood is one of anxiety. Christianity is perceived to be a good cause which is in danger of collapsing through lack of support. Or—in a quite different manifestation of the same fundamental atti-tude—there is a strident summons to more energetic efforts in evange-lism and social action. I do not mean by speaking in this way that it is not very important for Christians to be active in both evangelism and social action. But I do sense an underlying Pelagianism which lays too much stress on our own activities and is too little controlled by the sense of the greatness and majesty and sufficiency of God. I am saying that there can be a kind of Christian activity which only thinly masks a lack of confidence in the sufficiency of God.

I want to suggest the word "confidence" as the one which desig-nates the proper attitude. In a pluralist society, any confident affirma-tion of the truth is met by the response, "Why should I believe this rather than that?" Every statement of ultimate belief is liable to be met by this criticism, and—of course—if it is indeed an ultimate belief then it cannot be validated by something more ultimate. Our ultimate com-mitments are (as I have argued in an earlier chapter) always circular in structure. Having been brought (not by our own action but by the ac-tion of God) to the point of believing in Jesus as Lord and Savior, we seek to understand and cope with every kind of experience and every evidence of truth in the light of this faith. We are constantly called upon to rethink our faith in the light of these new experiences and evidences. We are prepared to recognize (as every human being has to recognize) that there are areas of mystery and that there are puzzles which are not solved for a long time. But we expect to find, and we do find, that the initial faith is confirmed, strengthened, and enlarged as we go on through life. And if, as always happens in a pluralist society, we are asked: "But why start with Jesus? Why not start somewhere else?" we have to answer that no rational thought is possible except by starting with something which is already given in some human tradition of ra-tional thought and discourse. Our immediate answer may well be, "Why not?" For the ultimate answer we have to wait for the end of all things. That expectant waiting is part of what it is to live a full human life.

I therefore believe that a Christian must welcome some measure of plurality but reject pluralism. We can and must welcome a plural society because it provides us with a wider range of experience and a

243

wider diversity of human responses to experience, and therefore richer opportunities for testing the sufficiency of our faith than are available in a monochrome society. As we confess Jesus as Lord in a plural society, and as the Church grows through the coming of people from many different cultural and religious traditions to faith in Christ, we are enabled to learn more of the length and breadth and height and depth of the love of God (Eph. 3:14-19) than we can in a monochrome society. But we must reject the ideology of pluralism. We must reject the invitation to live in a society where everything is subjective and relative, a society which has abandoned the belief that truth can be known and has settled for a purely subjective view of truth—"truth for you" but not truth for all. For one thing, I doubt whether such a society can long sustain its integrity in the face of the claims of those who have a firm commitment to some vision of truth. As I write, the press is full of the cries of outrage from Western liberal writers and critics in face of the Muslim reaction to Salman Rushdie's book *The Satanic Verses*. But it is doubtful whether these cries have behind them anything that can withstand the determined onslaught of those who hold firm beliefs about the truth. Freedom to think and say what you like will not provide the resources for a resolute grappling with false beliefs. The demand for freedom of thought and expression must itself rest on some firmly held belief about the origin, nature, and destiny of human life. If it has no such foundation it will prove powerless in the face of those who have firm beliefs about the truth.

In a pluralist society there is always a temptation to judge the importance of any statement of the truth by the number of people who believe it. Truth, for practical purposes, is what most people believe. Christians can fall into this trap. It may well be that for some decades, while churches grow rapidly in other parts of the world, Christians in Europe may continue to be a small and even shrinking minority. If this should be so, it must be seen as an example of that pruning which is promised to the Church in order that it may bear more fruit (John 15:1ff.). When that happens it is painful. But Jesus assures us, "My Father is the gardener." He knows what he is doing, and we can trust him. Such experience is a summons to self-searching, to repentance, and to fresh commitment. It is not an occasion for anxiety. God is faithful, and he will complete what he has begun.